BEYOND
LIBERALISM

The Political Thought of
F. A. HAYEK &
MICHAEL POLANYI

BEYOND
LIBERALISM

R. T. ALLEN

Transaction Publishers
New Brunswick (U.S.A.) and London (U.K.)

Library of Congress Catalog Number: 98-23204
ISBN: 1-56000-355-3
Printed in the United States of America

Library of Congress Cataloging-in-Publication Data

Allen, R. T., 1941–
    Beyond liberalism: the political thought of F.A. Hayek and Michael
Polanyi / R.T. Allen.
        p. cm.
    Includes bibliographical references and index.
    ISBN 1-56000-355-3 (alk. paper)
    1. Liberty. 2. Liberalism. I. Title.
JC585.A385   1998
320.51—dc21   98-23204
                                                          CIP

Contents

Acknowledgments

First and foremost I would like to express my thanks to my friends in the Michael Polanyi Liberal Philosophical Association (Polányi Mihály Szabadelvü Filozofiai Társaság) of Hungary for inviting me to join their research project, "The Tradition of Central European Liberal Philosophy," to which this study is a contribution.

Secondly, I must thank the Research Support Scheme of the Central European University for the financial support which it has given to this project and for its grant to me.

I have also to thank the Special Collections Department of the Joseph Regenstein Library of the University of Chicago for permission to quote from the unpublished papers of Michael Polanyi.

Mr. Lee Congdon kindly suggested several books on Hungarian and Austrian thinkers in the earlier part of this century, and Dr. Francis Dunlop kindly lent me the copies of some of Aurel Kolnai's later political articles which I have used for the Appendix.

A summary and chapters 12, 13, and 14 appeared in *Polanyiana*, vol. 5, no. 1, 1996.

—R.T. Allen, January 1994

Foreword

To avoid a mass of footnotes I shall give in the text references to the books most frequently cited, using the abbreviations listed below. Hayek and Polanyi often expressed the same ideas in more than one place. I shall not attempt to give all the relevant references and shall confine myself mostly to citing either the latest or the most generally accessible.

Abbreviations

Author	Abbreviation	Title
I. Berlin	FEOL	*Four Essays on Liberty*
F.A. Hayek	CL	*The Constitution of Liberty*
	CRS	*The Counter-Revolution of Science*
	FC	*The Fatal Conceit*
	LLL	*Law, Liberty and Legislation*, 3 vols.
	NSPPE	*New Studies in Philosophy, Politics and Economics*
	RS	*The Road to Serfdom*
	SPPE	*Studies in Philosophy, Politics and Economics*
L. von Mises	HA	*Human Action*
	S	*Socialism*
M. Polanyi	KB	*Knowing and Being*
	LL	*The Logic of Liberty*
	PK	*Personal Knowledge*
	SFS	*Science, Faith and Society*
	SMS	*The Struggle of Man in Society* (unpublished: box 26, folder 2*)
	TD	*The Tacit Dimension*
K. Popper	CAR	*Conjectures and Refutations*
	POH	*The Poverty of Historicism*
	OS	*The Open Society and Its Enemies*, 2 vols.

*References to Polanyi's unpublished papers, in the Special Collections Department of the Joseph Regenstein Library of the University of Chicago, will be given by means of the title or opening words, as used in the Library's Bibliography of the Polanyi Papers, and the Box and Folder Numbers.

Introduction

But have I not said that this movement [for the central planning of science] has virtually petered out by this time? Have not even the socialist parties throughout Europe endorsed by now the usefulness of the market? Do we not hear the freedom and independence of scientific enquiry openly demanded today even in important centres within the Soviet domain? Why renew this discussion when it seems about to lose its point?

My answer is that you cannot base social wisdom on political disillusion. The more sober mood of public life today can be consolidated only if it is used as an opportunity for establishing the principles of a free society on firmer grounds.
—Polanyi, *Knowing and Being*, p. 69

Further beyond Nihilism

This study takes its title from Michael Polanyi's "Beyond Nihilism." Just as he argued that freedom was endangered by the nihilism implicit in the "suspended logic" of Anglo-American liberalism, I propose to show that the reformulation of liberalism which Polanyi deemed necessary and which he began, must go further than perhaps Polanyi anticipated and eventually beyond liberalism altogether. Liberty and liberalism, taken as the doctrine that liberty is the chief political good, transcend themselves, and if we try to stay there we shall find that sooner or later we shall lose them.

Polanyi, I shall argue, in his recasting of liberty and liberalism in a more "positive" and fiduciary direction, came to a distinctly conservative liberalism or liberal conservatism, and only upon such an understanding can liberty be secured.

As for Polanyi's own political position, in Britain he supported the Liberal party. Yet, when in 1940 he spoke as a representative of that party, alongside members of the Conservative and Labour parties, on

1

"The Liberal Conception of Freedom" at a conference of the Student Christian Movement, he said that he would concern himself only with criticism of socialism and central planning, for:

> Conservative means: traditionalist, empirical, averse to a comprehensive programme. I will have no quarrel with this philosophy, because there is too little of it, and anyhow in England tradition is Liberal.[1]

Later, he argued several times that the radicalism of Tom Paine must be tempered with the conservatism of Edmund Burke, though, I shall argue, his own position is really that of Burke and has nothing at all to do with Paine.

Along with Polanyi's essays, I shall also examine the political writings of his friend, F. A. Hayek, the most influential representative of classical liberalism in this century, whose works inspired Lady Thatcher's rejection of *dirigisme* and corporatism and her programme of privatisation which has been imitated in many other countries and now seems to be embraced even by "New Labour" in Britain. Though he refused the designation of "Conservative" and preferred that of "Old Whig" (CL, "Postscript: Why I am not a Conservative"), Hayek's works, I shall argue, also manifest, though not to the same extent as Polanyi's, a similar transition to a more Conservative position.

But why undertake such a study, except for a purely historical interest?

Firstly, because this study is not "merely historical." All history, as Polanyi and R.G. Collingwood taught, is indwelling or rethinking, and therefore evaluative or critical of its subject matter. It is because I think that Hayek and Polanyi were right in their movement to a more "positive" and conservative liberalism, that I have studied their political thinking and now present my conclusions. And with them, I shall refer to others as representing what they rejected, or the conclusion to which they tended, or as treating in more depth topics which they touched upon.

And secondly, because, as the opening quotations from Polanyi suggest, a mood of mere disillusionment with illiberal movements and policies is not enough. Socialist policies, for example, always fail, but few socialists have learned from their failures: rather they demand more of the same *dirigiste* disease in order to cure it, for yet more planning to correct the errors of previous plans. For the aspirations which animate them remain: they are at odds with the world and cannot adjust to it. I, for one, suspect that it is only the electoral failure of socialism that has motivated the creation of "New Labour" and not any appreciation of its intellectual and moral bankruptcy. We need to penetrate to the roots of politics and policies and to examine the fundamental assumptions and presuppositions that control them. That is my aim rather than the details of practical politics. Hence this is a philosophical rather than a more strictly political study.

Especially as we approach the end of the twentieth century, it is appropriate to study the lessons which, at great cost, it has taught us. For Europe, and the European world overseas, the nineteenth century was the age of liberalism. Not always of liberalism triumphant, but of the spread of liberal ideas and aspirations, and of their realisation to varying degrees in many parts of the continent and further abroad. But the twentieth century disappointed those hopes. The disasters of the First World War and the Great Depression turned many minds to collectivist answers to the problems of the age: to socialism and economic planning of one form or another, and to dictatorships, of the Party or the Leader. The deliverance of Western Europe in 1945 was accomplished at the cost of the subjection of Central and Eastern Europe to the Soviet Empire. Only now in its closing years, since 1989, has the twentieth century looked like redeeming the hopes invested in it. Although the collapse of the Soviet Empire released, in what was Yugoslavia and in Georgia, intercommunal tensions that the heavy hand of Communist rule had suppressed, and has painfully exposed the massive economic inefficiency of centrally controlled economies, Europe is no longer divided into two armed camps, and no régime, apart probably from that of Milosevic in Serbia, maintains itself by terror and force upon its own people. Outside Europe there have been some notable victories for liberal ideals. Constitutional politics have returned to most of Latin America. China, though crushing internal dissent, is opening itself further and further to trade and a market economy, has reverted to its traditional policy of simply maintaining "the Middle Kingdom," though with some ambitions off its coasts, and treats communism only as something to keep the present gerontocracy in power. Only in the ruling parties in North Korea and Cuba, and among the still active Khmer Rouge in Cambodia and the "Shining Path" in Peru, does anyone seriously believe in communism. And several African states have experienced movements of dissatisfaction with presidents-for-life and one-party régimes, some of which have been peacefully and constitutionally replaced in a continent mostly ruled, since the end of the colonial era, by despotism tempered by coup and corruption.

Yet life in this world is never without problems, and movements of ideas and the spirit, seemingly dead and buried, may prove to be only dormant and to revive if, as Polanyi suggests in the passage quoted above, the intellectual climate is one only of disillusion with collectivism and not one of positive faith in free institutions. Moreover, there may have been something wrong with liberalism after all, something which the twentieth century has had to struggle with at great cost, and which could return to plague us once again. Consequently, it is appropriate even now to study those, such as Polanyi and Hayek, who endeavoured to restate its principles when collectivism was intellectually and politically dominant.

Like other movements of thought, liberalism has included several and sometimes divergent trends, and shades off into other positions. We shall be primarily concerned with "classical liberalism," by which I mean adherence to the following principles:

1. That, in the words of Lord Acton, liberty is "not the means to a higher political end" but "is itself the highest political end."[2]
2. That this liberty is, as J.S. Mill put it, the liberty to live one's life in one's own way, without interference from private persons or public authorities.
3. That this liberty requires each person and group to respect and not to trespass upon the equal liberty of other individuals and groups.
4. That to enforce and defend that mutual respect and restraint, a public authority (the state) is needed, but its power should be limited, wholly or mostly, to that task and that it should act by general and known laws.

This is what in Britain was generally understood by "liberalism."

But even in the nineteenth century there were other elements within liberalism and rival interpretations of it. I suggest that frequently these resulted from the differing situations in which liberals found themselves. In Britain liberalism was largely a movement seeking to build upon and to extend existing institutions, rights and principles, such as representative and elected legislative bodies, the rule of law, and free trade. Consequently the more conservative tendencies with liberalism outweighed the more radical ones. Those more radical elements are to be found in Bentham, who took his ideas more from Continental thinkers such as Condorcet, Helvétius, and Beccaria. Those ideas include an aggressive individualism, a rejection of tradition and custom as such, an itch to change and reform, and an ambiguous attitude towards the use of the power of the State: on the one hand, instinctive opposition to it, yet, on the other, a willingness to use it to promote a much desired state of affairs. Consequently, for the one side of Bentham all law is an evil for it is an infraction of liberty,[3] but for the other it does not really matter so long as people are made happy. For Bentham, adopting the psychology of the French Sensationalists, regarded people as centres of pleasure or pain and thus as easily manipulatable by means of carrots and sticks, not just to keep each from injuring others but to bring about any determinate state of affairs which would yield a greater balance of pleasure over pain. Voegelin quotes the opening of the *Memoire*, approved by Bentham, on the French translation of his *Panopticon*:

> If one could find a method of becoming master of everything which might happen to a certain number of men, to arrange everything around them so as to produce on them the impression that one wishes to produce, to make sure of their actions, of their connections, and of all the circumstances of their lives, so that nothing could escape, nor could oppose the desired effect, it cannot be doubted that a method of this kind would be a very powerful and a very useful instrument which governments might apply to various objects of the utmost importance.[4]

In the *Panopticon* itself Bentham answers objections to his proposed "inspection-school":

> Whether the liberal spirit and energy of a free citizen would not be exchanged for the mechanical discipline of a soldier, or the austerity of a monk?—and whether the result of this high-wrought contrivance might not be constructing a set of *machines* under the similitude of *men*?

Bentham's answer is

> Would *happiness* be most likely to be increased or diminished by this discipline?— Call them soldiers, call them monks, call them machines: so be it they were but happy ones, I should not care.[5]

The itch to do things *to and for* the people overcomes the belief in allowing them to lead their own lives.

Nor is this a result only of Bentham's substitution of a material notion of pleasure for the formal one of happiness, which individuals and groups could be allowed to specify for themselves. At least two other motives can be discerned in Bentham and elsewhere, especially Rousseau. The second motive is the oscillation of the "alienated" intellectual, uprooted from tradition and not at home in his *milieu*, between extending that "alienation" to all men in a war against tradition, authority, and all external powers that limit his "authentic" self, and longing for release from the loneliness of that state into a new, "authentic" and total community. Rousseau himself condemned the existing French society of his time, and by implication all society, yet found an image of freedom in ancient Sparta, a revived but distant Poland, and in the General Will of the Social Contract. Heidegger, in his Existentialist phase, rejected the "fallenness" of contemporary individuals into the "idle chatter" of *das mann*, yet yearned for a "resolute community," and, for a while, thought he had found it in the Nazi régime, which he never seriously repudiated. Sartre likewise, although he argued in *Being and Nothingness* that we are condemned to the "objectifying gaze" of the Other, the "bad faith" of allowing ourselves to be defined by our social roles, and the impossibility of achieving the coincidence of being and "nothingness" or radical freedom which we seek, nevertheless sought escape from meaningless and futility in the Communist party and tried to re-establish Marxism on an Existentialist basis. Radical and asocial individualism, one form of liberalism, swings over, as Hegel's dialectic predicts that it should, into totalitarian communalism. Polanyi noted how Marxism unmasked the "bourgeois" status of the alienated intellectual and then provided him with the chance to maintain his antibourgeois stance and to regain a sense of meaning in working for the proletariat via submission to the Party (PK, pp. 236–7). And Aurel Kolnai, in *The War against the West*, showed how many German professors, along with Heidegger, succumbed to the temptation to lose themselves in a *Volksgemeinschaft*, before 1933 as well as afterwards.

The third motive is like the first. It too is found in Bentham and Rousseau. It is the fateful temptation "to force men to be free." As we shall see, Sir Isaiah Berlin thought that this was a temptation principally for what he called doctrines of "positive liberty," in which freedom is thought to be found in living within a specific set of institutions or pattern of life. But classical liberalism, with its doctrine of "negative" liberty (freedom from interference and coercion) can also be affected by it and succumb to it. For example, J.S. Mill himself, in *On Liberty*, conceded that liberalism applies only to "human beings in the maturity of their faculties," whereas a very different policy is needed in

> backward states of society in which the race itself may be considered as it is nonage [and where] the early difficulties in the way of spontaneous improvement are so great that...a ruler full of the spirit of improvement is warranted in the use of any expedient that will attain an end, perhaps otherwise unattainable...Despotism is a legitimate mode of government with barbarians, provided the end be their improvement, and the means justified by actually effecting that end.[6]

It seems to me that the real import of this passage has often been overlooked. Mill does not mean that despotism over "barbarians" is justified *faute de mieux* as would be usually understood: that is, as a firm rule maintaining order in society and control of the streets, but otherwise letting the population get on with its customary way of life and enforcing its customary laws, like a traditional ruler or a British or French colonial government over the "natives." No, Mill means something more than that. He has in mind a *dynamic* régime "full of the spirit of improvement," which is justified in its exercise of despotism only as it aims at the *improvement* of the populace. Indeed, so long as that is its object, it is justified in using "any expedient." What more could a Communist party in power want? After all, the Dictatorship of the Proletariat, or of the Party and its Leader in its name, is aimed ultimately at the withering away of the state, class oppression and exploitation, and the final overcoming of "alienation" when "commodity production," and thus private property and the division of labour, have been abolished. That really would be liberation.

Both these motives are joined in the desire to use the power of the State to emancipate the individual from the fetters of custom, tradition, and all other groups and associations, such as family, Church, guild, "estate," class, local community, and informal public opinion. Hence the dual development in the nineteenth century of both the liberation of the individual from inherited restraints and the growth of the modern sovereign, rationalised, bureaucratic, and omnicompetent state. These were not so much conflicting tendencies as two sides of the one process.[7]

That process began in the eighteenth century, and was greater where there was a patchwork of local and provincial customs, laws, assemblies, Estates, and privileges. "Enlightened" rulers and régimes, including Louis XVI, sometimes found themselves frustrated by the representative organs of their provinces when they tried to introduce uniform and national or imperial codes of law and systems of taxation. Louis XVI's ministers, seeking to implement the maxim of "one king, one law," resorted to the use of *lits de justice* (appearances of the king in the *parlements* which then had no choice but to ratify his legislation) and *lettres de cachet* (warrants of arrest on the sole authority of the royal prerogative), and so abused the royal prerogative and made it "despotic." In Austria, whereas Maria Theresa sent her minister, Haugwitz, to persuade the provincial bodies to remove noble and clerical exemptions from taxation and to introduce a new decennial tax, and used her *jure regio* only in Carinthia, Joseph II bypassed them only to have his policies fail. This manifested the contradiction within "Enlightened" policies: on the one hand, to introduce rational and uniform laws and taxes and more individual rights especially of religion, expression and publication; yet, on the other, willingness to use "despotic" or arbitrary means in order to implement them instead of gaining the consent and co-operation of customary institutions. Under "Enlightened" influence, liberalism inevitably took a more radical and innovating form, as it also did in Britain after 1832 and would have done so yet more had not the more conservative persons and groups restrained it. Consequently, there arose within it those radical movements which rejected the *status quo* entirely and wished to liberate men from the chains of all tradition, custom and religion, movements which, in France in 1789, took over the momentum of reform *within* the scope and functionings of the *ancien régime*, and transformed it into the Revolution. Elsewhere, Continental liberalism was also tempted, not just to legislate away existing constrictions upon liberty, but also to legislate positively to promote its own favoured mode of life. For example, in education, not just to offer alternatives to Church schools, but to abolish them and to institute a system of secularist, anti-religious education. Likewise, in addition to or instead of abolishing interventionist economic policies and legislation, it sometimes continued and extended them in order to introduce "from above" the economic and industrial developments which in Britain had occurred spontaneously and "from below." (One notices the same policy in postcolonial Africa.)

There are two interpretations of this dual process. The one is to say that what mattered to the *philosophes* and other Enlightened intellectuals, and to those who acted upon their ideas, was more the particular reforms and not the way they were introduced. Undoubtedly that was often the case. The other, and to my mind the more profound, is to see both processes as one process of releasing the essentially independent and separate individual from the fetters of inherited authorities, associations, and institutions in order that he might find freedom in a new, impersonal, rational State to which has been transferred all authority and power. On the one hand, individuals uprooted from customary allegiances can find participation and community only in the organisations of the new State, which often created the nations (especially Germany and Italy) which it purported to represent, and, on the other, to bind them more closer to it, the new State aimed to do things for the people, such as to enlarge the franchise and provide schemes of welfare. It follows from this interpretation that the totalitarian régimes of the twentieth century were not so much departures but consummations of the liberalism of the nineteenth century, or of one significant form of it.[8]

The Self-Transcendence of Liberty and Liberalism

Finally, before embarking on the argument itself, I would like first to characterise its principal line in a little more detail. Liberty, I hold, like everything else in human life, is self-transcending. A familiar example of self-transcendence is the paradox of happiness: that, in order to attain happiness, you must give yourself up to something else and hope to achieve happiness as a by-product. Liberty, I shall argue, cannot be coherently defended nor securely enjoyed in and for itself but only as a condition for and by-product of something more important. I propose to show that in Hayek and especially Polanyi we see an awareness of this fact, and of it at several levels. Indeed, this is nothing new to liberalism. In the very statement by Lord Acton (the greatest of liberals according to Hayek), which was used above to define classical liberalism, we find him continuing: "It is not for the sake of good public administration that it is required, but for security in the pursuit of the highest objects of civil society, and of private life." And again:

> By liberty I mean the assurance that every man shall be protected in doing what he believes his duty against the influence of authority and majorities, custom and opinion. The State is competent to assign duties and draw the line between good and evil in its immediate sphere. Beyond the limits of things necessary for its well-being, it can only give indirect help to fight the battle of life by promoting the influences which prevail against temptation: religion, education, and the distribution of wealth.[9]

Acton's is not, after all, the "negative" liberty of doing as we please but the "positive" liberty needed for doing our duty. So too we shall find Polanyi defending the liberty of self-dedication to transcendent ideals. Yes, both count as liberals in making freedom the highest *political* good, but both see the political is transcended by the moral. And once that is admitted, so too must it be allowed that, in principle, liberty can at times be overruled when that higher good requires it. For example, there can no longer be a blanket rejection of censorship nor acceptance of any "experiment in living."

It is clear from what I have already said, that I regard Liberalism as a complex and ambiguous movement. Therefore my first task will be to outline the principal versions of Liberalism and to show how the original, moderate, and classical varieties slide into the radical ones which destroy liberty unless they transcend themselves in a definitely conservative direction. In order to illustrate these tendencies, I shall contrast with Hayek and Polanyi, and take as the *terminus ab quo* of the movement that I am tracing in their work, two of Hayek's fellow Austrians, Ludwig von Mises and Sir Karl Popper, who represent that fatal suspension of logic which Polanyi found in the Anglo-American liberalism that descends from Locke and through J.S. Mill. On the other side, I would have liked to complete that movement with a study of the Christian conservatism of Polanyi's fellow Hungarian, Aurel Kolnai. But my lack of German and Hungarian has prevented me from reading his more positive and earlier political essays, and so I have had to confine myself to an outline, in the Appendix, of the themes of his later writings in Spanish, French, and English. Also, to mark the *terminus ad quem* of my argument, I shall define and illustrate Conservative politics by continued reference to the works of Edmund Burke, to whom both Hayek and Polanyi refer. Conservatism is primarily the conservation of a traditional way of life, and not of the *status quo* whatever it is. The conservation of socialism is socialism, and of communism, communism. It was, indeed, a sign of capitulation to leftist ideology to call "conservatives" those in Russia who wished to maintain and then to restore the communist régime. When a traditional way of life has been overthrown and suppressed, conservatism means restoration. But life does not stand still nor does it return exactly to the same place. Burke, the Father of articulate Conservatism, recognised that "a state without the means of some change is without the means of its conservation."[10] Merely standing still proves self-destructive in the end. In particular, in order to conserve a traditional order of society, it is necessary to accommodate rising sections of the population into it, to give them a stake in it and in its continuance.

Now it is possible for the conserving and reforming, or, rather, adapting, functions to be divided between different parties or groups. In such a case they need to recognise their dialectical relationship to each other. R.G. Collingwood, referring to the "aristocratic" function of testing candidates for inclusion into the ruling class and the "democratic" one of proposing such candidates, remarked that, contrary to what J.S. Mill once said, it was the Liberals who were "the stupid party" for they forgot the equal necessity of the former function.[11] Any viable conservatism in the European world must embody a certain liberalism within itself. Conversely, any viable liberalism must recognise its dependence upon a living conservatism.

The argument itself will fall into three parts focusing, respectively, upon the nature, value, and foundations of liberty. In Part 1 and in order to refine some of the principal problems, I propose to begin with Sir Isaiah Berlin's well-known essay, "Two Concepts of Liberty," in which he distinguishes the "negative," that of liberalism as usually understood, from the "positive" one, and argues that frequently the elaboration of the latter has endangered and suppressed the liberties upheld by those who favour the "negative" sense. Although that distinction is mistaken, Berlin does raise important questions about the ways in which liberalism can be turned upon itself. I shall then attempt to clarify the issues at stake in any discussion of liberty, and to specify more precisely the principles of classical liberalism and to mark them off against other contemporary political positions styled "Liberal" but manifestly illiberal in content or implication.

I shall next take up Hayek's account of liberty as constitutional order, a *Rechstaat*. That embodies a great deal of truth but is not finally adequate. The difficulties found in attempting to define liberty suggest that the attempt is itself mistaken, that liberty can be really known only tacitly from lived experience of a tradition of liberty. Such was Polanyi's conclusion, and also Burke's. It means that in the very definition of liberty, liberalism transcends itself and rests upon tradition.

Turning, in Part 2, to the question of the value of liberty, we shall begin with von Mises's positive arguments, which are sceptical and utilitarian, and thus subject to Polanyi's exposure of their self-destructive basis. Utilitarianism either destroys what it is used to justify as useful or must transcend itself in recognising that the utility of human activities is a by-product of pursuing those activities for the sake of their inherent value. Next we shall turn to Popper's arguments, where we shall find continuing elements of that rationalism, scientism, and constructivism which Hayek was led to repudiate. Popper's Open Society, founded on his "critical dualism" of facts and standards which leaves the latter without any rational basis and which admits its own irrationality, cannot accredit itself and its freedom with any value. Hayek provides more complex and subtle arguments for the value of freedom. His utilitarianism is one of institutions and whole bodies of law, not of single actions nor even of types of action. His argument leads him to acknowledge that the practice of justice, on which liberty depends, must be performed as a value in and by itself and not for its benefits, of peace, freedom, and prosperity. Yet even he does not fully overcome the limitations of scepticism and utilitarianism. Only in Polanyi do we find a clear statement of the self-transcending value of liberty as the necessary basis for self-dedication to the pursuit of transcendent ideals and not just for doing as one pleases so long as one does not tread on the toes of others.

In Part 3 we shall examine the social and political foundations of liberty. Whereas earlier Liberals often took them for granted, Hayek and Polanyi did not. We shall look at their models of a free society, and shall see that it rests upon "prescription," or custom and tradition. With Polanyi, we shall find that a free society is not an "open" one, and that it imposes positive and not just negative obligations upon its citizens. Furthermore, it depends upon emotional bonds on at least two levels, of a general capacity for sympathy with our fellows which founds the Great Society, and upon particular attachments which hold together particular societies. Here I shall supplement Hayek and Polanyi with references to Max Scheler and R.G. Collingwood. As already indicated, it is only a definitely conservative liberalism that proves viable, as the history of the twentieth century should have taught us. And it proves viable only as it is passionately held as, or as a part of, a religious faith. Even Polanyi's self-transcending view of freedom cannot by itself give the individual person that unique value which his political liberty presupposes. We have to go beyond politics to morality and then beyond the moral order to the metaphysical and thence the theological, to the Christian conservatism of Burke and Kolnai.

Throughout this study I shall take for granted Hayek's and Polanyi's arguments against collectivism and totalitarianism (and likewise those of von Mises and Popper), and shall focus instead upon their proposed alternatives, their arguments for them, and the assumptions underlying them.

Notes

1. "The Liberal Conception of Freedom," p. 1, Papers, box 26, folder 8.
2. *Essays on Freedom and Power*, p. 74.
3. "No law can ever be made but what trenches upon liberty: if it stops there, it is so much pure evil...It may be a necessary evil: but still at any rate it is an evil. To make a law is to do evil that good may come" (*Of Laws in General*, p. 54). Note how that last sentence paves the way for a collectivist and *dirigiste* utilitarianism—see below, note 3.

   Compare Bentham on government: "All government is in the very essence of it an evil: for government can not be carried on but in proportion as obligation is created; and taken by itself all obligation is evil" (*First Principles Preparatory to a Constitutional Code*, p. 4).

   These passages reveal a severe *désordre du coeur*, a resentment of any discipline of the self's wilful desires and inclinations.

4. *Traités de Législation Civile et Pénale*, ed. Dumont (1802), vol. 3, p. 209, quoted Voegelin, *From Enlightenment to Revolution*, p. 60.
5. *Panopticon, Works*, vol. 4, p. 64, quoted Voegelin, ibid. p. 67 note.
6. *On Liberty*, pp. 15–16.
7. G.M. Tamás ("Austrian Conservatives and Hungarian Liberals," in *Polanyiana*, vol. 2), noting how Hungarian thinkers such as Oszkár Jászi, Aurel Kolnai, Karl Mannheim and Michael Polanyi appear more conservative when writing for an Austrian, German, British, or American audience, and more radical when writing for Hungarian readers, has suggested that the explanation lies in the differing political contexts. The former was one of familiarity with liberal and modern institutions, the latter one in which they were yet to be introduced. That illustrates what I have suggested about the context of liberalism. We might well expect that Hungarian Liberals at the beginning of the twentieth century to have viewed Hungary as a "backward" nation in urgent need of social, political, and economic reform and modernisation in order to make it more like the states of Western Europe. Such reform would have to be introduced "from above," by an intellectual and political élite, and perhaps imposed by them. To some extent, we may suppose, they would have seen themselves as justifiably forcing their compatriots to be free. Their liberalism, therefore, could easily take a radical, constructive, and somewhat collectivist form.

I myself am not in a position to test that hypothesis in respect of the earlier work of Jászi, Kolnai, and Mannheim (For details of their earlier careers and thought, see L. Congdon, *Exile and Social Thought*. On Jászi, see also, L. Congdon, "The Moralist as Social Thinker" in *Historians in Politics* edited by W. Laquer and G.L. Mosse; and *Liberty and Socialism*, edited by J. M. Bák.) Moreover, in the case of Michael Polanyi, there is little direct evident about his early political and social thinking. Before his visit to the U.S.S.R. in 1935 he published only two political articles, "A békeszerzköhötz" ("To the Peacemakers," 1917) and "Uj szkepticizmus" ("New Scepticism," 1919). (Both were reprinted in *Polanyiana*, vol. 1, no. 1, Autumn, 1991. English translations will be found in *Society, Economics and Philosophy: Selected Articles*.) And there is little that is relevant among his unpublished papers for the years between 1919 and 1935. What I would argue, if I were in a position to do so, is that the difference that Tamás has noticed, is rather one of time than place. That is, that the course of events after 1917 brought about a change of attitude from a radical to a conservative liberalism in reaction against revolution and the collectivist régimes that became established between 1917 and 1939. I have found two relevant passages in Polanyi's published work, of which the former supports Tamás's thesis, whereas the latter, along with one from Hayek, supports mine:

"[The Sociological Society, founded by Jászi, and its journal, *Huszadik Szászad/Twentieth Century*] jointly opened up the first barrage of resolute social criticism in Hungary. In heavy fighting against the combined pressures of an overbearing aristocracy, a narrow-minded clergy, a small nobility entrenched in government offices and a blindly complacent new business class, this movement established during the first two decades of this century a first foothold for democratic ideals in Hungary" ("Oscar Jászi and Hungarian Liberalism," *Science and Freedom*, 1, 1957, p. 7).

"When I was a boy and preparing to become a scientist I used to cherish great hopes for a new world organised by science. At that time, about forty years ago, I was living in Budapest. I was a great reader of Mr Wells's novels. I devoured them almost as they came from the press in England. They made me impatient with traditional statesmanship and I firmly determined to follow Mr Wells in sweeping aside all this gimcrack world as he thought it was putting in its place a new world run on scientific lines. However, two great wars and a number of revolutions have taught me to look upon human affairs in a different light. I still remain grateful to Mr Wells for his bold inspiration and I share his enthusiasm for radical reform...but I no longer believe...that the decisive problems of our world can be solved by applying the methods of science." ("Can Science Bring Peace?" *The Listener*35 (902), 25 April 1946, p. 531)

"These rationalist views [of "scientism" and "constructivism"] that I have been examining now for so many years are those on which I, in common with most nonreligious European thinkers of my generation, formed my own outlook in the early part of this century. At that time they appeared self-evident, and following them seemed the way to escape pernicious superstitions of all sorts." (FC, p. 53)

8. This is the argument of R.A. Nesbit's *The Quest for Community*, especially from chapter 5 onwards. Nesbit (pp. 189–90) quotes the prophetic words of Tocqueville's *Democracy in America* on the conjunction of a mass of dissociated individuals and above them the omnicompetent and omniprovident state.

9. Op. cit., p. 55.

10. *Reflections on the Revolution in France, Works*, vol. 5, p. 59; cf. ibid. p. 79, *Corr.*, vol. 4, p. 465. (Hereafter, I shall refer to this book simply as "Reflections," and all references to Burke's published works will be to the volumes of the Rivington edition, except as when otherwise stated.)

11. *The New Leviathan*, ch. 27, §§27:5ff.

Part I

The Nature of Liberty

There are people who have split and anatomised the doctrine of free government as if it were an abstract question concerning metaphysical liberty and necessity, and not a matter of moral prudence and natural feeling. They have disputed whether liberty be a positive or negative idea; whether it does not consist in being governed by laws without considering what are the laws or who are the makers; whether man has any rights by nature; and whether all the property he enjoys be not the alms of his government, and his life itself their favour and indulgence.
—Edmund Burke, *A Letter to the Sheriffs of Bristol,* vol. 3, p. 184

1

Berlin and Positive and Negative Liberty

"Negative" Liberty

Liberty has been understood in several divergent ways, some of which work against others. One of the central tasks for classical liberalism in the twentieth century has been the clearer definition of its notion of liberty against other ones. We shall begin, as others have done, with Berlin's "Two Concepts of Liberty," in which he distinguished "negative" liberty and "positive" liberty. Classical liberalism's idea of liberty is generally supposed to be a "negative" one. Berlin argued that "positive" conceptions have too easily been invoked to suppress genuine liberty, the "negative" liberty of the individual to live his own life in his own way.

We shall see that the distinction between two types of liberty cannot be sustained, and should be replaced by one between two inseparable aspects of liberty. Furthermore, as suggested in the Introduction, all forms of liberalism are liable to the temptation to "force men to be free."

The negative concept is an answer to "What is the area within which the subject a person or group of persons is or should be left to do what he is able to do or be, without interference by other persons?" It is the idea of a minimum area of individual liberty necessary for a person to remain human. It is liberty *from*, from deliberate interference with, in J.S. Mill's words, the individual "pursuing his own good in his own way." Liberty is itself and *not* other goods, such as justice, equality, and culture. If it is curtailed to secure or promote other goods, then there is an absolute loss of freedom, and not a gain of freedom of another sort or by other persons. It is compatible with autocracy if the ruler leaves a wide area of freedom to his subjects. For the question, "Who governs me?" is separate from "How far does the government interfere with me?" (FEOL, pp. 121–31).[1]

This is the familiar Anglo-Saxon idea of individual liberty. But I suggest that Berlin is wrong to define it as *negative* liberty. Rather, all liberty has its negative and positive aspects: a liberty *from* interference and a liberty *to* do certain things, the former being defined by reference to the latter.[2] We see this in the quotation from Mill. The liberty that is prized is a liberty to live one's own life as one pleases, and therefore to be free from interference, especially by public authorities, in living as one pleases. Interference can be only interference *with* something, something active in its own right. I cannot interfere with the plans and actions of someone in a deep coma, but only with his bodily functioning. Political and civil liberty presupposes that persons and groups have, or can have, plans and intentions of their own which other persons and groups can allow or prevent.[3]

In his Introduction, written after the four essays themselves, Berlin replies to this objection. He states that one can struggle against something without a conscious aim at a definite further state, that someone may not know how he will use his freedom but only that he wishes to remove the yoke that constrains him (FEOL, p.xliii). That is very true, and often, when restraints have been removed, people find themselves at a loss as to what to do. Nevertheless implicit in the idea of a restraint is the idea of that activity which it restrains. If I feel something to be a yoke, then I feel that it restricts me in doing something which I wish to do. That, as with the prisoner and the slave, may be a general freedom to live as I choose, or to do a range of things rather than just one. Often attention is focused upon the constraint and the effort to remove it, rather than upon the freedom which it restricts and how one intends to use it. Similarly, someone trying to escape from danger implicitly seeks somewhere less dangerous, though he may pay no heed to where he is actually going. This Berlin recognised a few pages before when he corrected his definition of liberty as the absence of obstacles to the fulfilment of desires. For, as in Stoicism, one can extend liberty thus defined by eliminating frustrated desires as well as by removing what blocks them. Civil and political freedom is the absence of obstacles to possible choices and desires (FEOL, pp. xxxviii–ix). That redefinition of freedom still includes a reference to choices, desires, plans, and intentions. And particular restrictions and interferences can be characterised only with reference to classes of choices, desires, plans, and intentions. For example, American "liberals," and the members of the British Liberal and Labour parties, favour removal of restrictions, governmental and social, upon one set of activities and wish to promote them upon others, respectively, private life and publication, on the one hand, and economic concerns on the other. Those in America who call themselves "libertarians" favour the removal of both sets of restrictions. And there has been a radical liberalism which has called for men to be liberated from restrictions *per se*, and not from specific ones, and thus to enjoy an indefinite and indeterminate liberty to do and to be anything.

What Berlin means by the "negative concept" of liberty is the general freedom *to* live as one pleases and therefore a general freedom *from* governmental and other forms of restriction upon it. It can be put equally in negative or positive terms: respectively, "freedom from interference by the state (and the public)" and "freedom to live as we please." That the former was usually preferred was, I suggest, due to the historical situation of classical liberalism as it was formulated in Britain, where a desire for a general positive freedom of the individual could be taken for granted and where the attention of Liberal reformers could be focused upon the inherited restraints upon it, or the new ones of public opinion, which they wished to be removed.

But Gray denies that this conception of liberty was unequivocally upheld by classical Liberalism. Locke and Kant, he states, held liberty to be reduced by the imposition of arbitrary will and to be enlarged by conformity to rational law, while J.S. Mill was as much concerned with the autonomous man (who decides for himself and does not bow to public opinion).[4] It is true that Mill was concerned not just with allowing individuals to live as they please free from governmental and other interference, but also with definitely encouraging nonconformity, diversity, and "experiments in living." Voluntary and uncoerced convergence would not have gained his wholehearted approval. As for Locke and Kant, they took rational systems of law and absence of arbitrary will to be conditions of freedom: respectively, "for liberty is to be free from restraint and violence from others, which cannot be where there is no law,"[5] and the hindrance of another's freedom, if it can coexist with that of others in accordance with universal law, is wrong.[6] Locke presents more of the negative side (and denies, against Hobbes, that freedom is doing simply as one likes), and Kant more of the positive:

> Any action is *right* if it can co-exist with everyone's freedom in accordance with a universal law, or if on its maxim the freedom of choice of each can coexist with everyone's freedom in accordance with universal law.[7]

For there cannot be a merely negative, nor a simply positive, concept of liberty. The point is that Locke, Kant, Mill (but not all of the time) and other classical Liberals, favoured a general freedom of individuals to live as they wished within a system of law which made that possible for all and which protected them against arbitrary interference. That is what Berlin, on the whole, was also concerned to defend, as against conscription into a particular arrangement of society which is supposed to liberate one's real or true self from enslavement to a lower or false self.

Positive Liberty

Positive liberty Berlin defines as an answer to, "What, or who, is the source of control or interference that can determine someone to do, or be, this rather than that?" (FEOL, p.122). It is the answer that I myself should be that source, that I should be my own master (FEOL, p. 131).

That can be understood in at least two ways: "politically," I as distinct from others, and, "psychologically," I as distinct from forces acting within me and perhaps originating from forces without me. The former sense can itself be developed in two ways: that of individualist liberalism, I individually by charting my own way through society and life making free contracts with other individuals and groups as I meet them; and that of collectivist liberalism and totalitarian democracy, I with everyone else negotiating a common pattern of life which we shall all then lead together. But Berlin largely neglects the "political" interpretation, and especially the collectivist version of it, and goes straight into a discussion of the "psychological" answer and of how it has been interpreted so as to come into conflict with "negative" liberty. Or, perhaps, he assumes that the political interpretation has already been taken care of in the concept of "negative" liberty. For the moment, I shall set aside the "political" interpretation and follow Berlin's "psychological" account of "positive" liberty. In fact he develops several concepts of "positive" liberty, and, as we follow him, we shall find that there are others.

The basic formula of positive freedom is self-mastery. I feel free when I am conscious of directing myself by my own will, and feel unfree if and when I realise that my choices are after all made for me. I, as master of myself, distinguish a higher self, free and rational, which I truly am, over a lower self through which I can be enslaved. Such is a common pattern of thought.

Now, argues Berlin, that higher self can be identified as a "real self" as already knowing and choosing a real good rejected by the lower self.

Consequently, coercion by another of that lower self in order to adapt it to the higher self is no restriction of one's freedom. Indeed, someone may be too blinded by his lower self that he cannot even see what is really good for him, and so coercion for his own good would not really be coercion after all. These dialectical transitions from freedom to coercion and back again (freedom for the lower self is freedom to coerce the higher self; the right form of coercion of the lower self means freedom for the higher and real self) could, says Berlin, be applied to "negative" freedom, but have in fact occurred in respect of "positive" freedom. And there they have taken two directions: self-abnegation to attain independence, and self-realisation or total self-identification with a specific principle to attain the same end (FEOL, pp. 132–3).

In the Introduction (FEOL, pp. xliv–xlv) Berlin states that it was mostly the real and higher self which was seen as realised in institutions, traditions, and forms of life wider than the individual, and thus it was mostly the "positive" conception of freedom that lead to tyranny via the compulsion of men to fit the requirements of those institutions, traditions, and forms of life wherein they would find their real selves. Only infrequently, as by some early liberal, anarchist, and populist writers, was the "lower self" thought to be incarnated in institutions that enslave the real self. That was a way in which the "negative" concept could have led to the destruction of freedom. Presumably, that would have been via the forcible liberation of men from such institutions.

Now it strikes me that this is, in most cases, the "positive" concept and its threat seen from the other side. For what is Marxism but the claim that present institutions indeed, all institutions, all divisions of labour "alienate" mankind and engender forms of "false consciousness" in which we endorse our slavery, and the promise of liberation from them into a completely unstructured liberty to be and to be anything we wish, but together and collectively? Likewise Rousseau revolted against man's enslavement by institutions and traditions and sought only a vaguely structured liberty in the "general will." The straightforward anarchist seeks immediate "liberation" from institutions *now* and directly, though that often leads him to use force and terror in an effort "to smash the system" and to force men to be free of what oppresses them.

Another possibility, invoking the notion of what people really want, is the argument presented by von Mises that a liberal social order, of private property, the private control of capital and no government interference in the market, is in people's own interests, that what most people want is peace and prosperity and that is how to secure both (HA, pp. 154, 156). Von Mises holds that, if men do not see that Liberal policies and a free market are in their own long-term interests, then no more can be done. But it could be argued that, if necessary, people should be forced to accept such an order. As already suggested, limited democracy has proved quite compatible with dynamic market economies in several parts of the Far East, while in Russia Mr. Yeltsin's government has had to rule mostly by decree in order to replace the centralised command economy by private ownership and a free market.

Conversely, conceptions of "positive" freedom can be combined with limited government, and need not lead to the coercive realisation of a specific state of affairs. For example, Bosanquet argued that the implications of what a person actually wants require an organised and cooperative social life, maintained by public authority, a "real" will which he may not recognise and against which his "average" or "indolent" self may rebel, but which, as rational, we all recognise as imperative upon us and as what we are trying to become. Liberty, as the condition of being ourselves and therefore of becoming more what we have already become, is thus a structured, ordered, and social liberty.[8] But, he continued, the State cannot directly bring this about by its distinctive activity of the use of force which can secure only "external actions," those which are necessary whether or not performed from the motives which would give them "immediate value and durable certainty." Hence the State's activity is inherently limited to "hindering hindrances," although it can secure those material conditions of a better life, such as housing, wages, and the apparatus of education, which are between the hindering of hindrances and the "actual stimulation of mind and will."[9] Although Bosanquet represented and helped to bring about that shift in British Liberalism from a policy of removing existing restrictions to one of the active pursuit of specific goals, he nevertheless, by his doctrine of the limits of State action, reared a largely liberal politics upon Hegelian foundations, and he went in his recommendations for policy no further than Hayek.

We now return to Berlin's discussion and the specific forms of "positive" freedom which he distinguishes.

Self-abnegation

There are two ways of overcoming the frustration of unsatisfied desires: to act upon the world so as to make it meet or at least approximate to what one wishes; and to act upon oneself so as to reduce and finally to eliminate the frustrated desire. If you no longer want X, you will not be upset or disappointed at not obtaining it nor at losing it. The former is the "naive" or "natural" attitude of mankind. The latter is that of a world-weary sophistication, which has given up the hope of fulfilment and seeks only to avoid suffering. It is the perennial teaching of Hindu asceticisms and Buddhism, and, in Europe, appeared in the Hellenistic world as the common doctrine of Epicureans, Cynics, and Stoics. It is primarily apolitical, a retreat into the self, a withdrawal from attachment to the world so as not to be affected and disturbed. The sage wishes for privacy to cultivate his Epicurean garden, or to go into the forest to prepare himself for final release from the world. If freedom is, as Leibniz and Voltaire defined it, the power to do as one wants, or as Rousseau put it, desiring what one can perform and doing what one desires, then it can be increased either by acquiring more power or by wanting less.[10] Berlin comments that a tyrant, if he could manipulate his subjects into giving up their original desires and into embracing his own, would on these definitions, echoed by Mill, have liberated them. They would certainly feel free, as, we may add, do the citizens of *Brave New World*. Berlin considers that this retreat of the ascetic may be a source of integrity or inner strength but is hardly an increase of freedom and its logical conclusion is the contraction of the self to zero and thus to death. (That was precisely the conclusion drawn by Hindu asceticism, especially Advaita Vedantism, and Buddhism: what causes suffering is attachment to the world and, ultimately, to the illusion of one's own reality.) But, Berlin notes, one political conse-quence of detachment is collective autarky and isolationism. This, we shall see, is a motive for and corollary of collectivist policies, which nevertheless can be seen as a version of Liberalism, the desire that we together should be masters of our destiny and not subject to forces we cannot control.

Autonomous Self-legislation

With the way of self-abnegation Berlin associates self-mastery as the obeying of one's own autonomous laws, and neither one's passions nor another's laws. The political consequence of this conception is for-bearance from treating people as subject to causal forces, acting upon their "passions," which the rulers can manipulate, the method of Helvétius and Bentham, and, we may add, of *Brave New World*, B.F.

Skinner, and the whole intention behind what the Americans revealingly call "the behavioural sciences."

But Berlin does not consider other political consequences of autonomy, the assumption that there is no authoritative Law, Natural or Divine, or Way to which we must obediently respond and which defines the order of the soul within and of society and the state without. From that it is inferred that, individually or collectively, we are to formulate our own laws. For Kant, there is but one Law, the Categorical Imperative, the form of the rational will, out of which, he believed, Pure Practical Reason could spin, by pure logic alone, a content to fill it, and one that would coincide with the generally recognised duties of mankind. But today no one believes in the possibility of a Pure Practical Reason, and it is admitted that an arbitrary filling is needed for the Kantian form of "universalisability." This yields an individualist liberalism of scepticism: because there is no substantive moral law, we *should* respect each other's freedom to legislate his own. It also opens the way for the freedom of the creative or merely dominant minority to impose its arbitrarily chosen ideals upon the rest.

Freedom as Recognition of Necessity

Freedom as the following of one's reason can also take the form of recognition of necessity, but Berlin, somewhat misleadingly, discusses it under the heading of "self-realisation." Seeing that things cannot be otherwise, we rid ourselves of frustrating desires and irrational fears. We identify ourselves with the rational order of the world and society, and understand the parts we play in them. This conception of liberty can be accommodated by a view of the world as a process, a rational and necessary process whose laws of development and thus its future path can be understood, as, in their different ways, Hegel and Marx claimed.

Freedom as a Rational and Harmonious Coordination of Individual Wills

As well as the recognition of existing rationality, there is also, although Berlin does not explicitly distinguish it, the possibility of the deliberate creation of a rational society in which all individual wills could be coordinated and which all rational men would accept. If such a pattern can be formulated, then those who are now irrational, or like children are subrational, can be legitimately coerced so as to make them conform to it. Domination in itself is irrational, but not so the domination needed to educate men into understanding and accepting the rational society that has been made for them, a society that they really want.

A subform of this conception is the imposition of the ruler's own plan upon the ruled, whereby he can raise them to heights they would not have achieved by themselves. Berlin does not refer to Nietzsche, perhaps because Nietzsche's "overmen" explicitly create values which have no rational basis, whereas what Berlin has in mind is a pattern of life which is supposed to be a rational necessity and about which there can be no legitimate argument. The wise live it spontaneously, and the unwise are to be compelled to live it and to understand that later they will understand it.

The Dangers of Positive Liberty

This is what Berlin takes to be the general danger in "positive" freedom: the assumptions that there is one true solution to the problems of human life and society, that all men have one and only one real purpose of rational self-direction, that all rational aims necessarily fit into one harmonious pattern, which some can discern more clearly than others; that all conflict and tragedy arise from irrational divergences from that pattern and so, in principle, can be avoided; and that when men are made rational, they will be obey the rational laws of their own nature and so be wholly law-abiding and free. This set of assumptions generates a transition from individual self-responsibility and self-perfection to an authoritarian state ruled by an élite of Platonic guardians. For a government formed by such persons can reasonably claim that they cannot consult everyone, nor wait until everyone is ready, but must act upon their own knowledge of that rational pattern (FEOL, pp. 151–4).

But there is at least one other route from individual liberty to totalitarianism: the recognition that control of one's life is not possible so long as others confront me with their own choices and plans. Only by coming together to form a common plan can we be masters of our fate. Berlin, as noted, recognised this in the form of political autarky, the control by the state of all its relations with the outside world, especially trade, so as to maintain its independence and not to be subject to the chances and changes of international markets, as in the drive towards European Monetary Union.

Yet Berlin goes on to outline a somewhat similar desire for a collective liberty, that of the whole group, which arises from the desire for a recognised status. Not itself a form of either "negative" or "positive" liberty, the desire to be recognised can take the form of recognition as a member of a respected group. It is a desire for solidarity, common dependence and sacrifice, status and understanding, a desire for self-assertion by the group, rather than for individual self-assertion and recognition by others as expressed by Mill. One's own identity can be affirmed, even though the ruler may be a bully, when he is seen as "one of us" (FEOL, pp. 156–9).

Collective liberty, as the sovereignty of the people, can, as Mill said, be opposed to the liberty of individuals. The doctrine of absolute sovereignty is itself tyrannical. It is rights, the rights of individuals, and not power which is absolute for the classical liberalism of Constant, Mill, and Tocqueville. The difference between "negative" and "positive" liberty is that between those who want to curb power as such and those who want to have it for themselves (FEOL, pp. 163–6).

Berlin concludes with what he regards as the greatest threat to life and liberty, the belief that somewhere and somehow there is a final solution, a unity of all positive values. In contrast he argues that we must recognise the heterogeneity and plurality of ends, conflicts among them, and the need to choose. That makes freedom an end itself, one amongst others, and not a temporary means to something beyond itself. We must accept this plurality ends and the "negative" liberty which it entails and reject the temptation to constrain men and society into conformity with one ideal pattern (FEOL, pp. 167–71).

Yet, let us note, this is something of a paradox: freedom, as the highest political good, requires that we regard it as but one good among many. At the most it can be only a *primus inter pares*. I suggest that here we have a hint of the self-transcendence of liberty, of a way in which it points beyond itself. Here it points to other and more or less equal values. When, in Part 2, we examine Polanyi's account of the value of liberty, we shall see that the meaning and value of liberty lies in its use to serve other values. That is a more thoroughgoing self-transcendence.

As we have seen, Berlin in fact distinguishes more than one form of what he calls "positive" liberty, and I have suggested that there is at least one other way in which it can threaten "negative" liberty. And, indeed, at one point Berlin embarks upon another road which leads from classical liberalism to the radical and collectivist reconstruction of society. The negative side of freedom is freedom from interference. And, generally, we take interference to be deliberate interference via physical obstruction, the making of threats, or the imposition of legal restrictions or obligations with penalties for noncompliance. (Other forms of interference, such as poking and prying, are resented as being invasions of privacy, a specific freedom to have a time and a place apart from the public gaze.) Although at one point (FEOL, p. 122) Berlin states that coercion implies deliberate interference, yet, on the next page, he disavows that condition. The test of lack of freedom, he states, is:

> the part that I believe to be played by other human beings, directly or indirectly, with or without the intention of doing so, in preventing me from doing what I otherwise might do.

Consequently, social institutions and arrangements, whether deliberately designed to do so or not, can be properly said to restrict freedom if they could be so altered that they did not. Hence my inability to buy something, whereas others can, can be rightly taken to be a result of coercion if, according to a particular theory, my poverty or weakness is something that could be changed.

Now this immediately opens the door to the total transformation of society by a deliberately constructed plan, agreed to or imposed upon all, whereupon all their actions are to be coordinated. For if intentions are irrelevant, then everything we do, with or without the aid of a social or economic theory, can be shown to prevent some others from doing what they might otherwise do. Each of my actions incurs what economists call "opportunity costs": spending £1 on a bus fare means I don't have it to spend on anything else nor to save. But opportunity costs apply to others as well as to oneself. If John marries Jane, not only does he give up the chance of marrying Susan but he also prevents Bill from marrying Jane; if you outbid me at an auction, you prevent me from obtaining that article; if you get permission to build a house next to my cottage, you prevent me from enjoying the isolation I formerly enjoyed there; if my neighbours all leave so as not to interfere with me, then they deprive me of opportunities of doing things together with them, even though it be only to argue with and moan at them. We hardly need semi-Marxist theories that see all social arrangements as conspiracies and all events as deliberately intended,[11] in order to regard whatever happens as an infringement of liberty, *unless we all get together to plan what will happen to us.* The last is precisely what Karl Mannheim argued in his *Man and Society in an Age of Reconstruction*, though, it turns out and as we may have suspected, the plan will be drawn up by some and imposed upon the rest, and, indeed, the tastes and aspirations of the many will have to be standardised so that they can fit into the plan.

Berlin in the passage in question has fallen into the trap of identifying liberty with power or the ability to do as one wishes, and lack of
freedom with lack of power or the inability to do as one wishes and
thus also with obstacles of any sort to what one might wish to do. That
generates a desire for a total and radical liberty, to be and to do anything, which resents and is perpetually at war with human finitude. For
we can only do this or that. We therefore need to examine this further,
so as to be able to demarcate those forms of interference and prevention which classical liberalism rules out, and those which, reluctantly
perhaps, it must allow, unless liberty is not to be totally lost in a totalitarian state or a destruction of all institutions and society. That means
that we must further define the varying interpretations of liberty and
associated notions. Moreover, the "negative" liberty of classical, individualist liberalism can be defended in more than one way, and the
differing arguments for it can recoil upon it and perhaps undermine it.
Let us now see what these possibilities are.

Notes

1. As we shall see in chapter 4, Hayek also sharply separates these two questions,
    and therefore liberty or the lack of it from forms of government. He and Berlin
    are right so to do. For example, there has been more economic liberty in Hong
    Kong, Taiwan, South Korea, and Singapore than there was in Socialist Britain
    from 1945 to 1952. Yet the last was more democratic than any of the others have
    been until recently. (It seems as if Chinese people, and those culturally related
    to them, generally have less interest in taking part in government than in being
    free to get on with their own business, an attitude the reverse of that of Athenian
    democracy, according to Pericles' Funeral Oration.)
       One author who does join the two is G.G. Brenkert, (*Political Freedom*, ch.
    6), who extends it also to participation in the running of other important institu-
    tions such as companies and trades-unions. It seems to me that such persons
    assume a largely interventionist policy on the part of government, and therefore
    argue that the self-determination of the individual requires him to participate in
    the forming of collective policies. It is true that the complexities of modern life
    do require more governmental supervision, but this can be done by means of
    regulation, and not direction: i.e., the enactment of laws which lay down re-
    quirements for or restrictions upon what individuals, groups or corporations may
    do or the manner in which they do it, such as standards of safety and hygiene.
    People are then free to act as they themselves choose within such legal frame-
    works. It is quite possible that a régime with little popular participation may lay
    down only a minimum of such regulations, as appears to be the case in the states
    just mentioned, whereas ones where there is much more popular participation
    may both enact many more regulations, as is generally the case in Europe and
    with more threatened in the EEC under the Maastricht Treaty, and also run
    organisations themselves and compel persons to join them or use them, as with
    nationalised industries and state monopolies of power supply, schooling, health
    care, and so on. Given such intervention, it seems that "democratic control is the

only way of extending self-determination. Likewise with private organisations. If trades-unions are given privileges by government, then it may seem right to compel them to be more accountable to their members. That has been the policy of the recent Conservative administrations in Britain. But how an organisation runs itself is its own affair. The Government should have repealed the 1906 Trades Dispute Act, which set trades-unions above the law, and should have made illegal the closed shop, or, rather, let the courts apply to it the Common Law prohibition of restraints on trade. Then trades-unions really would have been voluntary associations like the rest and with no coercive powers. Similarly, if the system of interlocking large companies in Japan gives those who run them great power over their employees, the rest of the economy, and the country generally, then the simple answer would be so to amend company law as to detach them from each other and thus to remove or greatly to lessen that power.

2. These two aspects can be equated with two forms of rights: the positive aspect corresponds to what I shall call a "competence," a right to do something, and the negative to what I shall call an "immunity," a right not to be interfered with by others. Each of these types of right entails the other, as do the two aspects of liberty.

3. I am endorsing the triadic analysis given by G.C. MacCullum ("Negative and Positive Freedom," *Philosophical Review*, vol. 76, 1967): "X is (is not) free from Y to do (not do, become, not become) Z." This has been criticised by John Gray (*Liberalisms*, pp. 48–50) and G.G. Brenkert (*Political Freedom*, p. 148 and p. 255 n.15), who have restated Berlin's objection that one need not have an alternative state of affairs in mind, either consciously or unconsciously, when struggling against something regarded as a restriction. An individual or a group may simply carry on as before. One may simply want to get rid of one's chains. But something cannot just be an impediment, restriction, or obstacle: it can be such only in relation to something else which it thwarts or threatens to thwart. As for those who carry on as before, they did have an alternative state of affairs in mind: namely, to do what they were doing *entirely of their own volition*. They were free, both before and after, to do the particular things in question or live their preferred way of life. But previously they were told to do it or not to do anything else. What they have gained, and what they aimed at, was freedom from being told what to do. There was, we may note, always the possibility that they would be told not to do what they wanted to do or to do what they did not want to do. (This is the state of mind of rebellious adolescents and colonies: they may want to do what in fact they are told to do, and not want to do what in fact they are told not to do; but that, in their eyes, is irrelevant; for it is being told and being dependent which they resent.) Likewise the man who simply wants to be free of his chains: he may have no specific alternative in mind but he aims at being free to do as he pleases and that, in general, is what his chains prevent. Being subject to Queen's Regulations as a volunteer who does not regret having enlisted is not at all the same as being subject to them as a resentful conscript.

Gray also argues that this triadic analysis can hardly accommodate freedom as a social status, such as being a free man as opposed to a slave, which originally meant being entitled to take part in political life. But, while that may have been what people had in mind, freedom as a status still has its positive and negative aspects. A free man was free to take part in political life, whereas the slave (along with the resident foreigner) wasn't, and the free man was therefore legally *free* from interference with his exercise of that right, and any actual interference was illegal. Conversely, there were many things which slaves or serfs were not free to do and others which they could be forced to do.

Let us also note a meaning of "free," especially as a verb, which is wholly negative: namely, to be free or rid of anything that one dislikes or resents, without any implication that it is a restraint upon one's freedom. In this sense I can be free from disease or free my house from vermin. It is this sense that "liberation" movements usually have in mind, though they trade on the other meaning. They seek to free the people or some group from something which is disliked or resented, that is, to rid them of it. Such action in no way implies, as their subsequent policies usually prove, that the people or the group will be free in the other sense, free to live as they chose. They may indeed be free of their colonial masters but only to be even more subject to home-grown ones.

4. *Libralisms*, pp. 62–3.
5. *Second Treatise*, p. 57.
6. *The Metaphysics of Morals*, p. 56/231. All references to Kant's works will give first the page number of the relevant English translation and then that of the edition of the Royal Prussian Academy.
7. Ibid., p.56/230.
8. *The Philosophical Theory of the State*, pp. 111–2, 117–9.
9. Ibid., pp. 173–84.
10. See also B. de Jouvenel, *Sovereignty*, pp. 248–9.
11. For example, a favourite in sociology of education, "schools select pupils for jobs": one has a picture of a staff meeting at which they send Alan into the army, Betty to the bakery, Carol to be a cosmetics saleswoman, and so on. The whole subject is replete with that personification of "society" and social events which Hayek has rightly and frequently castigated.

2

Aspects and Notions of Liberty

The Dimensions of Liberty

Liberalism I have taken to be the belief that liberty is the most important political good. That clearly leaves open the possibilities of divergence as to what liberty is, why it is the most important good, what are the other political goods, and how liberty is related to them. As we have seen, some understandings of liberty can turn out to be destructive of what classical, individualist Liberals understand by liberty. I propose first to distinguish some of the "dimensions" of liberty or ways in which liberty can be defined and what it can be applied to: liberty to do what, from what, for whom, and how far. After that we shall consider some questions about the relation of liberty to desires, choice, power, and opportunities, and then to rights. That will enable us to give a more specific determination of what classical liberals have taken liberty to be and of how their understanding has differed from others.

Starting from Berlin's account, and from the criticisms made of it, I shall now elaborate certain dimensions of liberty. Different concepts of liberty stress some of these and ignore others, but they also differ as to the ways in which they relate liberty to other notions, as we shall see in the second and third sections of this chapter.

Positive and Negative Aspects

Berlin's distinction between "negative" and "positive" liberty breaks down. As we have seen, liberty is always a simultaneous freedom *from* and freedom *to*. Berlin's "negative" freedom is a general freedom for the individual, and his "positive" freedom is a more specific freedom for either the individual or the group. In respect to every discussion of liberty we need to ask, "Liberty *from* what, and liberty *to do* what?"

Either of these aspects may be largely implicit and taken for granted. Nevertheless each implies the other.

*Outer, Interpersonal, Civil, Social, and Political Liberty in
Contrast to Inner, Intrapersonal, and Psychological Liberty*

Berlin's distinction between "negative" and "positive" liberty, while wrongly severing these twin aspects of all forms of liberty, also conflates them, respectively, with "outer," interpersonal, civil, social and political liberty, and "inner," intrapersonal or psychological liberty. Those to whom he ascribes a "negative" concept are in fact concerned primarily with social and political liberties, liberties possessed or lacked by one person or group in relation to others, especially those between subjects and rulers or citizens and governments. Conversely, some of those to whom he imputes a "positive" concept, such as Bosanquet, start off with an intrapersonal concept, the freedom of the higher, real, true or rational self in relation to an lower, unreal, false or irrational self. Then they relate that liberty to social order, law, and government, and argue that particular forms of the latter can liberate the higher self from the lower one. Berlin argues that the application of such theories promotes "positive" liberty at the expense of "negative" liberty. That thesis is better stated in terms of the threat to interpersonal or social and political liberties posed by policies supposed to promote, by political means, specific interpretations of intrapersonal or psychological liberty.

These two forms or applications of liberty are not the same. That is the whole point of the Epicurean freedom of the "apathetic" slave and the slavery of his passion-ridden master. To say of either that he is *really* free or unfree is not just a matter of substituting one notion of liberty for another but of valuing it over the other. Epicurus, and Hellenistic sages of all four schools, valued psychological liberty—self-mastery—over civil liberty. Somewhat similarly, those Jews under the Nazi régime who tried to practice "inner emigration" substituted an inner detachment and emotional freedom from involvement in events around them for physical escape to civil freedom outside the Nazi domains. Disputes about which is *really* freedom are disputes about which is the more valuable, or which value and which has none at all.

Nor is it a mere equivocation to call both by the same term. There is a definite and clear analogy between them. Let us assume that the civil or interpersonal is the original meaning, and that the intrapersonal or psychological meaning is an extension of it. Now just as one of the clearest examples of lack of civil freedom is being a slave or a prisoner, in the former case being wholly or mostly under the will of another and not living according to one's own choice and in the latter physically prevented from doing nearly everything that one wants to do and could do, so also does the man who experiences a conflict within himself between what he really wants to do and impulses that counter it, aptly consider himself a slave to or prisoner of those impulses if and when they overcome him. He wants to be free to do what he really wants to do and so to be free from the impulses, habits, compulsions, and addictions that frustrate the former desires.

Let us note that there can be four basic relations between the theories of these two sets of liberties:

1. J.S. Mill, at the beginning of *On Liberty*, simply set aside inner liberty, as the freedom of the will, as an pseudo-problem and concerned himself solely with interpersonal liberties.

2. Others, principally concerned with interpersonal liberty, have recognised that the enjoyment of it depends upon temperance and self-mastery, and thus upon some form of intrapersonal liberty. As Edmund Burke said, "It is ordained in the eternal constitution of things that men of intemperate minds cannot be free. Their passions forge their fetters."[1] That is, the neighbours of such persons have no security in the enjoyment of their own liberty, and so such persons have to be forcibly restrained and have their social and political liberties restricted.

3. The theorists about whom Berlin is worried start with intrapersonal liberty and then propose social and governmental policies and institutions which they believe to promote it but which often turn out to be destructive of interpersonal liberty.

4. As did Epicurus and the Indian ascetics, one can focus upon intrapersonal liberty and be indifferent to interpersonal liberties. Indeed, for the Non-Dualist Vedantins, concern with the latter would be proof of one's enslavement to the illusion of the reality of the world and of oneself along with it.

We need also to note that Berlin's account deals with only one specific range of theories of intrapersonal liberty: namely, those that divide the self "vertically" into higher and lower, real and unreal, true and false, or rational and irrational selves. Such divisions are held to apply to all men, whether or not they recognise them in themselves. Indeed, a mark of slavery to the lower self is that complete domination by it which prevents any consciousness of the higher self. Yet, although the notion of intrapersonal liberty presupposes a division in the self, it does not presuppose the specific divisions which he mentions, but only a division of some sort or other between desires, purposes, and emotions which can conflict with and frustrate one another and a preference for one or one set against another. In such a state of mind, a person can feel himself bound or fettered by the impulses that conflict with those which he prefers. He says that he really wants to give up smoking, or not to upset other people, but he cannot resist the urge to have another cigarette or the impulse to utter a snide remark. At such times he feels himself to be a prisoner to the force of habit, a compulsion, or an addiction, from which he cannot free himself. In what he himself regards as his wiser moments, he dissociates himself from those impulses which he then regards as acting upon and within him, *making* him do things which he does not really want to do. But, unlike the theorists to whom Berlin refers, we may well think that every one suffers from intemperance and lack of complete self-mastery but not from the same sort of internal division. And, of course, there are those, like D.H. Lawrence in some of his moods, who favour the lower and instinctive or irrational self over the higher and rational one, "thinking with the blood" over "living from the head."

General and Specific Liberty

As Burke said, "abstract liberty, like other mere abstractions, is not to be found."[2] Liberty must be concrete and have a content, a liberty to do something or other and a liberty from something or other. The question, "Is X free or unfree?" has no meaning except in relation to a set of liberties or actions. But those liberties or actions may be more generally or more specifically conceived. In classical liberalism, both the positive and the negative aspects are *general*: a general liberty to live as we please, provided we respect that of others to live likewise, and a general liberty from interference with living as we please, both by private persons and, especially, by public authorities. Traditionalist thinkers, such as Burke, are wary of very general notions of liberty, which can become so wide as to make all laws and institutions restrictive of freedom. Consequently they think more in terms of specific liberties and especially inherited liberties. We shall see that Hayek, despite an explicit statement to the opposite effect, in fact defined the general notion of (interpersonal) liberty in terms of certain more specific ones.

The Extent of Liberty, Wider and Narrower Conceptions

The contrast between general and specific liberty is not identical with that between a wider and a narrower extent of liberty, though the latter has a definite bearing upon it. A conception of general liberty is necessarily wide in extent, but a set of more specific liberties could be equally as wide in total. Persons may be more or less free, more or less enslaved, with respect to both civil and intrapersonal liberties. There can be more or less things one is not allowed to do, or is required to do, by public authority, custom, public opinion, or one's master. And likewise the grip of an unwanted habit or desire can more or less intrusive, extensive, or tight. There can be no computation of the extent of liberty, but there are clear differences between in some cases at least, as, for example, between a régime of genuinely free trade and one of controls, licences, and a plethora of regulations.

Individual, Corporate, and Communal
Forms of Interpersonal Liberty

Groups and corporate bodies, like individuals, can be free or coerced, and more or less free, with regard to public authorities, other groups and associations, and individuals. In totalitarian states they are allowed to exist only as a function of the state and thus under the control of the Party. Similarly, the French National Assembly in 1792 abolished all corporations except business partnerships. Conversely, anarcho-syndicalist theories would replace the state by a collection of syndicates. And corporativist theories would build the state upon them, although in fact every attempt to enact corporativism has made them organs of the state or of the Party that runs it.

Because of its importance later on, let us note that Liberal theorists have tended to think in terms only of the individual, society, and the state. Indeed, they have sometimes assumed there to be some inherent contrast or even opposition between the individual, on the one side, and society and government, on the other, such that the latter represents a threat to the liberty of the former. As for groups and organisations within the wider society, liberalism has tended to treat them all as "associations," created deliberately by their founding members for specific purposes. Indeed, it has often interpreted the wider society itself as an association based upon a contract of association, "the social contract." Consequently, it has had little specific concern for groups, associations, and corporations and their specific liberties, for it has regarded them as a collection of freely contracting individuals and their liberties as a function of those of the individual. Again, it is point of contrast between conservative and liberal theorists that the former do pay specific attention to them, to what Burke called "the little platoon." And in chapter 9 we shall see that Polanyi explicitly valued them and their role in fostering the uses to which freedom should be put.

Likewise, the members of groups and associations can be more or less free in respect of the groups and associations to which they belong. Schools can have more or fewer rules; firms can make more or fewer demands upon their employees; parents can have more or less authority over their children, and exercise it more or less tyrannically; and trades-unions can operate genuine ballots or simply order and coerce their members into going on strike, and, yet worse, they can make membership of themselves compulsory for anyone wishing to purse the relevant trade or work for a relevant employer.

These groups and corporations within the wider society are diverse among themselves. We can distinguish the following principal types that have appeared so far:

1. Associations or corporate bodies, usually with definite constitutions or terms or articles of agreement, which come into being to further a more or less specific set of aims (e.g., business partnerships and corporations, professional associations, trades-unions, political parties, learned societies, local "clubs and societies," members of a class or profession who meet in an assembly or "estate" and make corporate representations to the government and have recognised corporate rights and responsibilities). These are bodies which paradigmatically the members *join* or *institute*, voluntarily or involuntarily. They are composed of individuals.

2. Families and groups of families (clans) in which the members share a common life. Each individual is born into one such grouping and by marriage or adoption may join or form or be taken into another.

3. Local, religious, or ethnic "communities," without formal terms of membership or constitutions, to which the individuals concerned spontaneously conceived themselves as belonging. Rather, they are composed of families, and, by being born into a family, one is born into the relevant "community." It may be possible to leave one and join another, either by entering or starting another family or individually. Purely local "communities," defined only by geographical location, can be left or joined simply by moving, provided that the locals cease to treat the newcomer as a stranger or "foreigner."

4. Classes, ranks, or "estates," differentiated by political, social, and economic functions, which may or may not also have a definite corporate character as in (1). As with "communities," they are composed of families, and individuals enter them by being born into their constituent families, though it may be possible to move from one to another. "Communities" are related "horizontally" and "classes" "vertically," though they can overlap, as when certain functions are confined or not open to a particular

class. The more movement there is among "communities" and classes, and the less that individuals remain in those into which they were born, then the less they are "communities" or classes.

Each of these has its own rights and liberties, either by custom or by statute. Conversely, custom and statute can restrict or deny these corporate or communal rights and liberties. Again custom and statute can open, compel, restrict or deny entry into associations, and movement among families, "communities" and classes.

Individual and Collective Liberty

Civil liberty is often understood as "allowing people to choose for themselves." But that formula is equivocal: it can mean either "allowing each to choose for himself" or "each to choose together with others." We can each go our own chosen way, and our choices may happen to coincide as when people follow a fashion, or we can act collectively and together choose what we shall all do, as when members of a sports club meet to decide what their team colours will be.

It is important to distinguish collective liberty from corporate and communal liberty. The group itself can enjoy corporate liberty from other groups and to manage itself, but within the group its affairs can be left to the separate choices and decisions of the individual members or be made for all. Two clear examples of the latter are monasteries and kibbutzim, where the individual members live a coordinated and mostly communal life. The pupils of a day school mostly go each his own way after lessons, but those in a boarding school stay and live together in groups.

Both classical liberalism and libertarianism have been concerned with individual liberty. But, as we have noted, there has been an influential collectivist interpretation of liberty as the central choice and coordination of what all are to do and which has motivated socialism and communism.

These, then, are some of the dimensions of liberty. It is a mistake to think and talk about liberty without specifying which of these dimensions or applications we have in mind. But what of liberty in the abstract, and its relation to other notions such as rights and power?

Liberty and Desires, Choices and Opportunities

Both interpersonal and intrapersonal liberty presuppose the existence of desires, wants and intentions. Being free is being free to do something, and a only a being with desires and intentions can do things. We experience lack of freedom when we are frustrated in doing what we want. It therefore seems appropriate to define liberty in terms of the ability to do as one wants. But any such definition raises the following problems:

1. The *ability* to do as one wants includes having (a) opportunities, (b) resources, (c) skill and knowledge, and (d) such natural virtues as self-mastery and patience, that is, intrapersonal liberty. Liberty could therefore be increased by increasing any of these. Consequently there arise demands and schemes for political action to provide people with *real* opportunities in the form of money, aid-in-kind, education, and training. Those demands and schemes, in the eyes of strict liberals (or libertarians), generate a slide into collectivism and the loss of real civil liberty because of the regulations, taxation, and bureaucracy needed to implement them, apart from any egalitarian aims to deny to any what cannot be enjoyed by all, that may accompany such schemes.[3]

2. Liberty, thus defined, may be increased in the converse way by limiting or erasing desires and intentions. If I do not want to do it, then I shall not feel unfree if I am unable to do it. The whole point of *Brave New World* is that the inhabitants are satisfied by the way their society is organised and at the end of *1984* Winston Smith is made to love Big Brother.

3. Thus there arises the problem of the contented slave who never has to do anything he does not want to do nor is barred from doing what he wants to do. If freedom is the absence of obstacles to doing what one wants, even to doing what one might want, then it follows that the contented slave is free. Likewise his options are not foreclosed because he does not wish to do anything other than what he is told or allowed to do. Nor is this a merely theoretical possibility. There are ex-convicts and ex-servicemen who cannot settle down to life outside prison or the army where they had their lives organised for them and did not have to worry about what to do. So is the reconvicted and happy prisoner freer in jail then when he was outside?

4. The slave, within this definition, can be said to be unfree only if we operate with a notion of a set of fundamental human desires, such that either the slave at some point in his life *would* want to do something which he cannot, or he is defectively human in not wanting to exercise his own will and power of choice but is perfectly content to have another choose everything for him. But that is to make liberty an essentially contestable concept, for different views of human nature will produce different lists of fundamental wants, and there are views, such as behaviourism, which dismiss the whole idea of choice and self-determination at the start.[4]

Similar problems arise when liberty is defined by reference to choices and opportunities, as for example, the nonrestriction of options. In such a case I leave you free when I do not restrict your options, and I make you unfree when I do restrict your choices or opportunities. But consider the many types of action, event, and outcome that the latter can mean:

1. I capture you and keep you locked up in a room.
2. Not knowing that you are in the shed, I lock it and walk away.
3. I deliberately park my car across your drive and so prevent you from driving out.
4. When parking my car, I fail to notice that I have left it across your drive.
5. At an auction, knowing that you want a particular lot to complete your collection, I outbid you just to spite you.
6. I am immediately before you in the queue and manage to buy the last ticket for the show.
7. By design or accident, I drive into you. You lose the use of your legs and become confined to a wheelchair.
8. John and Jeremy both love Jill; John has to go abroad; he returns to find that Jeremy has already married her.

In all eight examples, what the one person does restricts the options of the other. All are therefore examples of decreasing the latter's freedom, if freedom is the nonrestriction of options. Whatever we do in one way or another restricts the options and thus the freedom of each other. By buying the house next door, I prevent you from having someone else as your neighbor. By coming round frequently, even when I know you have company, asking questions and generally by poking and prying, I prevent you from living privately and unobserved. By keeping to myself and leaving you alone, I prevent you from having a chatty and friendly neighbour. Again, I can, by indirect means, prevent you from doing something and so restrict our options. As well as locking you in your room, I can give you false information about the time of auction, so that you turn up too late to bid for the lot you want.[5]

I suggest that this is either a useless or a Gnostic notion of freedom. On the one hand, everything we do, including leaving others alone, can then be said to restrict their freedom in one way or another, and so it cannot be used to discriminate between actions and policies that do restrict freedom and those that do not. On the other, such a notion makes all finite existence, all situations, restrictive of freedom, which therefore can be found only in an escape from finitude and the world, to reabsorption in the One Light whence we have fallen, according to the Gnostic mythology.

Furthermore, such interpretations of liberty lead once again to the idea of a collective plan that will coordinate our wishes and choices, and so minimise our mutual obstructions and deprivations of each other's liberty. In turn that leads into totalitarian democracy and Karl Mannheim's "planning for freedom."

We also need to note that the notion of "a choice" is ambiguous, for it can refer either to the agent's *acts of choosing*, the choices that he makes or perhaps also to his range of preferences, or to *that which he chooses or is available for him to choose*, the possibilities and opportunities of his situation. Choice, as the act of choosing, presupposes:

1. On the side of the situation, a range of opportunities or possibilities, that is, real and not merely notional possibilities, lines of action that the agent could succeed in beginning. Of course, even there is no such range but only one thing that can be done, a menu that is *table d'hôte* and not *à la carte*, there is always the higher level option of "Hobson's choice": "take it or leave it" and "like it or lump it."
2. On the side of the chooser, knowledge of those possibilities (you can't choose what you have no idea of), a set of preferences (you cannot choose if you are indifferent to all, including the higher level option of any one of them or none at all, the neglect of which led to the fallacy of Buriden's ass), and, to execute that choice in many cases, the intrapersonal liberty given by the natural virtues of patience, resolution, and persistence.

It follows that liberty can be extended, as before, by extending either or both of the individual's or group's range of real possibilities and its knowledge of them, preferences in relation to them, and natural virtues. But equally liberty can be extended, also as before, by contracting its preferences to match the options available. Thus Karl Mannheim, in *Man and Society in an Age of Reconstruction*, proposed that consumer products be standardised and with them consumers' tastes and desires. If my preferences do not outrun the possibilities before me, I shall not feel frustrated. It could be easier to reduce people's wants than to formulate a plan that would result in the maximal satisfaction of their existing ones.

The theoretical equivalent of the actual reduction of desires is to limit the ones that are to be allowed to count, and so only those of them which are involved in the options opened up or restricted. It is restriction of possibilities for fulfilling the central set of human desires that will count as deprivation of liberty. But, whether or not we can draw up such a list, it still means that the second, seventh, and probably the eighth cases given above are ones of depriving another of his liberty. And our spontaneous actions will still close off some options for others in respect of those fundamental desires. In the nineteenth century, the rise and decline of the fashion for wearing ostrich feathers meant boom and then bust for ostrich farmers in South Africa, and in turn that meant a great expansion and then contraction of their opportunities for fulfilling at least some of their important desires, unless our notions of central desires are altogether unworldly. In consequence, the road to "planning for liberty," as advocated by Mannheim, beckons once more. Moreover, what classical liberals, and libertarians, value is the general liberty to live as we please, which includes the liberty to do trivial things. And many people will put up with regulation in respect of fulfilling some of what they themselves take to be their important desires, as with rationing in times of scarcity and requisitioning of property in emergencies, yet would resent other people poking and prying into less important matters which they regard as no one else's business precisely because they are less important.

When the idea of liberty is directly construed in terms of opportunities, choices, options, and their nonrestriction, then the converse idea of restriction or deprivation of liberty inevitably expands to cover everything that we do, or forbear from doing, towards others, as we can see from the list of eight examples given above. It is impossible to mark off any actions as definitely restricting another's freedom from other actions which definitely do not.

Five Notions of Liberty

Brenkert, in his *Political Freedom*, outlines three distinct ideas of liberty—conservative, liberal, and radical—and then his own of liberty as empowerment. I propose to follow his typology, with one addition and two changes of nomenclature. This revised typology will enable us to set off classical liberalism from other accounts of liberty, and to see how it shades off, on the one side, to the conservative, and, on the other, to the libertarian or radically individualist. Indeed, it is my argument that it must transform itself into the former if it is not to destroy itself by becoming the latter or opening the way to radical collectivism, and that we see this happening in Hayek and Polanyi.

Conservative Liberty

Brenkert, with reference to Burke, Tocqueville, Oakeshott, and others, defines Conservative freedom as "those traditional rights and liberties by which power is dispersed in ways such that it is not exercise arbitrarily by members of society."[6] As we shall see, Hayek would endorse the latter part of this definition of freedom, and would accept that political freedom does rest on tradition and custom. But Conservative liberty differs from Liberal liberty in not being "negative," for it does not simply spell out an area within which one person is free from interference by others nor is it only a limit on coercion and a freedom from power. It is a freedom of reciprocal rights and obligations, and of balancing powers. Moreover, it cannot be abstractly defined but is known only in the actual and prescriptive rights and duties carried by tradition and custom. It will therefore vary from nation to nation.[7] It is that set of practical arrangements which in fact make it possible for a given society to live freely.

To this characterisation I would add a further element: it is also the freedom, a primarily communal freedom, to live according to a traditional way of life, which may cut across some individual freedoms. I would also repeat that Conservative freedom is a matter more of sets of concrete and specific liberties than an abstract and very general freedom.

Brenkert objects that this notion cannot offer a theoretical means for distinguishing those customs and traditions which do form the basis of political freedom, and that it presupposes a common and shared history, and common views about natural moral laws, which are in doubt today. Since this is the notion of liberty which I propose to endorse as the only viable one, I shall now answer these objections by admitting them. Firstly, as in the rest of human life there is no algorithm or checklist for mechanically determining what is in fact the case. It is always a matter of informed judgement in the concrete situation. Indeed, as Hayek argues (LLL, vol. 1, p. 100 n.7), it may be the case that the people concerned do not know to which particular tradition or traditions they owe their liberty. As I shall argue in chapter 4, liberty cannot be adequately defined in the abstract but is known tacitly from within and from living it, that it is always a concrete liberty or set of liberties, and so inevitably varies from place to place and time to time. This feature is, rather, a merit of the conservative conception. And as for the latter objection, that is indeed the case, as will be argued in chapters 12 and 13. If such conditions are not present today, or not sufficiently present, then liberty is imperilled and we need to recognise the danger.

Liberal Freedom

I shall pass over this notion for it is what we are concerned with all along and for which, in its classical form, a definition has already been given, except to add that it seeks an abstract definition of freedom and wishes to see attained a general freedom to live as one pleases while respecting the rights of others to do the same. I shall also call attention to two recent developments of it, which Brenkert mentions and which are not to found in the authors we are studying: namely, on the one hand, that freedom, as the reduction of constraints, leads to an enlargement of the notion of constraint and thus, on the one hand, makes the world a "terribly threatening place, ever seeking to impose itself upon us" (a paranoia which I have observed in several students, especially those who have been subjected to sociology); whereas, on the other, there arises a heightened sensitivity that increasingly distances people from each other and inhibits their words and deeds lest they interfere with and intrude upon each other, so that "only within a diminishing private realm, behind a fence that must be constantly enlarged, can one enjoy perfect freedom."[8] One only has to look at the constraints imposed by "political correctness" in America to see how people can become trapped within severe bounds lest they offend by their speech the members of an increasing number of hypersensitive "communities." This development is a self-defeating form of liberty.

Libertarian or Individualist Radical Freedom

In addition to Brenkert's typology, I wish to distinguish what I shall call libertarian freedom or the individualist form of radical freedom. By this I mean that extension of classical liberalism which results in a suspicion of or antipathy to most or even all forms of custom, tradition, law, and government, and wants law and government radically remodelled and reduced to a minimum so as to liberate the individual from them so that he may define himself and his life for and by himself. It is typified by Tom Paine, one side of Bentham, and contemporary libertarian movements in America, where its more moderate and most sophisticated expression is R. Nozick's *Anarchy, State and Utopia.*

It is my general argument that libertarian freedom is self-destructive and that, to avoid collapsing into it, classical liberalism must return to a conservative notion of freedom, and that in fact Hayek and Polanyi set out in that direction. We shall examine some of the salient features of libertarianism in chapter 3, specifically the notion of natural rights.

Collectivist Radical Freedom

What Brenkert calls "radical freedom" I prefer further to specify as *collectivist radical freedom,* or *collectivist freedom.* Like libertarianism, it seeks liberation from the past and the present order of things so that people may define themselves and their lives.[9] But, unlike libertarianism, it seeks to do this collectively: we shall together define and decide what we together are to be and to do. For, correctly, it sees that if individuals are liberated each to go his own way, then they will arbitrarily set limits to what others can be and do, as we have noted above in "Liberty and Desires, Choices and Opportunities." Only a collective decision to formulate a collective way of life can provide for self-definition and self-determination of men living together. It is therefore more radical than libertarianism, and proximately seeks greater or total centralisation and collectivism in order to attain ultimate liberty. Brenkert exemplifies it with reference to Marx, Engels, Lenin, and Marcuse. But Rousseau originated it and the Jacobins were the first to try to practise it.

The desire wholly to determine oneself, and therefore the community, in a collectively determined plan for a collective life, results politically either in autarky, "socialism in one country in isolation," or a collectivist world government. But beyond that, as already indicated, it could only be satisfied by a Gnostic flight from the world, differentiation, determination, and finitude, to the merging of all back into the One.[10]

Welfarist Freedom

This is exemplified by Brenkert's own model of liberty as empowerment, which also includes political involvement, not only in the activities of public authority but also in other important institutions such as commercial organisations and trades-unions, and the provision of the conditions, means, and opportunities needed for individuals effectively to exercise their right to political self-determination, which means a conjoint self-determination, which is cooperative rather than collective.[11] Brenkert thus follows an increasingly frequent tendency to define freedom in terms of one or more of choices, powers, and opportunities. His version is more moderate than some and he recognises some of its difficulties. For convenience I shall call this *welfarist freedom*, for it entails an extensive system of benefits, in cash or kind, to provide people with the means and powers needed for them to be able to choose and to carry out their choices. One problem that Brenkert does not address is that the more there are of these provisions, the less people have of their own money to spend as they wish. People end up paying high proportions of their income, either overtly via direct and indirect taxation or covertly via inflation, only to receive it back, less that needed to support the bureaucracy needed to make all these transfers. There just aren't enough "rich" who can be taxed to support or "enable" the "poor." Freedom to spend one's own money in one's own way is an important part of freedom for most people. Hence if they vote for welfarist policies, they also tend to vote against the taxes needed to pay for them. The result is a chronic deficit and inflation as the only way of reducing it. These policies are favoured by those in America who now call themselves "liberals" (not "libertarians") and by the Labour and Liberal Democrat parties in Britain, often also with egalitarian ambitions.

We shall now turn, to the problems with which Hayek grapples in trying abstractly to define the general liberty that classical liberalism cherishes. Curiously, Hayek involves himself at one point in the same difficulties as are entailed by the welfarist freedom of empowerment, for both seek abstract definitions of liberty. In the same chapter we shall note the fundamental difficulty of libertarian freedom. That will lead us, in chapter 4, to look, with Burke and Polanyi, to an essentially conservative notion of freedom as the answer to these problems of definition.

Notes

1. *Letter to a Member of the National Assembly*, vol. 6, p. 64.
2. *Speech on Conciliation with America* (I do not have the Rivington reference for this: it can be found in *Speeches and Letters on American Affairs*, p. 91).
3. We shall glance at one example in "Welfarist Freedom" below.
4. See further, J. Gray, *Liberalisms*, ch. 5, and below, ch. 4 §§1 and 2.
5. For an example of this notion of freedom, see G.A. Cohen, "Capitalism, Freedom and the Proletariat" in *The Idea of Freedom*, edited by A. Ryan. Cohen thinks that this mutual frustration of freedom as doing what one likes occurs only with private property and under capitalism. But it must occur in all finite situations: see, on Cohen, J. Gray, *Post-Liberalism*, ch. 11.
6. *Political Freedom*, p. 32.
7. See the quotation on p. 34 above (n. 2). Burke continues: "Liberty inheres in some sensible object; and every nation has formed to itself some favourite point, which by way of eminence becomes the criterion of their happiness." His particular point is the English, and hence American, objection to taxation without consent and representation.
8. *Political Freedom*, p. 80.
9. An element common to both forms, but often more accentuated in the collectivist one, is hostility to roles. For they limit the self and are unchosen templates into which society makes us fit. Ultimately this hostility is the Gnostic desire to escape from determinateness and finitude, being this and not that. The self is, in Sartre's words, a "nothingness" or "fold in being," in which existence precedes essence, and which in the world is overladen and "objectified" by the roles which it can never be but can only play at, although in bad faith it may persuade itself that it is them. (On the Gnostic elements in Heidegger's *Sein und Zeit* and Sartre's

L'Être et le néant, see the Appendix to Hans Jonas's *The Gnostic Religion*.) This Gnostic resentment of differentiation can be seen in the contemporary demand, not only to decide for oneself what roles one is to fulfil, to make them all "achieved" and not "ascribed," but also to decide, or to negotiate with one's counterparts, what the role is to consist of.

An additional element, also Gnostic in origin, is the belief that one either has become divine and need no longer be burdened by a conscience (see the account of some of the Brethren of the Free Spirit in N. Cohn's *The Pursuit of the Millennium,* chs. 8 and 9, and, in the Appendix, of the Ranters of the seventeenth century) or is an amoral superman, "beyond good and evil," and superior to the "herd" and its laws. St. Paul, in his Epistle to the Galatians, dealt with both attitudes. In effect, the latter was the attitude of Keynes and the Bloomsbury Group: see Hayek, LLL, vol. 1, pp. 25–6, 162.

As Hayek again points out (FC, p. 51), the mediaeval Gnostics (the Bogomils and the Cathars) also attacked property and the family upon which liberty rests. For details see, S. Runciman, *The Mediaeval Manichee.*

10. See my "Flew, Marx and Gnosticism," *Philosophy* vol. 68, no. 263, Jan. 1993. It is this Gnostic element, rejecting everything which limits the individual and makes him *this* rather than *that*—roles, relationships, the accidents of time and place of birth and upbringing, customs, traditions, the plans and actions of others, which principally accounts for the destructivism of radical libertarians. For, not only are their positive plans bound to fail and to bring disappointment, but they are primarily orientated to destroying whatever exists just because of its finite nature. Secular Gnosticism has no way of escape from the world, and so its hatred of the world can be expressed only in "smashing the system." Burke (*Reflections, Works*, vol. 5, p. 303) quotes Rabaud de St. Etienne as saying in the National Assembly: "Toutes les établissements en France courennent le malheur du peuple: pour le rendre heureux il faut le renouveler; changer ses idées; changer ses loix; changer ses moeurs;…changer les hommes; changer les choses; changer les mots…tout détruire, oui, tout détruire, puis-que tout est à recréer."

11. *Political Freedom*, chs 5–7.

3

Hayek and Liberty under Law

Freedom as the Absence of Coercion and Interference

A weakness in classical liberalism, and in more ways than one, is its "negative" notion of liberty as freedom from coercion and interference. Today that has become liberty as the nonrestriction of options. But such a notion can eliminate liberty altogether, for what action or abstention from action cannot be construed, in one way or another, as restricting another's options? Even going away leaving him to himself prevents him doing things with you.

Let us consider again the list, in chapter 2, of eight actions or events which foreclose someone's options. Which of those eight actions can properly be described as restricting another's freedom?

My answer is, firstly, that only the first can count as a restriction of a person's *general* liberty, unless the ideas of freedom and its restriction are to become so wide as to be either useless or Gnostic. But a policy of performing actions like the third can amount in time to restriction of another's general freedom, although no single action in such a series does. A gang of toughs can so terrorise a block of flats or a street that those who live there dare not venture out and in effect are made prisoners in their own homes.

Secondly, a single action is likely not to deprive someone of his liberty in general but to thwart his exercise of a specific liberty or competence. In the third of our eight examples, parking a car across someone's drive prevents him from exercising his right of way from his drive onto the road. This is the point of distinguishing specific liberties from general liberty. It is misleading to describe such an act as "restricting his liberty," because virtually everything we do can do that in one way or another. The question is, Does it thwart the exercise of a specific liberty or competence, and how important is it? After all, to repair the front of a house that opens directly onto the street, one has to block people's right of way along the pavement or even the road as well. Apart from imprisonment and enslavement, and what we may call "constructive" forms of them, as in the example in the previous paragraph, what matters is not general liberty but specific liberties and how the exercise of one can block or limit the exercise of another, and the practical provisions that can be made to minimise conflict or to provide compensation. It is precisely because people talk about liberty in general that they land themselves with these puzzles as to whether, as the intended or unintended result of another's single action, someone can be said to have been deprived of his liberty.

And, finally, as was suggested in chapter 2, it does not matter, in "constructive" imprisonment, just at what point in the series their freedom is really restricted, for the acts in question are ones which, simply because they are hostile, ought to be prohibited, by criminal law or court injunction, at least after a while if not in the first instance. The same applies to a policy of annoying, interfering with, or frustrating people in other ways, and sometimes to single actions of those types. There is no need to construe them as restrictions on freedom in order to assert that they should not be performed and are misuses of one's own freedom. They are to be regarded as morally wrong, and perhaps be made crimes or torts, on their own account. The same applies to acts of negligence. One paralysed as a result of another's careless driving has a claim for damages because of his injury, and we do not need to say that he has been made "unfree" in order to acknowledge and to provide for his claim. Furthermore, if all hostile acts are to be made crimes or torts *only because* they restrict liberty, then the kidnapper who beats his victim would not commit an offence additional to the act of kidnapping.

This current tendency to try to construe all mischievous actions as infringements of freedom is, curiously, set forth as a criticism of and alternative to the "negative" liberty of classical liberalism yet is, in effect, derived from it. For what classical liberalism maintains is that we should be free to act as we please so long as we do not infringe the similar freedom of others. Consequently, any action or policy which is already regarded as objectionable and impermissible has to be interpreted as an infringement of the victim's liberty. But to extend the notions of liberty and its restriction to such acts usually means that many other actions would have to be prohibited for the same or similar reasons, so that in the end no one can do anything lest he restrict the liberty of some other. Liberty as thus understood ends up as no liberty at all when each one of us becomes confined in an ever-narrowing enclosure. Or, because it applies to all actions in one way or another, the idea of restricting another's freedom is rendered useless in this world. Furthermore, we are prevented from recognising how provision for other undesirable events and conditions can, sooner or later, eat into people's liberty to dispose of their own money. Perhaps that is a cost we ought to incur. The point is that we should be clear that we are going to incur it. And we should recognise other undesirable actions for what they are without having to twist them into infringements of freedom.

Even Hayek, in seeking to define liberty as freedom from coercion, makes that mistake precisely because he tries to give a definition of liberty in the abstract and of a general liberty at that. But that is just what classical liberalism is committed to, because it makes liberty the prime political good and, conversely, infringement of liberty the prime political evil. We shall now see how Hayek lands himself in this difficulty.

Hayek's fullest account of the nature of liberty is in *The Constitution of Liberty*. In *Law, Liberty and Legislation*, for example, he refers back to that account, except to modify the basic formula to "the state in which each can use his own knowledge for his own purposes," which, he thinks, is preferable to Adam Smith's "to pursue his own interest in his own way" which has egoistic overtones (LLL vol. 1, pp. 55–6; vol. 2, p. 153 n.7).

Setting aside as dangerous equivocations those equations of liberty with ability, power, and available options, and marking off individual (i.e., interpersonal) freedom from both inner freedom and participation in government or the selection of those who govern, Hayek recalls the earliest meaning of freedom, that of the free man as opposed to the slave: namely, "independence of the arbitrary will of another." Freedom, therefore, is an *interpersonal* affair, and the only infringement on it is coercion by men (CL, p. 12). It is also a "negative" idea, like peace, security, and quiet. It connotes the absence of coercion by other men. That can be seen in what a slave in Greece received upon being freed: legal status as a member of the *polis*, immunity from arbitrary arrest, the right to work at whatever he chose, and the right to move wherever he chose. With the right to own property, which the slave already had in practice, those rights are what the individual needs in order to be secure against coercion, and what classical liberalism has always advocated. The right to vote, "inner freedom," luxury, and power over other men or nature, will not alter a slave's dependence upon the arbitrary will of his master or an aparatchik's dependence on his superiors. But, with the four rights already listed, he cannot be coerced by others (CL, pp. 19–20).

This seems refreshingly clear after all the intricacies which we have so far investigated in defining liberty, problems which Berlin did not wholly escape. Interpersonal liberty is, then, the absence of coercion, "the state in which a man is not subject to coercion by the arbitrary will of another" (CL, p. 11). It remains further to clarify what coercion is and is not. Hayek's preliminary definition of that is:

> such control of the environment or circumstances of a person that, in order to avoid a greater evil, he is forced to act not according to a coherent plan of his own but to serve the ends of another. (CL, pp. 20–1)

The problem is that, later on, Hayek has to admit that coercion is as troublesome as liberty for the same reason, namely, the illegitimate and obfuscating extension of the idea. Hayek then gives a fuller definition of coercion (CL, pp. 133–4) which can be summarised as follows:

1. Coercion is a personal act, of one person towards another, and not an effect of physical circumstances, which compel us, and with which the former are confused.
2. Coercion is arranging matters so that the other person's least painful option is that which one wants him to take.
3. It therefore issues in personal acts, of choice, decision and execution, on the part of the one coerced. Forcibly to move his body or a part of it against his will, is as bad as coercion but is not itself coercion.
4. Coercion "implies both the threat of inflicting harm and the intention thereby to bring about certain conduct." Consequently, it does not include all ways of influencing another, nor even all ways of threatening harm in order to get him to change his intentions, for example, blocking his path or driving him away by making unpleasant noises.
5. The coerced person uses his knowledge and intelligence but is deprived of the possibility of using them for his own purposes and instead uses them for those of the one who coerces him. His action does not fit into any wider plan or project of his own but into that of the other.

This account enables Hayek to mark off as not coercive what others ask us to do in exchange for the benefits we wish to have from them, save where someone does have a monopoly of something essential to life, such as the owner of the only spring in an oasis or of all the opportunities of employment in a town, and then makes burdensome demands as a condition of conferring that benefit. Examples of authentic coercion are: enforced labour, extortion of protection money, blackmail by the threat to publish an evil secret, and threats by the state to inflict punishment and to use force to secure obedience (CL, p. 137). But the issue, Hayek admits, is rendered less clear by the differences among individuals in respect of their strength of will. Because a threat that will cow one person may provoke only scorn in another, it would seem to follow that what counts as coercion depends upon the psychology, the inner freedom of self-mastery, of the intended victim. It would in turn follow that what counts as restriction or deprivation of liberty depends upon the same condition, and that therefore no clear and general rules about liberty could be formulated. Hayek circumvents this consequence by appealing to the notion of the average person. Coercion usually takes the form of a threat of bodily harm to him or his dear ones or of damage to a valued possession. But, he continues, it could also consist of placing many but minor obstacles about him or inflicting a continuous serious of petty irritations (as we mentioned above). All close associations of persons provide opportunities for coercion, which, however law and public authority can hardly prevent. It is therefore only the more severe rather than the milder forms of coercion that are to count, that we should try to prevent and the absence of which constitutes liberty (CL, pp. 138–9).

One consequence of Hayek's account is that coercion and therefore liberty are to some extent relativised despite his intentions. For the average person in one society is not the same as the average person in another society. This is not to deny some constants that constitute a common humanity, but only to deny that they take the same specific forms. For example, the Chinese and Japanese are much more sensitive to shame and "losing face" than are Europeans, and, as a result, can be more easily coerced by threats of being shown up, put down or worsted in public. Generally, people feel less oppressed by hardships and restrictions which they have grown up with and are accustomed to than new ones. The same actions, laws, and institutions are unlikely to be felt as equally oppressive by members of different societies. One often remarked difference between the English and the French is that the former will put up with and pay taxes but will not tolerate conscription in peace-time, whereas the latter have the reverse attitudes.

Apart from that, Hayek's account of coercion neither covers all cases of definite coercion nor all cases of deprivation of liberty. Let us consider three examples:

1. A prisoner who is chained to a wall, bench, or post which he is never allowed to leave, and indeed who may be so chained and manacled that he cannot move his arms or legs at all. He surely is the most coerced and unfree of all persons. But no threats at all are used upon him, nor is he

made to do anything. Rather, he is prevented from doing anything except merely to think and to flex his muscles. As it stands, Hayek's definition of coercion does not cover this condition.

2. A trusted convict in an open prison, who has considerable freedom of movement around the prison, periods of leave from prison, and a fair chance of being able to escape should he try. Again, the point is that he is prevented from doing many things rather than being made to do something specific. With him we may contrast the condition of the slave, whether physically restrained like the galley-slave or not, who is deprived of his freedom in order to work. (We presume that, unlike our first prisoner, what keeps the second one in the open prison is not so much the physical means—walls, fences, locks—as the threat of coercion, of being pursued, caught, and physically forced back if necessary. He therefore fits that part of Hayek's definition.)

3. But what about the prisoner who has no intention of escaping, because he accepts the justice of his conviction and punishment, or thinks that he ought not to resist them even though he is innocent, or prefers the order and routine of prison where he does not have the burden of planning his own life? In none of these cases is such a person *coerced* in any way into staying in prison: no physical means nor any threats are necessary. It follows that, on Hayek's account, he is not deprived of his liberty. The old lag who offends again in order to return to prison is not *deprived* of his liberty, but he is no longer free. He wishes not to be free and deliberately seeks re-incarceration.

4. Consequently, coercion is one thing and loss of liberty another. For liberty can be voluntarily surrendered without coercion and coercion can be used *in order to* deprive someone of his liberty. The former possibility Hayek has already acknowledged with the example of someone who freely but irrevocably enters the Foreign Legion for a long period (CL, p. 14). Of course, the Foreign Legion will use coercion, if necessary, to keep him there or to bring him back if he deserts. But, in the same place, Hayek cites also the example of the Jesuit who lives up to the ideals of his order and regards himself, in the words of the Founder, as "a corpse which has neither intelligence [n]or will." In such a case the use of coercion is excluded *ex hypothesi*. We may also mention the example of the contented slave, discussed by Gray and others with reference to the equation of liberty with nonrestriction of options.[1] The actual and likely desires of such a slave are not frustrated, for he is quite content with his lot and to do his master's bidding. It follows that he is free and not unfree. Nor can we dismiss this as a merely theoretical or abnormal case, for, surely, among domestic slaves there must have been some who were as contented with their lot as some free people who suffered destitution. We may also recall St. Paul's advice to Christian slaves to accept their lot.[2] Some, we may presume, did so. Again, Hayek half acknowledges this possibility when he says that no degree of luxury and comfort, nor of power over other men, will make a slave any less dependent on the arbitrary will of his master (CL, p. 20). The question is, Is the slave who does not mind being

so dependent, and so who does not need to be *coerced* into remaining in that state, therefore free after all?

5. Finally, let us reconsider one of the examples of genuine coercion, namely, being blackmailed. Of course, blackmail can be resisted, as by the Duke of Wellington who replied, "Publish and be damned." It is success in blackmail, or the intention of the blackmailer, that matters. It is coercion or an attempt to coerce; it is an evil; but will it, in and by itself, bring about a loss of liberty if it is successful? What it usually brings about is a loss of money. One can be blackmailed into loss of liberty, as for example into confessing a crime that one has not committed and being sent to prison for it. But is being a victim of blackmail always and inherently being deprived of one's liberty? It seems to me to be a forced and artificial claim that it is.

Those last remarks reveal that there is after all some similarity between Hayek's attempt to define liberty in terms of coercion and definitions in terms of fulfilment of desires and nonrestriction of opportunities, with the same result of trying to make other evils or undesirable events fit the schema of liberty and loss of liberty, in this case liberty and coercion. The significant difference is that, by using the notion of "coercion," Hayek limits the frustrations that are to count to (a) actions of persons, which (b) are deliberately aimed at such frustration, which (c) are backed up by force or threats of some kind, and which (d) are aimed at getting the victim to do something which the one who coerces him wants him to do. But these restrictions are sufficient neither to demarcate the loss of interpersonal liberty nor the use of coercion.

Hayek also considers an equal opposite of liberty, namely, oppression, a state of continuous acts of coercion (CL, p. 135). Coercion can be a single act, and, as such, is not necessarily a deprivation of liberty. But oppression, as a series of such acts, is much more likely to be. This fits our examples of the deliberate blocking of someone's drive and of a series of actions by a gang of toughs which in effect imprisons people in their own homes. Yet, if we forget about general liberty and think about specific liberties, we can say that a single act can block the exercise of a specific liberty, such as that to use a given right of way.

Nevertheless there is still a difference between oppression and freedom. Consider some of the other examples that Hayek gives: the oppression that can be exercised towards an employee whom he dislikes by a manager in a town dependent on one principal employer, by the captain of a ship, by the employer of domestic servants (especially when there was little alternative employment and servants needed good references from their present employers in order to be employed in another household), by any monopolist of something essential to life, and by a morose husband or nagging wife. These forms of oppression consist in a series of deliberately inflicted annoyances, insults, obstacles, and inconveniences. They do not constitute deprivation of liberty, though the victims dearly wish to be free or rid of them. In one way or another the victims have few other choices, and so are open to oppression. The sailors on the *Bounty* were constrained both by their physical confinement to the ship and by the severe penalties against mutiny enacted in the Articles of War; the miner and the servant have few other ways to earn a living; the victims of other monopolists have nowhere else to go to obtain what they need; and law, conscience, or psychological subservience, keeps the oppressed spouse tied to his or her bane. Hayek states that usually all that the law can do in cases like the last is to make the association a voluntary one in the first place. And that is not possible with respect to children: take them away from their parents, and they can be even more oppressed in the institutions into which they are put, as recent cases in England have all too tragically proved. By definition, the relation of children to parents, guardians, or anyone else who may be responsible for them, is not a voluntary one. The oppressed persons in Hayek's example are confined more by circumstances than by human will, and it is this which makes it difficult or impossible to escape from their oppressors. Certainly, except for the sailors until their term of service has expired, they are all legally free. Hayek, it seems, is himself extending the notion of liberty too far.

As I have already stated, I think that the basic mistake is twofold: seeking an abstract definition in the first place, and thinking, in the second, of a general liberty and not a set of specific liberties. Some other strands in Hayek's discussion point us in the right direction. But first I propose to reflect upon some other important questions that have arisen both in our preceding investigations and in our study of Hayek.

Being Free and Feeling Free

What Hayek seeks is a general set of conditions which constitute liberty or its absence and which can be universally applied. I think that is what anyone who is unequivocally and unqualifiedly a liberal is committed to doing. Perhaps there is no such set, as our comments upon the notion of "the average person" have suggested. What is coercion, or serious coercion, for one person or for a typical member of one society may not be so serious or even coercive at all for another person or for a typical member of another society.

That points us towards a distinction which clears up the problems of the contented slave and of the old lag anxious to return to prison: namely, the distinction, ignored by all those we have mentioned so far, between *being free* and *feeling free*. An unqualified liberal, surely, must be concerned with the former, whether or not those who have it realise and appreciate it, and whether or not those who lack it realise and resent that fact. After all, what Berlin and Hayek are concerned with are those specious arguments which seek to show that we have not really given up (interpersonal) liberty in return for self-fulfilment, power, voting rights, prosperity, real opportunities and options, or other things. If people are convinced by them, then they may think themselves free when they are half-way into slavery, or, while they are still free, they may be persuaded that they are not and so be seduced out of real freedom into an illusory one. And, from what I have read, this distinction is not stressed and is perhaps obfuscated, by those who are not markedly in favour of individual, interpersonal freedom but are concerned with the achievement of other states of affairs which they still propose to call "liberty."

The contented slave, the old lag happy to have got himself back into prison where what he is to do is decided for him, and the regular soldier who prefers military discipline to civilian freedom, are not free, although the soldier may be free to leave the army on certain conditions, but they do not feel unfree. They either like or do not resent their conditions. For their desires are either fulfilled or not noticeably disappointed. No options which matter to them are foreclosed. Rather, the convict and the soldier in question are glad that options are foreclosed for them by others. That is just what they want. It follows that, if liberty is defined in terms of nonfrustration of desires and nonrestriction of options, such persons are free, *interpersonally* free.

Only by appealing to desires and options, for autonomy and self-direction, which they do not feel or which they wish not to exercise, but which we take to be central to human existence, can we say that, after all and in the terms in question, they are nevertheless not interpersonally free.[3] What that amounts to is a concession that they are not free, along with a disapproval of their wish not to be free or of their contentment with lack of freedom. Therefore, instead of recognising these facts, the meanings of "liberty" and "lack of liberty" are tacitly changed in order to apply to them.

The appeal to central desires constituitive of our humanity, whether particular persons recognise them or not, can issue into a further appeal to a "real will" to be free which people have although they may not know it or wish to be rid of it. They could then be "forced to be free" by being turned out to fend for themselves and not being allowed back into dependence on others. After all, that is what needs to be done with children who cling to their mothers' apron strings or who allow themselves to be dominated by friends with stronger personalities. If we do that, are we coercing them, causing them frustration, blocking off their opportunities or restricting their options? Clearly, we are, and not just with respect to mere possibilities but to ones that they definitely want to realise and have been realising. And certainly in respect of children and adolescents, less knowledgeable about themselves and the world and less able to control themselves than mature adults, we can be right so to coerce them, to push them away or to tell them to have less to do with so-and-so. And it may be the duty of those concerned to use something like coercion to prevent weak-minded adults from excessive dependence or to wean them away from it. But there are other cases where the issue is not so clear.

In particular, there is the problem, for classical liberalism, of a people who have a comparatively restrictive set of institutions and laws, customary and statutory, yet with which they appear to be generally content. Their accustomed way of life permits few "experiments in living," frowns on most, and reacts with horror and affront at some. Clearly, they generally feel free since *ex hypothesi* they are on the whole content with, and do not feel particularly oppressed by, their laws and institutions. But equally clearly they have much less interpersonal freedom than J.S. Mill would want them to have. Would it be right for a ruler over them to "force them to be free" and by law and the use of legal coercion to legitimise and protect "experiments in living" among them? The majority, at least, would then feel oppressed and coerced in having their secure institutions overturned. And surely they would have some justification. The freedom to enjoy secure institutions and to live an undisturbed customary way of life is as much freedom as freedom to indulge in any "experiments in living" that could unsettle them. It may not be so easy as to formulate a universally applicable set of conditions that would constitute liberty, and to some extent the notion may have to be relativised. We may have to allow with Burke that, for practical purposes, a people is free if generally they feel themselves to be free.[4] We should also note that, in so doing, we are invoking a more communal dimension of freedom, the freedom of the group or, rather, of the individuals as members of the group and as sharing a common pattern of life, rather than a purely individual freedom.

Liberty and Rights

We now turn to the second strand in Hayek's account of liberty: namely, liberty as a set of rights.

Hayek repudiates the idea that freedom, as interpersonal and individual freedom, can be divided into several freedoms. Though it permits of degrees, it is one (CL, p. 12). This, I suggest, reflects his desire to define a universally applicable condition and thus a general liberty. Yet, as we have seen, he appeals to the original application of the term, the freedom of the free man in ancient Greece which the slave did not possess and which was in fact a sum of distinct freedoms. Hayek specifies them himself, as we have seen: legal status as a protected member of the community, immunity from arbitrary arrest, the right to work at whatsoever he wished and the right to move wheresoever he wished. Those were what the slave lacked, though he possessed the right to own property. Other slaves and prisoners have not had, or were deprived of that right. In the Middle Ages, serfs could not be bought or sold, and their compulsory services were more or less fixed by custom, but they were tied to their manors, yet free men could not take up any trade at will but only what the guilds would allow them to. Today, in some of the free states of Europe young men are still subject to compulsory military service in peace-time, and only recently in Britain has the closed shop been abolished, except for university undergraduates, actors, lawyers, and doctors. As we have already seen in some cases, it is more helpful to speak of freedoms rather than freedom in general, and thus of the ways in which given persons are free or not free. I now suggest that it is better to do so in all cases.

Moreover, by citing the four freedoms gained by liberated slaves in Greece, plus that of owning property which they already had, as containing most of what classical liberals regarded as the conditions of freedom (CL, p. 20), Hayek virtually resolves an otherwise general liberty into these five more specific ones.

It will be noticed that they are explicable via the notion of "a right." But "a right" has proved to be as slippery as "liberty" and "coercion." We need therefore to clarify the meaning which the word has in this context. Here it will suffice to distinguish "liberties" from "powers" and "entitlements." Liberties comprise *competences* to perform certain actions and *immunities* from certain actions by other parties. Competences impose upon others only obligations of noninterference, "negative duties": that is, they entail immunities from obstruction of their exercise. In contrast "powers" and "entitlements" impose obligations to perform definite actions, "positive duties." For by "powers" I mean rights to direct certain other persons to perform certain actions or to determine what they may or may not do, as electors have the right to determine which candidate will fulfil the office in question and as parents have a general right to control their children. And by an "entitlement" I mean a right to receive the relevant certain goods or services, which others are thereby obliged to provide. Manorial lords, for example, were entitled to so much labour, and other services and goods, from their serfs, and in some codes of law a man's widow and children are entitled to inherit certain proportions of his estate, irrespective of his wishes.

Classical liberalism has been principally concerned with the establishment and enforcement of certain key liberties (competences and immunities) along with the limitation in number and scope of powers, of private persons and especially governments, over others to which the last have not consented. Its aim, in other words, has been to secure and enlarge a sphere, or set of spheres, of discretion wherein the individual may act largely as he pleases.

Furthermore we can mark off classical liberalism from other varieties of liberalism, and other political movements that have grown out of it, by reference to the sorts of rights which each favours. On the one side, the more libertarian forms of liberalism seek even more to restrict those rights which are powers, or which entail powers, except insofar as they arise from freely agreed contracts and to enlarge those which are immunities. On the other, some liberals have stressed the importance of political rights, meaning thereby political powers. They have assumed that the core liberties which they prize are best secured by popular participation in government. But, as Hayek rightly argues, democracy is a matter of how the government is formed, and not of what it will or will not do. It may be the case that a majority will vote for parties and policies that seriously impinge upon the liberties of a minority or of all. And one may possess a power or many powers over others, and yet be subject, and in the very exercise of those powers, to the power of a superior with little security against arbitrary and harsh treatment, as Thomas Cromwell and many a Soviet *apparatchik* discovered. There has been a further shift within liberalism, from democracy to "social democracy" or egalitarian welfarism, which is, in effect, a move from rights as powers to rights as entitlements, entitlements both to shares in general welfare, as set out in Articles 22-5 of the United Nations Declaration of Universal Human Rights, and to equal shares in it.

It is clear that rights as powers and entitlements can conflict with rights as competences and immunities. Powers are powers to direct and thus to compel, and those over whom they are exercised have no immunities against them, though powers can be limited and those subject to them can have immunities against certain ways of exercising them. In general, the more powers that there are, the less the number and extent of liberties. The statement of a power usually indicates the persons over whom it is to be exercised: electors over candidates for public office; parents over their children; the police over those suspected of or charged with crimes and over the general public in certain circumstances; dictators over everyone. But although entitlements entail claims against someone or other to supply the goods or services to which one is entitled, it is possible to state them without at all indicating those against whom such claims rest. Consider Article 25.1 of the UN Declaration which states that everyone has a right to "a standard of living adequate for the health and well-being of himself and his family." It is clear that the rights there specified are not simply competences and immunities, the competence to acquire and retain resources for supporting oneself and one's family. For the Article explicitly states that the right to security holds when one cannot provide for oneself. Consequently, it must also be an entitlement to have these benefits supplied by others when one cannot do so oneself. But no indication is given of the identity of those others. When that happens, as is usually the case, it may not be so obvious that others are having claims stacked up against them. Yet if I am *entitled* to all that Article 25 states, someone must provide it if I cannot, and so I have a set of corresponding claims against that person or persons, claims that I or a third party must in the end be able to enforce unless my entitlement is to be an empty promise. And as claims pile up against other people, so their liberties decrease, especially their competences to spend or save their own money as they wish and their immunities against confiscation of their money and other resources.

It seems plausible, therefore, to interpret the claims of classical liberalism in terms of a certain set of liberties (competences and immunities) and the consequent restriction or elimination of powers and entitlements that would conflict with them.

Hayek, in effect, proceeds (CL, pp. 139–47) to define liberty in terms of immunity to coercion, a private and protected sphere wherein the individual has the competence generally to act as he pleases. In turn, such private spheres are to be defined by general rules, so that each can shape what in particular will constitute his own and can recognise what does and does not belong to his own and to those of others. An essential and central condition, or part, such private spheres is private or several property, whereby we can act effectively in the world, either by means of our own property or by contracts to employ that of others. That requires that property be dispersed and not centralised in one set of hands which then could exercise coercion over the rest. The foundations of liberty are therefore dispersed property rights and contract, and the legal protection of the one and enforcement of the other. To these are to be added other rights such as ones to privacy and secrecy (i.e., immunities to being watched and spied upon, now a dead letter as far as the tabloid press in Britain is concerned), and access to (i.e., competences to use) certain public and common facilities such as the highway (and the courts, we may add). In saying that he cannot there and then enumerate all those rights (CL, p. 142), Hayek admits that it is in terms of them that liberty is to be defined.

These private spheres are protected by the threat of coercion on the part of the state.[5] The state, in doing this, does not oblige citizens to perform specific actions, except as they have freely contracted so to do, but only to desist from actions that infringe on the protected spheres of others. This means that one can avoid that coercion by not putting oneself in the situations in which it will be exercised. (The criminal does not "will his punishment," but in an orderly state he voluntarily brings it upon himself, and likewise those who are made to fulfil their contracts or to pay damages for breach of them and for torts.) So long as the laws are framed in general terms, about types of person and types of action, one need never be coerced in fact for one can avoid it. Furthermore, those laws which oblige individuals to perform specific actions, such as to pay taxes and undergo military service, are at least known and predictable, and one can form one's own plans around them. One remains independent of the wills of particular persons, and is less unfree, for example, in having to undertake a known and limited period of military service than in being constantly liable to arbitrary arrest (CL, pp. 142–3).

As a consequence of having defined liberty in terms of protection from coercion, Hayek raises the question of whether the threat of coercion by the state is to be used only against coercion. He answers that forms of violence would count as coercion, but that fraud and deception might not. Yet both are like coercion in being the manipulation of the data on which another acts so as to make him do what the deceiver wants him to do, and thus his unwilling tool (CL, pp. 143–4). Again, we note the desire to bring undesirable actions under the heading of "coercion" rather than to deal with them in their own terms. And it is not all acts of deception that are made illegal, but those which are used to defraud people of their property or to subvert the political and legal order, such as "personation" at the polls, and impersonation of a police officer. It is simpler to define criminal deception in terms of rights, either as invading those of others or pretending to ones which one does not possess.

Liberty as the Rule of Law

We have found two strands in Hayek's characterisation of liberty: as freedom from coercion and as the possession of certain rights (principally competences and immunities). But there is also a third strand, which is elaborated in the remaining chapters of *The Constitution of Liberty* and again in *Law, Liberty and Legislation*. The need for the enforcement of the laws against coercion and for the protection of rights, and the desirability of restricting the powers of public authorities to known and general laws (as they were not under the Nazi and Communist régimes), leads Hayek finally to define liberty in terms of subjection only to such known, general and predictable laws.

It is not just the case that Hayek argues (CL, ch. 10) that general laws are necessary to liberty, whereas specific commands are inimical to it, but that he virtually defines liberty as subjection only to general laws that apply to all. Laws proper are "abstract" and state only certain conditions which actions in certain circumstances must satisfy. What in particular is to be done in any given situation is left to the judgment and discretion of the person involved. They neither specify detailed actions to be done nor command particular persons to do them. Consequently, they provide a framework within which people can formulate and carry out their own plans of actions. They allow people to pursue their own ends and do not subject them to serving another person's ends or to obeying his will. They are like laws of nature, of which we can make use for our own purposes. For they also specify consequences of our actions: if I do this, then that will follow; or, in order to do this,

I must do that. They may eliminate some choices, but do not usually prescribe actions that one must perform. Therefore, Hayek, concludes

> When we obey laws, in the sense of abstract rules laid down irrespective of their application to us, we are not subject to another man's will and are therefore free. (CL, p. 153)

Perhaps this is not so much another definition of freedom as the other side of freedom as freedom from coercion understood as arbitrary interference. A system of general laws is laid down in ignorance of whatever particular persons and actions it may apply to in the future, and is interpreted and applied without latitude for discretion by the judge. Therefore it is not arbitrary. (We may add that failure to prosecute, as in a recent case in Britain of incitement to murder, is as equally arbitrary as illegal arrest and detention, and likewise wide variations in sentencing are also resented as arbitrary.) Only within such a framework can we be free from arbitrary interference and subjection to another's will, whether it be that of private persons or public authorities.

Hayek quotes with approval a passage from Bracton cited by Polanyi:

> For that is an absolute villeinage from which an uncertain and indeterminate service is rendered, where it cannot be known in the evening what service is to be rendered in the morning, that is where a person is bound to whatever is enjoined to him. (CL, p. 133; LL, p. 158)

Polanyi points out that the transition from serfdom to freedom came about by the fixing of feudal dues, by custom, statute or written copy, and then by commutation of dues in terms of money, whence the copyholder became a tenant, "entitled to dispose freely of his own time and person, and to select according to his own judgment what is most congenial and profitable for him to do" (LL, p. 158). Hayek, in support, quotes a passage from Maitland on the greatest restraints being those which can be least anticipated (CL, p. 449). In contrast, Stalin created a régime in which no one knew where he stood:

> It has happened sometimes that a man goes to Stalin on his invitation as a friend. And when he sits with Stalin, he does not know where he will be sent next, home or to jail.[6]

In *Law, Liberty and Legislation*, liberty is in effect identified with the largely spontaneous and customary laws of just conduct (*nomos*). Yet, notwithstanding the importance of the distinction between general laws and specific commands, and the ranges of generality and specificity between them with both respect to the actions to be performed or not performed and the persons to whom they apply, it does not follow that the rule of law is thereby one of freedom. For one may be free from *arbitrary* interference by being subject to *regular* interference. Maitland, as quoted by Hayek in the passage cited above, also wrote, "Known general laws, however bad, interfere less with freedom than decisions based on no previously known rule." Such laws are a necessary but by no means sufficient condition for liberty.

Hayek himself recognises this in part, and adds two empirical conditions: that the laws are to apply as equally to those who make and enforce them as to the rest of the population; and that, if any law does single out a specific group, then there should be both a majority within that group and one outside it, in favour of it. I call these "empirical" provisos, because Hayek states that, if they apply in practice, then it is unlikely that any oppressive laws will be enacted (CL, pp. 154–5). The point to note is that Hayek therefore allows that a system of merely general laws could restrict liberty, and thus that liberty cannot be identified with living under such a order. He cites the example of a fanatical religious group which imposes its own restrictions upon everyone, and, in particular, Scottish Sabbatarianism, which he regards as innocuous compared to laws that are likely to be imposed only on some. But a more pertinent example would be the Islamic imposition of Sharia law. For Islam is both a Code, a sacralised way of life (specifically that of Arabs of the seventh century with some additions from Judaism and a ban on alcohol), and, unlike Judaism and Hinduism, a *missionary* religion. All peoples are to be brought into "submission" (*islam*) to Allah and his will as revealed to his Prophet and specified in the Koran and the *haddith*, the sayings attributed to Muhammad. It is not a Code which individuals may take upon themselves as they wish, but is to be the law of all, and is thus enforced in Islamic states such as Saudi Arabia, Pakistan, and the Sudan, in the last of which the Arab North is waging a war of Islamisation upon the Negro and Christian or animist South. Sharia law is a known and predictable system, if properly applied to all, yet its prohibitions and prescriptions hardly constitute a free social order as Hayek would understand it. Again, there can be universal conditions imposed upon transactions among people, which therefore are not regulations for the use of facilities provided by the government as are traffic regulations (LLL, vol. 1, p. 132), and which, while not prohibiting those transactions, certainly interfere with the ease with which people may exercise their freedom in those respects. It comes as a surprise to an Englishman to learn what a German has to do if he wishes to sell his house. Likewise, to go fishing in rivers and lakes an Englishman needs only to purchase a local licence available from shops selling angling gear, but a German must attend a course of evening classes for six months and then pass a set of detailed written examinations! And current legislation in Britain on health and safety is closing down hundreds of small businesses which cannot afford to comply with the regulations. A *Rechstaat*, of private law impersonally drawn up and impartially applied, could still be a very restrictive one, especially for those who do not have servants or subordinates to see that all the regulations are complied with. The European Union (EU), for example, is much more intent on creating a uniformly and highly regulated market than a free one. Likewise a system of taxation which left everyone with, say, only 20 percent of his income and virtually no capital, all by due process of law, would be a very serious restriction upon individual liberties. In contrast, a somnolent régime which only occasionally exercised some of the many discretionary powers that it possessed could well offer more liberty than one which impartially and universally applied a system of extensive but universal regulations and high levels of taxation.

This does not devalue at all Hayek's elaboration of the importance, conditions, and implications of the rule of law, which provides, as far as anything can, a secure legal framework for liberty and a set of constraints upon public authority instead of wide discretionary powers. It shows only that the formal conditions of generality of content and universality of application, are not sufficient conditions for freedom under the law, even when combined with the distinction between private law (including criminal law), applying to dealings among citizens, and public law, dealing with government agencies and their relations to the citizens, and the proviso that none or only a minimum of the latter is to compel the public to do or refrain from specific types of action. What also counts are the material conditions of how many areas of life, and how far in each case, are regulated beyond what is necessary for the populace freely and effectively to act within them. Indeed, Hayek partly recognises this deficiency when he discusses the guarantees provided by entrenched individual rights (CL, pp. 182–3), though even there he focuses upon those rights which are a part of the formal rule of law rather than substantive liberties independent of it, such as limits upon levels of taxation or rights (competences) of association and nonassociation. And later he explicitly acknowledged it, and quoted the example of the legal requirement of religious conformity as among the most severe restrictions of personal liberty yet applicable to all (LLL, vol. 1, pp. 101, 170 n. 10). His reply was that such rules are not rules limiting conduct towards others or protecting the private domains of individuals, except where it is believed that individual infractions of them may bring a supernatural punishment upon the whole community. The point is not that Hayek is seeking to revive or revise Mill's "very simple principle" for delimiting the sphere of legislation, but that there he aims to show that it is *nomos*, the body of spontaneously formed customary and case-law concerning just conduct (private and criminal law), which embodies liberty, as against *thesis*, the laws of deliberate legislation for specific purposes and organisations (public law). Only "actions towards others," and not "matters of command and obedience," are likely to come before a judge for settlement, and thus only about the former will judges declare, apply or modify existing law or state for the first time a law, appropriate to the case, entailed by or at least consonant with the existing body of law.

But that argument, while generally sound, has itself one deficiency: namely,that customary law usually includes more than general laws of just conduct. Rather, it defines a whole way of life, and therefore is likely to include both privileges for some and corresponding obligations upon others, as in feudal law, and laws about matters which do not directly affect others, such as modes of dress.[7] Disputes about both of these could come for settlement before a judge, or before the holder of power and who can enforce his decisions, and who may decide the case himself or appoint another to do so. Our interest is in the latter set of laws. For although they may be enforced by opinion and ostracism, there could be disputes as to whether an alleged deviation in dress or some other point of manners is in fact a deviation from the acknowledged law. It follows that a substantive restriction of the sphere of law, of *nomos* as well as *thesis*, could still be required.

Just what the important substantive or material rights are, and how far they extend and in what ways and in what circumstances they may be limited or even overridden, as in emergencies such as war and natural disasters, remains to be decided. Hayek was right to mention rights to private property, freedom of movement and occupation, plus access to certain public facilities such as the highways. In addition to them we have suggested access to the courts and some maximum amount or proportion of taxation, plus a general lack of regulations and controls beyond what is necessary for the effective carrying out of the ordinary business of life. But it is clear that there are limits upon the specification of such central rights. How far they apply, just what their boundaries are, how far one is compatible with another: none of these can be defined in the abstract. And what can be achieved and maintained with respect to them will vary from one time and place to another. An excitable and lawless population can be ruled only by a relatively heavy hand and a considerable amount of discretionary power. Likewise what counts as coercion, as we have seen, will vary from place to place. It is clear that liberty cannot be completely defined. It has tacit dimensions. Perhaps in the end it can be only tacitly comprehended. Such was the conclusion of Burke and Polanyi, to whom we now turn.

Notes

1. *Liberalisms*, ch. 5.
2. Eph. 6:5–8.
3. For examples of such appeals, see Gray, *Liberalisms*, chs. 4 and 5.
4. Cf. Burke: "If any ask me what a free government is, I answer, that, for any practical purpose, it is what the people think so—and that they, and not I, are the natural, lawful, and competent judges of this matter," *Letter to the Sheriffs of Bristol*, vol. 3, p. 183.
5. We may add that that is, in a large part, a modern achievement. Collingwood (*The New Leviathan*, ch. 28,§§ 28.74) points out that for most of history there was no criminal law (in the modern sense) nor any agency to enforce it, only a common knowledge of offensive actions and the right of individuals to defend themselves or others against them or to punish offenders. See also Hayek, LLL, vol. 1, ch. 5. On ways in which stateless societies enforce their laws, see M. Gluckman, *Politics, Law and Ritual in Tribal Societies*, ch. 3.
6. Bulganin to Khrushchev, in *Khrushchev Remembers*, quoted A. Bullock, *Hitler and Stalin: Parallel Lives*, p. 704.
7. Laws about dress may concern the differentiation of classes or sexes, and thus be both specific rather than general and also affect others by prohibiting implied claims to belong to another class or to confuse sexual identity. Yet they may be general and not directly concerned with conduct towards others: for example, those which, according to Mary Renault's *The Praise Singer*, on the island where Simonides was born, severely limited the decoration permitted upon a person's costume.

4

The Tacit Dimensions of Liberty

The Tacit Understanding of Freedom

The problems we have found in defining liberty suggest that it cannot be strictly defined in the abstract and that it is better to think in terms of more specific liberties than of a general liberty. In particular we have noted, in the previous chapter, a certain relativity in the notion of coercion and thus in freedom from it, and have consequently agreed with Burke that, for practical purposes, a people is free if, on the whole, they feel free, even though they may in fact live under a set of laws and customs which another people would find highly restrictive. A formal definition of interpersonal freedom as "freedom from coercion" might not mean very much if there is an extensive diversity in what is allowed to count as coercion and its absence, apart from the other difficulties which it incurs and which Hayek could not completely clear up.

We have only noted a very small part of the extensive contemporary discussion of freedom and its definition. Even so, we may well agree with Burke's reaction to a similar situation two centuries ago, which was quoted on the title page of Part 1. There is little new under the sun, and we could do worse than to continue to follow Burke.

As we shall see in Part 3, a significant part of the reformulation of liberalism by Hayek and Polanyi is a *rapprochement* between it and tradition and custom. Rather than conceiving liberalism rationalistically as essentially opposed to tradition and custom, they have recognised that liberty depends upon them, that a free society must be, to a large extent, one living by inherited traditions and institutions. What that further entails, and how far it takes us beyond liberalism itself, we shall have to explore. At present we are concerned, not with the realisation and maintenance of liberty, but with its definition. We seemed bound to conclude that liberty is understood in a largely tacit manner, with a focal and explicit group of important specific liberties such as several property, immunity to arbitrary arrest, and freedom of movement, occupation, worship, and speech. Furthermore, it follows that, because liberty cannot be explicitly and exactly defined, it can be properly understood only from within an experience of living in liberty and a tradition of freedom.

Such was the opinion of Burke:

> Nothing universal can rationally be affirmed on any moral or any political subject. Pure metaphysical abstraction does not belong to these matters. The lines of morality are not like ideal lines of mathematics. They are broad and deep as well as long. They admit of exceptions; they demand modifications.[1]

> The rules and definitions of prudence can rarely be exact; never universal.[2]

> No lines can be laid down for civil or political wisdom. They are a matter incapable of exact definition. But though no man can draw a stroke between the confines of day and night, yet light and darkness are upon the whole tolerably distinguishable.[3]

> The restraints on men, as well as their liberties are to be reckoned among their rights. But as the liberties and the restrictions vary with times and circumstances, and admit of infinite modifications, they cannot be settled upon any abstract rule; and nothing is so foolish as to discuss them upon that principle.[4]

> Civil freedom, gentlemen, is not, as many have endeavoured to persuade you, a thing that lies hid in the depth of abstruse science. It is a blessing and a benefit, not an abstract speculation; and all the just reasoning that can be upon it is of so coarse a texture as perfectly to suit the ordinary capacities of those who are to enjoy, and of those who are to defend it. Far from any resemblance to those propositions in geometry and metaphysics, which admit no medium, but must be true or false in all their latitude, social and civil freedom, like all other things in common life, are variously mixed and modified, enjoyed in very different degrees, and shaped into an infinite diversity of forms, according to the temper and circumstances of every community. The extreme of liberty (which is its abstract perfection, but its real fault) obtains nowhere, nor ought to obtain anywhere. Because extremes, as we all know, in every point which relates either to our duties or satisfactions in life, are destructive both to virtue and enjoyment. Liberty too must be limited in order to be possessed. The degree of restraint it is impossible in any case to settle precisely. But it ought to be the constant aim of every wise public council to find out, by cautious experiments and rational, cool endeavours, with how little, not how much, of this restraint the community can subsist. For liberty is a good to be improved, and not an evil to be lessened. It is not only a private blessing of the first order, but the vital spring and energy of the state itself, which has just so much life and vigour as there is liberty in it.[5]

I have quoted Burke at some length because it is precisely his idea of liberty to which the logic of Hayek's and Polanyi's positions will lead us.

One error that Burke had especially in mind was the insistence upon some one aspect or form of liberty to the endangering of the whole edifice. For example, security from imprisonment without public trial is one of the cornerstones of civil liberty. Yet, if the government of Eire had cooperated, the swift detention without trial of some 250 organisers of murder and violence in Northern Ireland would have done much for the peace, security and liberty of the rest of its inhabitants over these last twenty years or more. That example may be generalised. Every constitutional system requires for its preservation the power temporarily to suspend some of its central elements. Could the United States have held presidential and congressional elections in 1944, as its Constitution required, if it had been fighting the Axis powers on its doorstep and not three thousand or more miles away? The tragedy of the Weimar Republic was not that its Constitution did not provide for such powers in the form of presidential rule, but that those who did invoke them—firstly, Hindenburg and his advisors, and then Hitler—did so in order, respectively, to circumvent it and to overturn it. To deal with emergencies, such as natural disasters, terrorism, subversion, revolt, and invasion, a government must be able to employ discretionary powers of coercion: to commandeer or requisition property, to mobilise reserve troops, to conscript or direct labour, to impose censorship, to restrict the movement of people and goods, and so on. And whether or not a state of emergency exists can be decided only by the judgment of those in power. It is itself necessarily a matter of discretion to invoke such powers of discretion. But in a troubled and insecure world, no government can fulfil its duty without having such powers in reserve. It has often been a weakness of Liberal theory to take a peaceful and secure world for granted.[6]

Again, every system of law must have some indeterminate margins which seem incompatible with the rule of law. Hayek, with reference to the principle *nullum crimen, nulla poena sine lege*, remarks that "there probably exists no country where a person will not on certain occasions, such as when he disobeys a policeman, become liable to punishment for 'an act done to public mischief' or for 'disturbing the public order' or for 'obstructing the police'" (CL, p. 207). But for the law to be effectively enforced there must be a general duty of the public not to obstruct the police in the course of their duties and also one to render specific assistance as required, or reasonably required. And those are duties which cannot be further specified. Furthermore, the law must have certain vaguely defined prohibitions in order for the authorities to be able there and then to deal with activities that threaten people's lives, liberties, and property. We have in Britain the Common Law offences of "obstruction of the highway," "conduct liable to cause a breach of the peace" and "loitering with intent to commit a felony." Queen's Regulations include one concerning "conduct prejudicial to military order and discipline." When I was boy at the grammar school, we were all issued with a little book of school-rules, the last of which read, "Any breach of good manners is a breach of school rules." The total absence of any such laws can be as detrimental to liberty as is the presence of many of them.

Yet again, entrenched rights (competences and immunities), as in a Bill of Rights, can undercut their own purpose. I shall mention three current examples, two relating to the freedom of speech and publication and the third to the right to silence of the accused:

1. In the United States the former right has become, so it seems, a right *inter alia* to say anything about anyone accused of a crime and about a trial in progress, conduct which in Britain would swiftly incur severe penalties for contempt of court. To secure the right to a fair trial, the right to publish comment upon it, as opposed to straightforward reporting of the proceedings, must be curtailed.

2. In order to cut off the supply of "the oxygen of publicity" for the terrorists of the Irish Republican Army (IRA), and to remove the added insult to the relatives of their victims of hearing them justified by their "political wing," the British government banned the broadcasting of any speeches and interviews by members of the IRA and Sinn Fein. Broadcasters circumvented this law by having someone else read the words spoken by the leaders of Sinn Fein. I suggest it would have been better to ban Sinn Fein entirely as a subversive organisation.

3. In certain cases, where there were no independent witnesses or additional material evidence, parents suspected of injuring or killing their children have been able, by stubbornly refusing to say anything, to escape being charged and tried, and so the prosecution can now draw a jury's attention to the silence of the accused in such circumstances and to invite it to draw its own conclusions.

The general lesson to be learned from these examples is that we cannot tell in advance just how the implications of one liberty may conflict with those of another. Entrenched rights may be a safeguard, but they can also be a danger for the very same reason: namely, that they cannot be overruled. Moreover, since the specified rights are guaranteed, it may be inferred that the remainder are not, and thus that they do not exist, as in Continental systems of law where it is often assumed that what is not explicitly allowed is therefore prohibited.

Hayek, holding that what matters is a system of laws of just conduct which apply to all and to an unknown number of future cases, rightly concludes that a Bill of Rights would be unnecessary. The rights usually included in such enactments are not absolute and are or should be limited by general rules of law. Nor are they the only important ones for individual liberty. No exhaustive list of such rights can be drawn, and other rights may come to be equally or more important as the circumstances of life change (LLL, vol. 3, pp. 110–111). Also, as he points out, recent lists of basic rights, such as the UN Universal Declaration of Human Rights, incorporate what we have called "powers" and "entitlements." His specific objection to the latter is that they treat people as if they were always, and only to be considered as, members of organisations and not of a spontaneous and free society (LLL, vol. 2, pp. 104–6). They certainly require an organisational structure to be enforced and they lay positive obligations, probably many and large ones, upon others to supply them.

The yet more general conclusion to be drawn, as Burke urged, is that we can specify only some central features of a system of liberty, *even in peaceful and orderly times*; that those features themselves have limitations and any one or group of them may have to be modified as and when necessary for the preservation either of another specific liberty within that core or of the whole system; that such modifications and limitations cannot be specified in advance and in the abstract; and that it is necessarily a matter of judgment, at the time and the place, of what needs to be done.

If this is so, it follows that knowledge of liberty is primarily the lived knowledge of liberty embodied in specific institutions and practices, which cannot be abstractly codified and applied elsewhere. Polanyi argued on several occasions (e.g., PK, p. 54) that the French, who under "Absolutism" had lost a lived knowledge of liberty, could only receive the articulated doctrines of liberty and not the unspecifiable art of practising it.[7] Conversely he argued that, although the twentieth century has seen the working out of the consequences of scepticism and the nihilism in which it results, this sets problems only for the theory of liberalism which has combined moral idealism with scepticism. For, having gone the full circuit of political revolution, we now know liberty. "We again know with certainty freedom from servitude. No theoretical difficulty in the formulation of freedom can now shake our belief in the reality and value of freedom."[8] Any theory of freedom, or of any other aspect of social and political life, can only be a distillation of what has already been achieved in practice, and so a necessarily partial articulation of what we already and tacitly know.

Even more strongly, when contrasting totalitarian societies with those based on "free mental activities" (e.g., science, scholarship, justice, human sympathy, religion, sports), Polanyi wrote:

> The doctrine of liberty, which is realised by the fact of life being guided by such intuitively [i.e., tacitly] known principles as in science, law and language, and having as its aim the service to these principles which are immanent in "principled" practice; can only be transmitted by practice. If the art of discovery, the proper use of language, the principles of justice, can only be transmitted by that unbroken sequence of social experiences, commonly known as tradition, then the much more elusive, because far more polymorphous, art of liberty cannot be made articulate. Liberty, no doubt, is represented by certain institutions, customs, doctrines, literature, etc., but it is only in life by these institutions and according to these customs, and inspired by these doctrines and literature, that liberty can continue to exist. It is a local affair, an endemic achievement. (SMS, p. 59)

Again, two pages later he wrote that Liberal doctrine cannot be exactly stated. There is "no single rule which has no exception, not a single ideal which is to be pursued to its logical limit." For we cannot prejudge all cases without admitting a certain latitude of interpretation. Consequently, only an illiberal system, based on an authority from which no dissent is allowed, can claim finality.

Fifteen years later Polanyi restated the tacit dimensions of liberty. Having made the same points as we have just made, about the vulnerability of free institutions to misuse for the subversion of liberty and about the need sometimes to curtail liberty in order to defend it, Polanyi concluded:

> Just as the practice of freedom cannot be secured by any set of formal rules, so also the essential meaning of freedom will always escape any attempt at a formal definition. It must be defined in terms of specific examples, if it is to be distinguished from servitude. Only within a free society can free institutions preserve freedom.... and the very words "freedom" and "servitude" can carry their true connotations only when uttered within a free country.[9]

Polanyi then elaborated the implications of the essentially tacit knowledge of freedom: that freedom in fact does not rest upon the explicit content of the constitutional rules of free countries but upon the tacit interpretation of them; that all formulations of liberal principles derive their meaning from a widely diffused and inarticulate knowledge of what freedom is; and that freedom depends upon the presence and accredited authority of the liberal tradition. The point is that these are necessary preconditions for the *realisation* of freedom because they are also the necessary preconditions for the *understanding* of freedom, which cannot be reduced to a set of explicit statements. For example, as mentioned above, discretionary powers for use in emergencies are necessary under any constitution, in order *inter alia* to preserve the constitution itself. Yet it is necessarily a matter of discretion and judgment both as to whether any particular state of affairs or turn of events is a genuine emergency requiring the use of those powers, and also as to how and how far those powers are used properly to deal with the emergency rather than to use it as a pretext for permanent use of those powers. Opponents of constitutional order in the 1930s, such as Sir Oswald Mosely, regularly appealed to current problems and crises, such as extensive unemployment, in order to manifest the need for "efficiency" and thus dictatorial methods which would cut through the cumbersome delays of parliamentary processes. Only people brought up within and holding to traditions of freedom can safely handle emergency powers without subverting the liberty that they are meant to protect. One Ministry that the Communists in the coalition governments in Central and Eastern Europe after 1945 always insisted on having was that of the Interior, so that they could control the police and thus eventually everything else. Consequently, there has to be a shared and tacit understanding as to when, how and how far such powers can be invoked and used, and mutual trust that those exercising them will not misuse them. One only has to look at the very different histories, since independence, of North and Latin America, the former inheriting traditions of liberty and self-government and the latter not, to see what is required for the maintenance of liberty, the rule of law and constitutional order. With them a written constitution of specified and limited powers is not necessary, as in Britain, and without them a formal constitution is a worthless piece of paper.

And throughout Hayek's account of *nomos* (LLL, vol. 1, ch. 5), the mostly spontaneous evolving law of just conduct, upon which liberty depends, he emphasises time and time again that it never was nor never can be formulated and established at will. Codification is not the invention of a system of law, but the systematisation of existing law and removal of some of its discrepancies. In such a system of *nomoi*, it is enough to know how to act and unnecessary to be able to state the laws. In novel circumstances there is a need to appeal to experienced men, and later to recognised judges, who can give appropriate judgments and so make articulate and more precise the rules about which men differ or to supply new ones where none previously existed. All this depends upon an essentially tacit understanding of just conduct and a sense of the spirit of law whereby people can judge what is consonant and not consonant with it. Significantly he cites again the principle of *nulla poena sine lege*, which, he says, applies only to written law and not to those rules which would at once be accepted if they were stated. English Common Law, he notes, has not accepted it in this latter sense, and retains the conviction that a rule may exist which everyone is assumed to be capable of observing even though it has until now not been articulated (LLL, vol. 1, p. 117).

If this is so, it appears to follow that a people who have not known liberty in practice cannot have any idea of it therefore cannot desire it. But this is contrary to fact. For serfs and slaves do have ideas of what it would mean to be free and some definitely yearn for it. After all, slaves have masters, serfs manorial lords, and prisoners warders, and in each case the former can see and appreciate the freedom, or greater freedom, of the latter. Again, the slave and serf soon learn, by trying to do them or being told by others not to do them, that there are many things they are not allowed to do, just as does any child in any family. Men have imagination and are not limited to what they actually experience. Habituation can, among those who are timorous and subservient by nature, lead to an eventual loss of the desire for liberty. But that does not mean that they did not have it in the first place.

> I envy not in any moods
> The captive void of noble rage,
> The linnet born within the cage,
> That never knew the summer woods

A captive person may lose his rage at his loss of freedom, but none born to slavery or serfdom is like Tennyson's linnet and born without an idea of it.

That we must admit to be true. But all it means is that we all, no matter what our circumstances are, have an idea of, and at first a desire for, doing as we wish without being obstructed by others. This is the negative side of liberty. Having achieved freedom from the chains, walls, and constraints that bind us, we may then find ourselves with little definite idea of what actually we want to do. And "doing as we wish" and "not being obstructed by others" are insufficient as definitions of liberty, for they cannot be realised. Men in society cannot but obstruct each other in many ways, and one person's doing as he likes is bound to prevent some other from doing something that he likes to do. Inevitably, we have to go beyond these vague and extensive notions and further to specify what liberty can in fact mean. It is a *workable* idea of liberty, and not the merely abstract notion of freedom, that presupposes practical experience of an actual system of specific and concrete competences and immunities.

That in turn means that liberty necessarily has a communal dimension. The liberal model is always that of the individual determining his own way in life. Other people and their plans and actions provide the context, sometimes helpful and sometimes obstructive. Freedom is the freedom of each to negotiate his way in society. Hence the search for an abstract definition of liberty, applicable to every individual everywhere, and of a general liberty for the individual to choose his path in life. But the abstract individual, like abstract liberty, cannot exist. And each concrete individual lives in and is shaped by a concrete society. And thus what he understands to be freedom, its central elements and its limits, depends upon the traditions in which he has been brought up. Indeed, it is in large part, unless he has become a victim of ideology— the attempt to live by abstract ideas alone and not by attention to one's actual situation and the real nature of the world—the freedom to live the traditional life that he has inherited. For the most part, that is something taken for granted, until there is a threat to it. The knowledge and content of freedom—real, concrete freedom—derive from custom and tradition, and therefore include, and may mostly consist in, a freedom to live a shared, rather than a mostly individual and private, way of life: *our* liberties, the patterns of reciprocal relations, rights, and duties, in which we have been brought up and wish to live.

The Implications for Liberalism

We have now distinguished between merely abstract notions of liberty, which in principle can be projected by anyone at any time, and more concrete and practicable notions which embody the lived experience of liberty and whose contents therefore remain largely tacit and will vary with time and place. The former, I suggest, are likely to be rationalist and radical ideas of a general, wide, and structureless liberty because they are not informed by actual experience and so are primarily only negations of the restraints that are experienced and resented. That is, they will be ideas of a boundless liberty of doing as we please, either individually or collectively. As we have seen, such notions prove deeply problematic because of the inevitable frustrations of one sort or another that life among our fellows brings about. Every state of affairs opens some possibilities and forecloses others. That means that the abstract and wide notion of doing as one pleases, entailing not being obstructed, easily gives way to notions of freedom as power, opportunity and the nonrestriction of choices, and, in turn, collectivist notions of us all together deciding what we shall all do. Again, freedom projected as the negation of felt frustration and oppression can easily become the radical freedom of complete self-determination and autonomy, acknowledging no law nor any obligation that one has not laid down for oneself, a desire for a Gnostic emancipation and liberation from all external and unwilled determination and ultimately from finitude itself. None of these notions is realisable in human life in this world. Yet, as we have seen, attempts to define freedom have all too easily issued into them.

The conclusion to be drawn is, I suggest, that a viable idea of freedom is one that tacitly embodies or appeals to a lived experience of freedom, and thus has a positive content, a set of liberties, rights, practices, laws, and institutions, themselves largely tacitly known, understood, interpreted, and operated. Any formal definition of such an idea necessarily falls short of what is meant. Therefore, if the tacit details are left out of account, the further articulation of such an idea inevitably results in the quagmires of theory that we have surveyed, and, in practice, the destruction of real liberty and the imposition of some system of oppression. We may rephrase Berlin's suspicion of "positive liberty" in terms of the dangers of the specification of an *explicit* content for a notion of liberty that begins merely as the negation of experienced powerlessness and obstruction. Any idea of liberty must have a positive side (a set of competences) as well as a negative side (a set of immunities). The question is, How do we arrive at that positive side? The only practicable answer is, By reflection on a free (or relatively free) way of life that is already lived, and by constant awareness of the necessarily partial results of our reflections.

For the most part, classical liberalism has in fact rejected unviable notions of liberty although it has sought for an abstract definition of a general liberty rather than a concrete understanding of more specific liberties. For it has been based upon an experienced liberty which it has partly articulated and to which it tacitly referred for interpretation and practical guidance. What classical liberals primarily meant by "liberty" was the concrete set of liberties that they knew from having lived it.[10]

This means that liberalism is either the articulation, inevitably incomplete, of existing practices of liberty, or the projection of a merely imagined condition. As the former it has a greater chance of being a realistic and feasible doctrine than as the latter. Yet it also appears to entail that, as Gray claims,[11] liberalism is either only a summary of certain periods in the history of particular liberal societies or an ideology projecting spurious notions and norms upon all times and places. Moreover every political doctrine must likewise be either a more or less valid articulation of a local experience, with no validity beyond that experience, or an imposition of a set of abstract ideas upon diverse and recalcitrant realities, either as the result of an extension of a formulated tradition beyond its native sphere or as something dreamed up *de novo* and thus with no valid application anywhere. It further follows that the very attempt at a political philosophy is mistaken. All that can be done is to describe some part of the tradition wherein we stand, and that is a purely historical task. Indeed, all philosophy suffers the same fate. Now that it has abandoned the "foundationalist" and "critical" ambitions which have motivated it since Descartes, or earlier, there can be no systematic philosophy aimed at universal truths but only criticism of all systems.

But these conclusions present us with a set of false dilemmas:

1. All valid philosophy is the articulation, and then the explicit elaboration, of what we already know, as adult human beings living among our fellows in the world, though vaguely and inchoately, and not, as in the special sciences, the discovery of facts hitherto totally unknown. We all have knowledge and some idea of what counts as knowledge. Hence we all are in a position, *ceteris paribus*, to formulate a philosophical theory of knowledge. This is a constructive task for philosophy, but not a foundationalist nor critical one. Rather than searching for certainty in some indubitable bedrock, we start, as we must, with what we already know and seek to articulate what it presupposes and those ultimate beliefs which we cannot but hold to be true.[12]

2. Necessarily, the contents of philosophy vary according to what is already known. You cannot formulate the presuppositions of a form of knowledge, or of a practice, which you do not have. Forms of knowledge are "local affairs," in space and time. As Collingwood insisted, every attempt at philosophy is an "interim report." But this has no bearing on the truth and validity of the forms of knowledge and their presuppositions. Nor does it rule out the existence of a set of universal presuppositions of all knowledge whatsoever.

3. Likewise with political philosophy, which, as its history shows, is especially conditioned by the political experience of those who engage in it. Each particular political order is a "local affair" but that does not mean that it and its presuppositions have no wider validity. To practise modern

natural science you need a tradition of research, and the necessary equipment, which are not possessed by either every individual or nation. Nevertheless its methods and results have universal validity whereas those of astrology and "occult sciences" do not. So too a given political order may embody, more fully and effectively than others, universally valid ideals, even though it may not be possible to achieve or maintain it at other times and places.

Liberalism, therefore, can frankly admit that its realisation requires highly specific conditions, including a developing tradition of experienced liberty, without having to confess that its principles have no universal validity but are either merely local as Gray argues they must be[13] or an ideological attempt to constrain concrete and diverse reality to fit abstract and stereotyped ideas. It can make this claim more convincingly if it distinguishes between general principles and specific policies and institutions, indeed, between levels of more general and more specific forms of each.

My own suggestion is that the valid core of liberalism is an account of certain competences and immunities which have become recognised and established within the European world and can be enjoyed in similar circumstances. As Hayek has rightly argued, two fundamental presuppositions of liberty are the Rule of Law, that is, government according to known laws framed in general terms and applying to all, and a presumption that everything is permitted which is not specifically prohibited. The former alone is insufficient, as we have seen. As for the latter, Hayek quotes a Soviet legal theorist (Malitzki, writing in 1929) as stating:

> The fundamental principle of our legislation and our private law, which the bourgeois theorist will never recognise, is: everything is prohibited which is not specifically permitted. (CL, p. 240)

He also cites Aristotle (*Ethics*, 1138a): "Whatever [the law] does not bid it forbids" (CL, p. 495). The point is, not that the Soviet authorities prevented individuals from doing everything which they had not authorised, but that they gave themselves the right to interfere as and when they pleased. Indeed Polanyi, drawing upon a distinction between "private" liberties (concerning actions which either have are thought, by the authorities and the public, to have negligible social effects) and "public" ones which do have manifest effects, argues that they may be inversely related. People under a despotic régime may be allowed to do many things in private life which may be stamped out by social ostracism in a society living under public freedom. "Under Stalin the scope of private freedom remains much wider than it was in Victorian Britain, while that of public liberties is incomparably less" (LL, p. 158). What matters is that there be a general presumption by all that individuals have a general competence to act as they wish, along with a general immunity against arbitrary interference by the authorities. Similarly, Burke held Common Law and the statute of Habeas Corpus to be the sole securities of (English) liberty and justice.[14]

These general competences and immunities can be further specified, as noted in the previous chapter, in ways which Hayek has suggested, along with some limits upon the number and extent of regulations and the burden of taxation. But there can be no question of a simple checklist, nor of rigorous and unambiguous definitions of these liberties, nor any uniform pattern for realising them. Like everything else to do with human life, they admit exceptions and require modifications, especially mutual adjustments, lest the abstract perfection of one prove concretely injurious to the exercise of another.

The question, then, is, Why is liberty, understood mostly in terms of these competences and immunities, so important? We now turn to the answers provided by our authors, answers that, in some cases, bear back upon the understanding of liberty itself and can profoundly modify it.

Notes

1. *An Appeal from the Old Whigs to the New, Works*, vol. 6, p. 97.
2. *First Letter on a Regicide Peace*, vol. 8, p. 89.
3. *Thoughts on the Causes of Our Present Discontents*, vol. 2, p. 369.
4. *Reflections*, vol. 5, p. 123.
5. *Letter to the Sheriffs of Bristol*, vol. 3, pp. 145–6.
6. Hayek proposes, in his model constitution, to limit emergency powers by having them granted by one organ, the Legislative Assembly dealing only with *nomos*, to another, the government, formed from and by the Governmental Assembly, which will exercise them. Such powers would be defined in extent and duration, and the Legislative Assembly would be free to recall them (LLL, vol. 3, pp. 124–6). But one can easily envisage the government chafing at the restrictions of the Legislative Assembly, and possibly with some justification on some occasions. And no paper provisions could prevent a determined government from using its temporary powers either openly or covertly to remove, obstruct or undermine the Legislative Assembly, nor could it allow for a situation, such as invasion, in which the Legislative Assembly could not meet in order to renew those powers.
7. But see, N. Henshall, *The Myth of Absolutism*, on the factual inaccuracy of such a statement. "Absolute power" meant the royal prerogative over matters of state (peace and war, coinage, appointing counsellors and officials), in other words "public law." It did not apply to "private law," the protection of the life, liberty,

and property of the individual. That was governed by customary law. Where royal legislation impinged upon it, as with taxation, consent was necessary, by Parliament, Estates, *parlements*, and provincial, local, and corporate assemblies. To legislate and act in defiance of customary law and consensual organs was "despotism." And that was what Louis XVI resorted to under the influence of "Enlightened" ideas. In many important respects, two obvious exceptions being a national representative body and only the king's justice and no "seigneurial" justice, England did not differ from France and other Continental countries (although Henshall does overstate his case at this point). It was the impatience and abstract rationalism of "Enlightened" ideas which turned, in July 1789, a movement of reform of and within the institutions and practices of the *ancien régime* into a Revolution that sought to scrap it altogether and to begin from scratch.

Polanyi frequently attributes his own argument to Burke, and in one place ("On Liberalism and Liberty," *Encounter*, vol. 4, March 1955, p. 32; also in *Society, Economics, and Philosophy*) states that therefore Burke doomed most of Europe to unfreedom whereas in the nineteenth century there was notable progress in achieving liberty. But Polanyi misinterprets Burke and misses the depth of his indictment of revolutionary France. From the start Burke saw the need for reform in France, and had previously foreseen the financial crisis towards it was heading. But Burke saw that reform was turning to revolution because of the disordered intellects of the politicians who came to the fore, their false notions of liberty, their wish to start with a clean slate, their impious lack of humility amounting to "metaphysical madness" in their scorn for concrete reality, and their use, through religious indifference, of the *philosophes'* spurious morality of "benevolence" and religion of "humanity," motivated by hatred of God and man. Nowhere does he state that the French were ignorant of liberty except in the form of abstract ideas. On the contrary, he asserted that the old constitution of France, although dilapidated, was basically sound and was "suspended before it could be perfected." France had "the elements of a constitution very nearly as good as could be wished." Through its internal and local diversities and interests "general liberty had as many securities as there were separate views in the separate orders" (*Reflections*, vol. 5, pp. 81–2).

8. "This Age of Discovery," *The Twentieth Century*, March 1956, p. 234.
9. "On Liberalism and Liberty," *Encounter*, vol. 5, March 1955, p. 31.
10. Hayek (CL, pp. 55–6) points out that the English and the empirical idea of liberty is represented in France by Montesquieu, Constant, and Tocqueville, whereas the French and rationalist ideas are represented in England by Hobbes, and imported by Priestley, Price, Godwin, and Paine (and likewise by Jefferson to America), to whom we can add Bentham and the Mills. The point is that rationalist and radical ideas are more likely in situations in which there is less experienced liberty combined with a strong desire for it, and that in the same circumstances foreign ideas and models, which may be empirical and practicable in themselves, are likely to be misunderstood in rationalist and radical ways. This is yet more likely when the effort is made to introduce and thus to impose such a model "from above" and in defiance of local traditions.

R. Aron (*An Essay on Freedom*, pp. 18–9) comments on the circularity of Tocqueville's notion of a "civil and moral freedom which finds its strength in union and which the mission of power itself is to protect: this is the freedom to do without fear all that is just and good." Tocqueville contrasts it with the "corrupted" freedom of doing as one pleases, which is the enemy of all authority and suffers all rules impatiently (Bentham!). But, asks Aron, who is to determine what is just and good? "These statements take on a precise meaning only in a historic context where everyone knows what the state has the right to require or to forbid, and by the same token, what the individual is entitled to demand in the private sphere in which he reigns alone." As we shall see in chapter 9, Polanyi, also like Burke, gives a similar "positive" definition of liberty and rightly regards it as primarily a public and not a private one.

Similar, Brenkert (*Political Freedom*, p. 247 n. 8) quotes A. Hereth on Tocqueville: "It would not be possible to acquire the concept of freedom, if one does not know it through practice…For him freedom was a practical matter, which could be described in theoretical discourse only with the greatest difficulty."

11. *Liberalisms*, pp. 239–40.
12. See further, Collingwood, *An Essay on Philosophical Method* and *An Essay on Metaphysics*, and also his two essays, "Faith and Reason" and "Reason Is Faith Understanding Itself," reprinted in *Essays in the Philosophy of Religion*; and Polanyi, *Personal Knowledge*, especially Part 3.

Collingwood gave a strict and dichotomous distinction between "relative" and "absolute" presuppositions, which soon breaks down when applied. What is required is a notion of levels of presuppositions: for example, those of a particular phase in the development of a specific form of knowledge; those of the form of knowledge itself and thus manifested in all phases of its maturity; and those of all our knowledge, what Polanyi called "ultimate beliefs." Collingwood also denied that absolute presuppositions are truths: they are presupposed and not propounded. But to presuppose something is to presuppose it to be true and not false.

13. *Liberalisms*, pp. 261–4; a position modified somewhat in his *Post-Liberalism*, chapter 20, but radicalised again, as an "agonistic liberalism" based upon Berlin's value-pluralism, in his *Enlightenment's Wake*.
14. *Letter to the Sheriffs of Bristol*, vol. 3, pp. 145–6.

Part II

The Value of Liberty

Classical liberalism rested on the belief that there existed discoverable principles of just conduct of universal applicability which could be recognised as just irrespective of the effects of their application on particular groups.
—Hayek, *Law, Liberty and Legislation,* vol. 1, p. 141

The ideal of a free society is in the first place to be a good society; a body of men who respect truth, desire justice and love their fellows.
—Polanyi, *The Logic of Liberty,* pp. 29–30

A society refusing to be dedicated to transcendent ideals chooses to be subjected to servitude.
—Polanyi, *Science, Faith and Society,* pp. 79–80

5

Von Mises's Sceptical Utilitarianism

Arguments for Liberty

Any answer to the question, Why is liberty so valuable? presupposes that there are real values and that we can know them. Yet more than one argument for liberty has tacitly or explicitly rested upon scepticism about the reality and knowability of values. It is a familiar claim that, since there is nothing good or bad in itself, or because we cannot know that anything is really good or bad, we should be free to hold and express our own beliefs and to adopt our own ways of life. But such an argument manifests that suspended logic of which Polanyi complained. For it fails to recognise that, if indeed nothing is or can be known to be really good or bad, then there is nothing good or known to be good about liberty and nothing bad or known to be bad about tyranny and slavery. The liberalism of scepticism undercuts itself.

Yet the restatement of liberalism in the twentieth century has consisted mostly of a set of negative arguments against socialism and other collectivisms, which have shown that they are impossible, destructive of society, subversive of law and rights, economically inefficient, and liable to corruption. The case for a liberal social order has consequently been that it is the only possible and desirable alternative. Perhaps this reflects a largely "negative" conception of liberty, the liberty of doing as we wish, for which it seems difficult to state a positive argument other than that is what we like to do. And it is noticeable that Polanyi, whose principal concern is the positive aspect of liberty, the freedom to do certain things, explicitly stated that his was a "positive" idea of liberty. We shall not be concerned directly with the negative arguments but with such positive ones as our chosen authors have presented and with the presuppositions of both sorts of argument.

We have suggested that there are likely to be two types of positive argument for a social order of competences and immunities: that it is what people like and want, and that it embodies universal ideals or principles of conduct. In this chapter we shall consider von Mises's sceptical utilitarian arguments for liberty, as a contemporary example of that "suspended logic" which Polanyi sought to overcome, and they mostly fall into the former class. For utilitarians have largely also been hedonists, have assumed pleasure to be the only good, and so have regarded everything else as good, worthless or bad only as it may promote, be irrelevant to or detract from experiences of pleasure.

At this point we may note two ways of interpreting the notion of pleasure which can have very different consequences for human liberty. On the one hand, it can be understood materially as referring to a uniform experience such that one can directly compare one person's pleasure with another, as Beccaria and Bentham assumed. In this case it makes sense to think of "the greatest happiness of the greatest number." And then it becomes an open question whether that is to be achieved by each one of us acting upon his own initiative or by some grand, coordinating plan, devised either collectively by all, or by some group or individual and then imposed upon the rest. We have already noted Bentham's equivocal attitude to individual freedom, and in part it stems from his choice of a material notion of pleasure. On the other hand, one can regard "pleasure" or "happiness" as a formal notion, that is, as "whatever it is that makes a person happy or gives him pleasure," such that there may be wide diversities among groups and individuals, and therefore no way of comparing them nor of combining them in a comprehensive plan for their joint achievement. Consequently, the appropriate social order will be that of a common framework for individuals and groups to pursue their own material goals.

Furthermore, we need also to distinguish two forms of utility: (a) *instrumentality*, whereby one thing is valuable as a *disposable and substitutable* means to something else, and (b) *foundational value* whereby one thing is a nonsubstitutable and nondisposable foundation or necessary support for something else. Once I have emptied my flooded basement, I no longer need the fire-brigade and their pumps, and I could have emptied it by bailing it out with a bucket. But, in the sewerage and water systems, although one pump can replace another, pumps of some sort or other are permanently needed and in use.[1]

Therefore, if the value of liberty is said to be that of its efficacy in providing or maintaining something else, it is important to know if it is but one means among others, and thence if it is the most effective or not, or if it is the only possible one and so a foundation or necessary support. For example, Bentham was an unequivocal hedonistic utilitarian, with a material notion of pleasure, and so he could hold liberty to be of value only as serving pleasure. Consequently, he could have been an unequivocal liberal only if he had held liberty to be necessary support for people's pleasure. But, as we have noted,[2] he would have welcomed B.F. Skinner's claim to have found a technique for so shaping human behavior by controlling its conditioning circumstances that any desired outcome can be produced, nor did he care if men became machines instead of free and active citizens so long as they would be happy. Just as Dr. Johnson said that Hume, another utilitarian, was a "Tory only by chance," so too was Bentham only incidentally a liberal. He certainly wished to do away with inherited and existing controls, but he was strongly tempted to replace them with new, more numerous and far-reaching ones. J.S. Mill, whose heart was better than his logic, in effect abandoned hedonistic utilitarianism, and its material ideas of pleasure and happiness, and argued that interpersonal freedom was a necessary condition for human flourishing. Its value lay in what it supported and allowed, but no other political and social system, Mill implied, could be substituted for it.

The relation between utilitarianism and any political system is inevitably problematic because of the substitutability and disposability of mere means, unless the category of foundation-value is sharply distinguished, as it rarely is, from that of instrumentality. Yet utilitarian ways of thinking have so dominated modern thought, that many see no *tertium quid* between utilitarianism and "intuitionism." Mill, in his *Utilitarianism*, constantly assumes that the only alternative to the former is the latter and that there is no need to refute it. Conversely, H.A. Prichard, rightly rejecting the utilitarian devaluation of moral conduct as a mere means to something else, could only point to a series of disconnected intuitions of duty.[3] Such a dichotomy is totally erroneous, if only because utilitarians themselves must, on their own logic, "intuit" the noninstrumental value of the end or ends which they themselves set up as the source of all other values. Usually, at that point they waver and obfuscate, since they regard all "intuitions" as arbitrary and unfounded assertions. For utilitarianism is the refuge of ethics when the world has been reduced to mere factuality, devoid of value and meaning. "Value-judgments" consequently become projections of "subjective" valuations upon a neutral world and cannot be recognitions of values in it. Yet some things remain related to others as useful to their realisation or continued existence. Instrumentality is an obvious fact in a world in which there are agents striving towards goals. It is also a value for those agents in relation to their goals. Therefore, at this point many utilitarians seek to escape the consequences of the divorce of value from reality by referring to the *fact* that people favour and pursue this or that, most often happiness or pleasure, and thus things around them have value or disvalue as helping or hindering those goals. These "objective facts," of what people desire, are then tacitly endorsed as authentic values although, on the usual assumptions of utilitarians, there can be no such things. G.E. Moore, a non-hedonistic utilitarian, called that "the Naturalistic Fallacy," and explicitly acknowledged the "intuitive" nature of his own choice of aesthetic experiences and friendship as the valuable goals of human life.[4] One may wonder if such are appropriate foundations for human liberty. Polanyi definitely thought they were not. But von Mises could think of no other; Popper, in his few statements of his own position, apparently concurred; and Hayek presents a mixture of arguments for liberty, one of which is an utilitarian one based on similar assumptions. In this chapter, we shall review the distinctively utilitarian elements in von Mises's arguments, and, in the next shall study the assumptions on which those arguments rest and which Popper also made.

Von Mises's Value-Scepticism

Two tensions run throughout von Mises's *Socialism* and *Human Action*. He presents, in a clear and uncompromising form, a familiar empiricist, positivist, sceptical, and utilitarian case for individual liberty: values are personal preferences; only the individual can know what will make him happy; the only rationality of action is the taking of appropriate means to ends we adopt; therefore, individuals should be free to pursue their own goals with mutual respect for each other's endeavours; and, in the long run, a market economy in which the state does not intervene will best serve what the vast majority of men show by their persistent conduct to be their interests. Yet at the same time as he asserts the merely "subjective" character of value-judgments and the "value-free" character of science, including economics, he unhesitatingly expresses his own "value-judgments" upon many of the issues at stake and implies that they are not "merely subjective" (e.g., HA, p. 835; S, pp. 13, 310–11, 452, 582). That, of course, is a familiar contradiction. Much less familiar is his distinctively un-empiricist and anti-positivist thesis that economics, or rather "praxeology" of which it is a specific part, is a wholly *a priori* and deductive science, which, he implies, is informative and not as a set of mere tautologies. If, as he presupposes, nonempirical yet substantive knowledge is possible, one wonders why it should be confined, in the human sphere, to the explication of action as the taking of means to ends. Why could it not apply also to our knowledge of ends and values? Indeed, why should we not revise the empiricist and utilitarian assumption that action is always and only the adoption and execution of means to ends beyond themselves? That, for empiricist and utilitarian thinkers, is an *a priori* truth, one that they take wholly for granted, but they would probably say that it is a tautology. We shall not be able to pursue all these questions for ourselves, but they may indicate that an adequate account of the value of human liberty may require far-reaching adjustments in many of our assumptions.[5]

Let us then begin with von Mises's account of the scope of science, in the wide sense of that term, and his assumption that it is incompetent to deal with values.

It may be the case, that as well as imbibing general positivist assumptions, von Mises also made the common mistake of unwarranted generalisation from one's specialist study to other spheres and forms of knowledge. It was the achievement of the Austrian School of Economics, founded by Carl Menger, von Mises's teacher, to overcome the impasse in classical economics created by the lingering attachment to the assumption that economic values somehow rest in goods themselves quite apart from human desires and preferences, and specifically are a function of the labour that goes into producing them. But economic values are only what people are prepared to pay, combined with the availability of the goods in question. What no one wants, or what is immediately available to all, has no price. It is not simply that the economist brackets his own valuations and studies the facts of the valuations that others make, but that economic values are "subjective" facts in the first place. Whatever may be the aesthetic value of a painting, its economic value is only what it can be sold for, and thus what someone or other is prepared to pay. The subjectivity of values is an axiom of economics and of praxeology in general (HA, p. 21), yet it may be a grievous error elsewhere.

Whatever may be the reasons for his adoption of it, there is no doubt that von Mises took "science" and "values" to be mutually exclusive:

> To call something fair or unfair is always a subjective value judgment and as such purely personal and not liable to any verification or falsification. (HA, p. 243; cf. p. 172 on murder, and p. 95)

Masked as the benevolent paternal autocrat, the author's Ego is enshrined as the voice of the absolute moral law. (HA, p. 687; cf. p. 686)

[Philosophy of law and political science make] purely arbitrary assumptions concerning allegedly eternal and absolute values and perennial justice [and] misconstrue their own arbitrary value judgments derived from intuition as the voice of the Almighty or the nature of things.... There is, however, no such thing as natural law and a perennial standard of what is just and unjust. Nature is alien to the idea of right and wrong...The notion of right and wrong is a human device, a utilitarian precept designed to make social cooperation under the division of labour possible. All moral rules and human laws are means for the realization of definite ends. (HA, pp. 715–6)

Justice applies only to concrete conduct from the point of view of valid laws of the country. (HA, p. 717)

The question of whether society ought to be built up on the basis of private ownership of the means of production or on the basis of public ownership of the means of production is political. Science cannot decide it; Science cannot pronounce a judgment on the relative values of the forms of social organisation. But Science alone, by examining the effects of institutions, can lay the foundations for an understanding of society. (S, p. 31)

Against the assertion that all men should have equal incomes, as little can be said scientifically as can be said in support of it. Here is an ethical postulate which can only be evaluated subjectively. All science can do is to show what this aim would cost us, what other aims we should have to forego in striving to attain this one. (S, p. 436)

There is no such thing as a scientific ought. Science is competent to establish what is. It can never dictate what ought to be and what ends people should aim at. (S, p. 539; cf. pp. 581–2)

As the penultimate quotation indicates, von Mises's explicit line of argument is that the science of human action, as reason, can show us the effects of given actions and policies, and the means to be adopted for realising our desired ends, but cannot deal with the ends we seek (HA, p. 173). Given his beliefs that there can be an *a priori* praxeology and that it can demonstrate that complete collectivism is impossible because it cannot calculate, that a liberal social order and free-market economy are more productive than any restricted or hampered market, and that therefore they can provide more of what people actually want, then he is right to claim, as he does, that science and reason support liberalism and not any collectivism. Indeed, a limited state, the rule of law and a free economy are not just one means among others but the only means. They are more of a foundation than an instrument. Certainly von Mises acknowledges that social cooperation is a necessary support for human life (S, p. 298, n. 1; HA, p. 158). Liberalism is based a purely rational and scientific theory of social cooperation, and presupposes that as a matter of fact people prefer life, health, nourishment, and abundance (HA, pp. 153–4). Von Mises's praxeology, and consequently his liberalism, operates with a purely formal notion of happiness (HA, p. 15) and therefore is not susceptible to collectivist proposals for achieving a common and substantive goal by central direction. Society is the co-willing of one's own ends directly and of others' ends as the means or conditions of attaining one's own via the division of labour which alone is the effective way to realise them (S, pp. 297–8). It is an organism which spontaneously organises itself, a network of individually formed and coordinated plans and joint enterprises, not an organisation (S, pp. 296–7).

Von Mises's value-scepticism is an integral part of his argument. It entails that there cannot be a substantive common good which might be achieved by a collective and centrally directed effort. The only objects of value are what individuals choose as their goals. Yet is there not a danger that it undercuts the liberal social order that he advocates? Is he not in the same position as those Anglo-American liberals who, Polanyi maintained, prevented their assumptions from destroying liberty only by suspending their logic? We shall now answer those questions with reference first to von Mises's conception of science and to the social conditions of its existence, and then to his account of liberty in general.

Science, Scepticism, and Utilitarianism

As a utilitarian, von Mises can think only in terms of "utilitarianism or intuitionism," of "ends and means," and of all action as the bringing about of end states distinct from itself. All that matters, all we call good and evil, is the consequences of actions. Intentions, for example, have value only as leading to actions, and thus to the desired outcomes of those actions. And those desired outcomes are, necessarily, Happiness. All systems of ethics inevitably turn out to be eudaemonistic in the end, however much they may repudiate that notion (S, pp. 396–401).

It turns out that science is not neutral after all, for it shows that intuitionism is incompatible with scientific method and therefore baseless, leaving the field to be occupied wholly by utilitarianism, eudaemonism, and liberalism (S, p. 400). There is, after all, a scientific ethics or an ethics compatible with science, and there can be only one such ethics. Two erroneous assumptions bring about this paradoxical result: that, as a matter of fact, people do value actions, intentions, motives, habits, customs, and the like only as means to ends other than those things; and, that all action is the bringing about of something other than itself:

> Since action is never its own end, but rather the means to an end, we call an action good or evil only in respect of the consequences of the action. It is judged according to its place in the system of cause and effect. It is valued as a means. (S, p. 399)

If by "we," von Mises means all mankind, then this is simply wrong. For people manifestly do regard some actions, and likewise motives, intentions, thoughts, emotions, habits, and so forth, as good or bad "in themselves," irrespective of any consequences. "Intuitionism" is a fact, and science is supposed only to register facts and not to evaluate them. No matter if a man in fact does not steal or murder, many of us find him at fault for *thinking* about stealing from or murdering another. Indeed that what is really or ultimately good or evil about a person is his "heart," and that the goodness and evil or his actions is that of them as expressing his "heart." As a person von Mises may not agree with this, but as scientist he ought to recognise the fact.[6]

In addition, von Mises does not refrain from expressing his own "subjective value judgments" (e.g., HA, pp. 243, 686, 715; S, pp. 13, 310–1, 582). More importantly, both works are pervaded by, and obviously written from, a passionate desire to promote the cause of human liberty and happiness. It is not merely a personal fault of von Mises that he failed to observe the positivist ideal of scientific detachment, for that is a requirement which cannot be met:

1. No scientific or scholarly work can be done without attention to scientific and scholarly values and standards, those that define and guide success and failure within science and scholarship, and by which scientists and scholars monitor and assess their efforts and results.[7]

2. In turn, commitment to those values and standards requires some degree of commitment to the value of science and scholarship. True, routine work can be done with only a low degree of attention, interest, and commitment, but persons with such attitudes are parasitic upon people who have that real interest and commitment which enables them to establish, extend, and maintain the methods and standards that others can apply in a more routine manner.[8]

3. The sciences of life, technology, and mind study achievements, processes, and actions which go right or wrong, succeed or fail, and work or break down. The subject-matters of these sciences are themselves applications of or attempts to achieve certain values and standards, and the scientist or scholar cannot study them without evaluating the objects of his attention in terms of those values and standards, just as he evaluates his own en-

gagements in any activity. That, as Collingwood said, is "a criteriological activity," one in which we set ourselves an aim and monitor our attempts to achieve it. Actions can be understood only by rethinking them, by grasping what the agent was aiming at and therefore whether and how far he succeeded or failed. Neutral sciences of achievements are logically impossible.

Of particular interest for our inquiry is the positivist and utilitarian attitude towards the value of science and scholarship themselves. That can be only a "subjective value judgment," for science and scholarship, like everything else, can have no genuine value "in themselves." At the most they can have value only as people like practising them, and then only for those who do so, or as providing means for the satisfaction of generally felt wants. They therefore become either amusement or technology. What, then, will this mean, if actually lived upon, if people actually behave as positivism and utilitarian say that we do and must? For science and scholarship themselves it can mean only that their own internal standards and values are of no inherent importance. We can acknowledge and observe them if we wish, yet there is nothing inherently wrong with shoddy thinking, faked evidence, invalid inferences and arguments, bungled experiments and inaccurate observations. They can be said to be wrong only as they do not yield the results hoped for, that is, amusement for the practitioner and an increase in welfare for the majority. The institutions of science and scholarships—traditions of observation, experimentation, theorising, recording, and exchanging information; universities, libraries, laboratories, institutes, museums, archives, journals, and scholarly and scientific societies—all these would not have arisen nor would be maintained if a certain number of people did not both themselves passionately care about them and also gain the general support of society at large. Positivists themselves take that attitude towards science, or what they regard as science, and so did von Mises. The whole tone of his work evinces a profound respect for truth whatever it may turn out to be, and for the proper procedures for reaching it. Here is something that von Mises implicitly regards as no mere "subjective value judgment." His theory of science and its value is contradicted by his own attitude towards and practice of it. Science could not exist in the first place if the positivist theory of value were true and really believed.

As for the utilitarian account of its value, as a means to private pleasure or public welfare, that would also destroy science. For, again, with no inherent value commanding respect, there would be few efforts and no self-sacrifices to further and maintain it. It cannot exist for dilettantes and dabblers alone. And, were it somehow to come into existence, all that could be maintained and developed would be those parts of it which are manifestly related to providing means for the satisfaction of felt wants. Polanyi often argued that, when science is held to have no inherent value of its own, pure science will be abandoned in favour of applied science and the pursuit of material welfare. Whether or not the last is sought collectively by central planning, as the Marxists urged, or individually by private individuals and companies, is a secondary matter. Either way, without some people dedicated to its pursuit, and a general acknowledgment of its intrinsic importance, pure science will wither and with it much applied science. For the latter is often an accidental and unpredictable by-product of the former. The practical uses of a discovery cannot be foreseen before, nor often when, the discovery is made. And research guided by practical interests alone would not yield fundamental discoveries and the further practical applications of them.[9] Utilitarianism transcends itself, and by itself destroys or thwarts the very results that it seeks.

Scepticism and Liberty

What can a positivist and "value-free" science say about the value of liberty? Nothing. That von Mises explicitly accepts:

> Science cannot decide whether freedom is a good or an evil or a matter of indifference. It can inquire wherein freedom consists and where freedom resides. (S, p. 191)

Yet he also explicitly rejected the "democracy of scepticism," the frequently expressed but fallacious notion that, because there is no knowable good and hence no common good, no one person's or group's ideas of good and right are better than any other's, and that therefore we all should have the rights to live by our own and to determine public policy. For he realises that that undercuts itself:

> The demand for democracy is not the result of a policy of compromise or of a pandering to relativism in questions of world-philosophy, for Liberalism asserts the absolute validity of its doctrine. (S, p.83)

That doctrine is "peace and prosperity," the avoidance of war and revolution, keeping the peace, the protection of life and property, and the solidity of the economic interests of individuals and nations (S, p. 70;

HA, pp. 155–7). For those reasons it supports democracy, the legal equality of all citizens, the toleration of all parties and opinions, as the only ways of peacefully maintaining society and dismissing governments (S, pp. 71ff., 77, 82–3, 189). The question is, Can liberalism rightly assert its absolute validity on von Mises's premises?

He rejects the notions of Natural Law and natural rights (S, pp. 43, 72, 319f; HA, p. 174), in both the very different classical and rationalist versions, which he does not really distinguish. All value is utility, and no social arrangement can have value save as a means to peace and prosperity. But what about the latter? Wherein lies their value?

> Science, from the point of view of its valuational neutrality, does not blame the apostles of the gospel of violence for praising the frenzy of murder and the mad delights of sadism. Value judgments are subjective, and liberal society grants to everybody the right to express his sentiments freely. (HA, p. 172)

Science, we remember, cannot establish value judgments and can only clarify the conditions and consequences of courses of action. The utilitarian philosophy, based on this scepticism, can recommend tolerance, freedom, private property and popular government, only insofar as they are beneficial, and not because they are right or just (HA, pp. 173–4). But, we ask, beneficial to what or whom? To people in general, would be von Mises's reply. But why, on his assumptions, should they be valued, and thus what benefits them? To that there can be no answer. Science deals only with facts, and the facts are people do and do not value themselves and each other. And any statement that we all ought to value ourselves and each other is "merely subjective."[10] Thus there can be no foundation for liberalism in a "purely rational and scientific theory of social cooperation." It must begin with an arbitrary and "subjective" valuation of each individual and his rights.

What von Mises falls back upon is the fact that peace and prosperity is what people actually want, and that liberalism tells them the way to attain that end (HA, p. 154).[11] Yet he forswears the illusions of the simplistic psychology of hedonism, as held by Helvétius and Bentham, and is fully aware that human life is not wholly governed by calculations of pleasure and pain. He recognises that men are capable of self-sacrifice and suicide (HA, p. 19), and, as just quoted, also of violence, murder, and sadism. All that he can, and does say, in answer to the latter is that they are blind to their own interests, which lie in social cooperation and not in revolt against the social order, and that to restrain them the coercive power of the state is necessary, contrary to the teachings of anarchism (S, pp. 56–7, 398; HA, p. 149). But appeals to people's interests notoriously fall foul of "free-rider" arguments. Why should I put myself out to promote some common good if others will do it for me, or if my own share of the good gained, or loss prevented, is less than what it will cost me? "Rational game theory" has elaborated the permutations of such calculations, but ignores the point that the whole mentality of calculating egoism which it expresses, endangers social order and cooperation. Every cooperative enterprise requires a willingness, not only to give and take, but to give more than to take, to put oneself out and to do more than one's strict share. That is demonstrated by the practice of "working to rule" wherein people do only and everything that they are strictly required to do, and thus bring the enterprise to an eventual halt. Social cooperation requires at least some degree of disinterested self-dedication to the common welfare, a sense of identity and solidarity with others. As someone once remarked, the obvious course of action for a liberal, when his country is attacked, is to emigrate. Men may risk their lives for money, but no one will die for it. Equally appeals to our interests "in the long run," as when von Mises criticises the "short-run" attitudes of welfarists (HA, pp. 843-4), are defeated by Keynes's cynical rejoinder that in the long run we are all dead.[12] Moreover, some of us will be dead within a shorter run than others, and my interests, at any moment, may not be those of the rest: some people can make profits out of war, inflation, and fraud. Utilitarianism has never been able logically to move from my search for my happiness to my promotion of that of others, and, from Helvétius and Bentham onwards, it has offered only compulsion and "education" to change men's outlooks or the naive assumption that the interplay of individual egoisms inevitably produces the optimum outcome for all.

A utilitarianism of private interests either transcends or destroys itself. To attain the desired benefits we must aim beyond them and give at least some devotion to ideals of justice and humanity without thought as to what we personally shall get out of them. That means there must be genuine good, which can be recognised by all and is not a "subjective value judgment." And if there are no such values, then liberty itself has none. A coherent Liberalism cannot be based on scepticism about values. We shall now look at Popper's Liberalism and the scepticism on which it too is based in part.

Notes

1. See further my *The Structure of Value*, ch. 2.

2. See above, p. 2.
3. See his "Does Moral Philosophy Rest on a Mistake?" (*Mind* 1912). J.S. Mill (*Utilitarianism*, ch. 1) simply assumed that ethics is a matter of either *a priori* intuitions (Kant and "moral sense" theory) or of observation and experience (utilitarianism). As for the ends of utilitarianism, they cannot be proved to be good except by being shown to be means to something admitted to be good without proof.
4. *Principia Ethica* §113, p. 188.
5. In modern philosophy, a substantive and informative *a priori* has been expounded only by phenomenology, and, in particular, by Scheler in respect of ethics (*Formalism in Ethics*) and Reinach of law (*The A Priori Foundations of Civil Law*, Eng. trans. in *Aletheia*, vol. 3, 1983). So far as I know, a comparison between von Mises's *a priori* praxeology and the methods of phenomenology has yet to be made.
6. This is but one example of the utilitarian's systematic distortion of the facts of human life. We shall take this up when we come to Hayek and Hume and the values of customs and institutions. For the present we shall note that von Mises simply takes it for granted (HA, p. 716; S, p. 399) or regards it as a tautology (HA, p. 12), that human action is always an effort to achieve a state of affairs beyond itself. Von Mises does distinguish between "labour," as "effort" and "toil" to bring something else about, and "immediately gratifying activity," such as paddling a canoe on a Sunday afternoon, which is not a means to the attainment of an end (HA, p. 137). But von Mises pays no further attention to such activities for they do not come within the scope of "catallactics." Most utilitarians, being also hedonists, would interpret "immediately gratifying activities" as means to an end, namely, a state of pleasure which immediately follows on from the action and which the agent specifically has in view. They lack any conception of taking pleasure in the very performance of an activity, indeed of activity itself (Aristotle's *energeia*) and identify it with "process" (*genesis*) or change, and in turn identify all processes with self-terminating as opposed to continuing ones.
7. See Polanyi, PK, p. 183 and also p. 220 where he points out that science needs also the support of society at large and that for the sake of science's inherent value. See also, on this topic and that of (3), my *Structure of Value*, chs. 6–10, which develops the arguments of Collingwood and Polanyi.
8. See further my "Passivity and the Rationality of Emotion," *The Modern Schoolman*, vol. 68, no. 4, May 1991.
9. See below, ch. 9 §2.
10. Bentham, followed by J.S. Mill (*Utilitarianism*, ch. 5) and more recently by R.M. Hare (*Freedom and Reason*, p.118), asserted that "each to is count as one and not more than one," and thus tried to incorporate justice into utilitarianism. But why should we all be equally valued on utilitarian assumptions? On the contrary, if pleasure is the only good, then it follows that those more sensitive to pleasure and pain, and able to experience greater enjoyment or distress, must count as proportionally more than those less sensitive. X's average "score" of 10 units in similar circumstances must count for more than Y's average score of 5.

   Nietzsche, with better logic and valuing "life," had no time for weaklings and degenerates (*The Twilight of the Idols*, p. 534; *The Will to Power* §373, also §§287, 752, 784). The same goes for all external valuations of persons: for example, Hegel and the way in which the World Spirit uses and discards us (*Reason in History*, pp. 65, 69–71, 89, 90, 91), and Lenin's total detachment from any considerations other than bringing in and defending the Revolution. All that R.M. Hare can say about the value of human life and our duties towards each other, given his utter divorce of fact and value, is that they are not "derived from the 'essence of man' or from any philosophical mystification of that sort; they are acknowledged because we say, 'There, but for good fortune, go I'" (*Freedom and Reason*, p. 122).

11. This is occasionally reinforced by the insinuation that those who hold other doctrines compel people to adopt them: for example, "Masked as the benevolent paternal autocrat, the author's Ego is enshrined as the voice of the absolute moral law" (HA, p. 687). This comes near to what Polanyi analysed as "moral inversion." For non-sceptical and non-utilitarian doctrines are debunked by declaring them to be expressions of an imperialistic ego, and von Mises's own moral preferences are hidden behind what is claimed to be a value-neutral science.

12. It is notable that the electorates of Lithuania, Poland, Hungary, Bulgaria, and Russia, preferring security in the short term to greater prosperity in the longer term, after their first experience of freedom, returned to power or Parliament ex-Communists who dropped Marxism and offered varieties of socialist interventionism, though in some cases they have executed another about-turn. It may also be the case that other people active in politics lack experience, especially the experience of working together. The use of proportional representation in any case tends to fragment parties and to prevent the emergence of stable government.

6

The Open Society and Its Lack of Value

Open and Closed Societies

We have seen that von Mises leaves the liberty that he values without any rational foundation because of the dichotomy of fact and value to which he thinks science is committed. We now turn to Popper as a second example of "suspended logic" and shall endeavour to ascertain if and how far he overcame that dichotomy and so was able to give rational grounds for his preference of the Open over closed societies.

It is not Popper's presentations and criticisms of Plato, Hegel, and Marx, upon which most discussion of *The Open Society and Its Enemies*, has focused that concern us, but what Popper has positively to say about the Open Society, its liberty, and the value of that liberty. Yet *The Open Society and Its Enemies* tells us little directly about the former and why it should be defended against the latter, except, by implication, that, because closed societies are bad, an open one must be good.

We shall now try to clarify what the Open Society is supposed to be and thus the idea of liberty which it embodies. Popper largely defines the Open Society by contrast with a closed society. We may summarise and tabulate[1] the characteristics of each in Figure 1.

Popper implies that the attributes of the one do not apply to the other, although he acknowledges that the group-spirit of tribalism is not entirely lost in modern, open societies but remains in friendship, comradeship, "youthful tribalistic movements," certain clubs and adult societies, and in moments of conflict and crisis (OS, vol. 1, p. ix). And transition from the one to the other obviously takes time and there are intermediate stages which combine features of both. Popper dates the start of the transition from a closed to an open society in the seventeenth century (OS, vol. 1, p. ix). Popper thereby implies that mediaeval Europe was a closed society. Yet it is difficult to see how it could fit that description. Let us quickly consider the first five items listed above:

CLOSED SOCIETY	OPEN SOCIETY
Institutions and castes are sacrosanct	Tradition and established ways do not have absolute authority and can be criticised and changed
No competition for status	
Tribal, semi-organic unit, living together, sharing common efforts, experiences, and emotions	
Submissive to magical forces	
Totalitarian	
"Naively monist": no distinction between natural and normative laws, and natural mishaps and sanctions imposed by others	"Critically dualist": sharply distinguishes "facts" from "decisions"
"Naively conventionalist": natural and normative regulations both produced by will, human or divine	"Critically conventionalist": norms and normative laws made and alterable by man

Figure 1

1. Europe has never had castes, and therefore no "sacrosanct" ones. Classes there were, with differences of legal status. Yet it was possible for some at least to move from one class to another, and there was an increasing differentiation of classes and occupations in the towns. And the Church offered a career open to talents: Cardinal Wolsey was the son of an Ipswich draper.

2. One wonders where there has been no "competition for status," both among individuals and classes.

3. A closed society is also "tribal," living together, and sharing the same emotions. As we shall see in chapter 13, there is no society without shared emotions. But, while in some places, such as the Borders and Highlands of Scotland, people lived in clans, wherein they were linked by blood, acknowledged the leadership of a chief, and felt themselves to be distinct from, and often in conflict with, neighbouring clans, most of mediaeval Europe was not so organised, as Popper himself acknowledged (OS, vol. 2, p. 50).

4. As for being "submissive to magical forces," whether mediaeval Europe was or not, partly depends upon what one means by "magic." As we again shall see in chapter 13, every society is held together by what Collingwood called "magic," those rituals which engender and sustain the emotions needed for practical life. Undoubtedly, such forces are stronger in some societies and some periods than others. If today they are weaker, that may be an unsatisfactory state of affairs. By "magic" a rationalist could mean any elements of religious belief and practice, but that, of course, would be to beg the question. And by "magic" could be meant "witchcraft," the

practice of seeking to achieve results in the world by the invocation of spirits or the manipulation of occult forces. In that respect it is interesting to note that there was an increase in witchcraft in the sixteenth and early seventeenth centuries alongside, and sometimes indistinguishable from the new natural science, as in the case of Paracelsus, and that there has been another revival within the last twenty years or so, as the shelves of bookshops and public libraries will testify.

5. Mediaeval Europe could not be called "totalitarian," for there divisions of power among kings, barons, free cities, and Church and State. Also there were systems of law (customary, feudal, Roman, and statute), recognising rights and setting limits. Indeed, absolutism, to the extent that there was such a thing in the seventeenth and eighteenth centuries, weakened and sometimes destroyed those limitations upon power. Moreover, absolutism was often supported by "enlightened" and "critical" opinion in its revolt against tradition and established authority. Indeed, as we noted in the Introduction, the emancipation of the individual from the bonds of tradition and traditional associations and authorities was often part of the same process as the growth of the modern omnicompetent, impersonal, and bureaucratic state, the latter both forcibly bringing about the former and providing a substitute for the need to belong to and to participate in something greater than oneself.

So why should Popper apparently classify mediaeval Europe as a closed society? One could say that his attitude is perhaps an expression of the Enlightenment's rationalist impatience with and disdain for everything "superstitious" which prevented any serious historical study of the Middle Ages until the work of Edmund Burke and Sir Walter Scott.[2] Whether or not that may be so, a more definite reason can be seen in the last pair of contrasts between closed and open societies.

That between "naive monism," which does not distinguish between natural and normative laws, and "critical dualism," which does to the point of making it a dichotomy, is another version of the familiar antithesis endemic in empiricist and positivist philosophies, codified by G.E. Moore, and continued by analytic moral philosophy, between "naturalism" and "anti-naturalism." The former is the identification of values with facts, or some specific range of facts, and of *is* with *ought*, such that "good" is entailed by and can be strictly deduced from certain "natural" or factual attributes of things. That, say the anti-naturalists, is to make "good" and "ought" *mean*, say, "pleasure" or "promoting Evolution," and thus to deprive them of their meanings. One then utters a mere tautology in saying "pleasure is good" or "Evolution ought to be promoted." But it always does make sense to ask if pleasure is good or if Evolution ought to be promoted. Therefore, they conclude, fact and value, description and evaluation, *is* and *ought*, remain radically distinct. One always needs a separate moral or evaluative or prescriptive principle as the major premise for any valid moral syllogism:

> X is good (or ought to be done);
> This is an X (or has X-ness);
> Therefore this is good (or ought to be done).

At this point the later analytic philosophers diverge from Moore, who believed that he could simply "see" that certain states of mind, such as friendship and aesthetic experience, are good. On the contrary, say Hare and the rest, there is never any such connection, and the major premise is always a freely chosen postulate. In effect, theirs is a sceptical Kantianism: a purely formal system in which the Categorical Imperative is reduced to the merely formal requirement that all moral principles are "universalisable." Hare himself favoured utilitarianism as the substantive matter for this formalism to work upon and thought that all decently minded persons choose likewise, and that only "fanatics," such as Nazis and white South Africans (under *apartheid*), would choose principles which, if universalised, could rebound upon themselves were their circumstances to change.[3]

This moral theory takes it for granted that all reality is merely factual, just what it happens to be, human reality included. Although they eschew all metaphysics, and emphatically assert that ethics has nothing to do with it,[4] its proponents hold a distinct cosmology, that of man as a radically autonomous and self-defining subject in a mechanical and meaningless universe which does not set before him any Law or Way and wherein he must choose his own.[5]

We have seen how von Mises explicitly drew the consequences of this cosmology, that all judgments of value are "merely subjective," though like everyone else he could not consistently and coherently live that doctrine. Likewise Popper draws some consequences from "critical dualism" of "facts and decisions" but shies away from others. We make and change norms and normative laws ("critical conventionalism"), by decisions or conventions to observe or alter them. But, says Popper, they are not necessarily arbitrary. He denies that "convention implies arbitrariness." For we can compare existing conventions with standards which we have decided to be worthy of being realised. Yet, he admits and rightly so on his premises, that those standards are of our own making, for we decide to adopt them and they are not to be found in Nature, which consists of facts and regularities and is neither moral nor immoral. We impose standards upon Nature and introduce morals into the natural world. Decisions cannot be derived from facts, and we and we alone are responsible for adopting or rejecting any suggested moral laws (OS, vol. 1, pp. 61–4, 66). Facts as such are meaningless and receive it only via our decisions (OS, vol. 1, pp. 278–9). It follows that the normative elements in our decisions cannot be based upon facts, that I cannot decide to do X because X *is* good. Rather, X is good only as I decide that it is.

Theories about human life are formulated within human life and not outside it. Sooner or later they react back upon it. If it is thought that there is nothing good or right prior to our decisions, then the facts of social life appear differently. They cease to have any inherent weight and authority; laws are merely expressions of will; and customs and institutions shape us without our consent and without any reason of their own. Consequently, a society which is based upon the opposite conviction, "naive monism," that there are indeed laws and obligations prior to human will, can appear to be repressive in imposing upon its members customs, laws, and institutions which in reality have no inherent value which could command us. As did premodern Europe to Popper, it will appear to be a closed society to those who reject its fundamental beliefs. The belief that there are no obligations which one does not choose or legislate for oneself is likely to issue into a rejection of any that others and tradition set before one.

Indeed, in the full logic of "critical dualism" and man as a self-defining subject in a meaningless world, all society, all law and all institutions are arbitrary impositions upon a self which regards itself as radically autonomous. Thence can arise demands for the remaking of the social order in accord with the requirements of the will unconstrained by any external obligations. This has taken two principal forms: the individualist one of removal of restraints upon individuals who will then be free to arrange matters among themselves, with more or less of a legal framework within which to do so; and the collectivist one of democratic totalitarianism whereby all together are to decide what all should do. Each of these has its more impatient and therefore revolutionary forms. Thence arises the modern problem of stabilising society against a doctrine which undermines it if its logic is followed through and acted upon.

That is the problem that Popper sets himself. Our present discontents come from

> what is perhaps the greatest of all moral and spiritual revolutions of history, a movement which began three centuries ago. It is longing of uncounted and un-

known men to free themselves and their minds from the tutelage of authority and prejudice. It is their attempt to build up an open society which rejects the absolute authority of the merely established and the merely traditional while trying to preserve, to develop, and to establish traditions, old or new, that measure up to their standards of freedom, of humaneness, and of rational criticism. It is their unwillingness to sit back and leave the entire responsibility for ruling the world to human or superhuman authority, and their readiness to share the burden of responsibility for avoidable suffering, and to work for its avoidance. This revolution has created powers of appalling destructiveness; but they may yet be conquered. (OS, vol. 1, p. ix)

According to Popper, Plato in the ancient world and Hegel in the modern one, sought to counter and defeat these progressive forces, while Marx, via his holism and historicism, allowed his humanitarian sympathies to be derailed into a repressive system. Each of these three philosophies is, according to Popper, in intention or effect, a return to a closed and tribal society.[6] Instead of going for a total and simultaneous reconstruction of society, which will destroy the Open Society, we should act more temperately and slowly by the experimental and revisable methods of "piecemeal social engineering."

The Consequences of Critical Dualism

Popper, then, sets himself the same task as Polanyi. The passage just quoted is paralleled by many similar ones in Polanyi's numerous essays. So too is that where Popper says that historicist prophecies express a deep dissatisfaction with a world that does not and cannot live up to our moral ideals (OS, vol. 1, p. 5). On the one hand, they both accept the modern spirit of humanitarian reform, but, on the other, they are aware of great strains and dangers stemming from that very change in ideas which produced the spirit of reform. The problem for both is so to stabilise the situation that the latter is avoided while the former is maintained. Yet their answers to this question are deeply different. As we shall see in chapter 9, Polanyi rejects entirely the assumptions of Popper's "critical dualism" and the idea of an Open Society. We shall now ascertain how far Popper succeeded in stabilising the Open Society against its internal strains.

Popper is right to locate the problem in the very critical dualism which defines the Open Society.[7] In the addendum to *The Open Society and Its Enemies*, Popper, in line with Anglo-American liberalism rather than the *ésprits forts* of the Continent, tried to protect his critical dualism of facts and decisions or standards against the relativist self-destruction which it appears to engender. Though a decision to accept a proposal creates the corresponding standard but a decision to accept a proposition does not create the corresponding fact, both facts and standards can be discussed and criticised. And just as truth, the correspondence between a proposition and the relevant fact, is a regulative ideal to which we can approximate even though we can never reach it or be sure that we have reached it, so too can right or good correspond to certain standards, to which we can approximate even though we cannot say that we have found the absolute right or valid proposals that we seek. Just as there is no general criterion of truth, so there is none of absolute rightness, such as the *greatest happiness principle* or minimisation of misery. But we can make progress and discoveries. Cruelty is always "bad" and to be avoided wherever possible, and the Golden Rule is a good standard (OS, vol. 2, pp. 384–6). Liberalism is based on this dualism of facts and standards, and is the search for better standards (OS, vol. 2, p. 392).

But, if so, then it is based on shifting sands. For if proposals and standards are such only as we decide to accept them, and there is nothing in the world to limit or guide our choice, how then can we criticise them or look for better ones? To criticise one standard we need another by which to judge it, a second standard which we thereby accept as true and valid. But if all standards rest on our arbitrary decisions, then there can be only the semblance of criticism and appraisal, for that by which we are judging would be as unfounded and arbitrary as anything which we judge. Likewise for progress to be possible, there must a real good and right to which we can approximate. If there is no such unchanging and valid ideal, there is no measure of our greater nearness to it, nor distance from it. And when Popper says that right and good can conform to some standards or other, and that, in particular, cruelty is bad and the Golden Rule good, he is, on his own premises, stating only what he himself has simply decided or created. What we have here, I suggest, is an example of that suspended logic which, having undercut any rational basis for standards and values, and thence for moral principles and political policies, falls back upon and appeals to a conventional sense of what is right and good, which it takes for granted. Convention does imply arbitrariness, if there are no nonconventional standards.

It looks at times as if Popper falls into the common mistake of failing to distinguish two sorts of decisions: those which are decisions to accept or recognise that X *is* Y, and those which determine that X *shall be* Y. For example, he says that if someone accepts Christian ethics, not because he is commanded to, but because he thinks it right to do so, then that is his decision. "Whatever authority we may accept, it is we who accept it" (OS, vol. 1, pp. 2–3). Yes, of course it is the person's own decision to accept Christian ethics or any authority, and to live by the one and to heed the other. Those are decisions of the latter type, decisions to do something or that someone else should do something. In contrast, deciding that Christian ethics are the right ones, or that this is a genuine and trustworthy authority, is an act of recognition, a decision of the former type. We may illustrate this difference by a familiar example. The umpire's decisions are primarily of the former sort, for example, that the batsman *was* out of his crease when the ball hit the stumps. But those of the captain are of the latter sort, for example, that Smith and Jones *shall* open the batting. Consequently, by apparently aligning the decision to accept a way of life wholly with a decision to do something ("a proposal"), and by ignoring the elements of recognition within it, Popper implies that there is no element of recognition, no deciding that something is the case, and that therefore such a decision is entirely a matter of will—whim, rather—and without grounding. After all, the captain can decide that Smith and Jones *shall* open the batting because he has decided, after comparing them with the others, that they *are* the steadiest players of the new ball. In any case, Popper unequivocally states that a decision to accept a proposal *creates* the corresponding standard whereas one to accept a proposition does not create the corresponding fact (OS, vol. 2, p. 384). The latter, we may say, is one to *recognise* a fact, but the former is one to set up or adopt a standard.

Although Popper also sometimes acknowledges that decisions of the latter type are also involved in those of the former, as when he states that we have to decide if there is sufficient evidence for us tentatively to accept an hypothesis (OS, vol. 2, p. 380), and thus would not endorse any wholly "objectivist" account of an impersonal process of knowing, yet his formulation of his critical dualism, and the way he applies it to decisions about good, right, and duty, make that dualism into a dichotomy, the familiar one of bare and neutral facts over and against "subjective value judgments" and arbitrary decisions about matters of good, right, and duty. Facts, he states, have no meaning and gain it only through our decisions (OS, vol. 2, pp. 278–9). It follows that our decisions to act, or that something shall be so, cannot be based on recognitions of the values or significance of things.

Moreover, he dismisses what he calls "spiritual naturalism," that is, any account of a definite human nature which we ought to realise, because it can be used to endorse as "natural" any positive norm and anything that happens to men (OS, vol. 1, p. 73). He goes further and dismisses as meaningless and unprofitable all questions about what something is, about its nature or essence (OS, vol. 1, p. 109). Yet, if there is not an ideal human nature for us to achieve, then there can be no inherent standards for human conduct, no Natural Law for us to obey, no real good and harm which we can do to ourselves and our fellows. If there is no condition which is truly human, then we cannot fall short of it nor thwart others' endeavours to attain it. If there is no right way to act, then there can be no wrong way that deviates from and counters it. Where else but in a notion of a proper human life can we find a standard for conducting ourselves?

Popper realises that proposals to reform institutions require an answer to the question of the purposes they are to serve and the functions to which they are to be adapted. "Social engineers" must know what they are trying to bring about. To that he has his own answer, that of humanitarianism, which he specifies as protection for all from aggression by others, reform by law-abiding and peaceful means except where there is no legal provision for it, protection by government of that freedom which does not harm others, as equal limitations of everyone's freedom as is possible yet not going beyond what is necessary for that, a government that actively protects the citizens and their liberties, but one that does not try, inevitably counterproductively, to enforce morality which can be enforced only by one's own conscience unless it is to degenerate into tribalistic taboos (OS, vol. 1, pp. 109–13). This is quite a sizable and respectable list of demands. The question is, why these demands, and not those of the historicists, totalitarians, and tribalists whom he opposes? His very choice of "humanitarianism" indicates that, despite his explicit doctrine, he does have an ideal of human well-being, a good for man as man and thus for all men, and thus an idea of a proper and natural state or condition of human life. Especially notable is the last item in his list, the ethics of conscience in contrast to mere taboo. The former is manifestly taken to be superior to the latter. But, given the dichotomy of facts and decisions, these requirements for social policy are ones only that Popper has decided to make. Moreover, his preference for an ethics of conscience over taboos presupposes that there is a genuine good and right which we recognise and do not "decide" and of which conscience reminds us, as against the mere "you mustn't" of taboo. But that is a distinction which cannot be drawn on Popper's assumptions.

Furthermore, Popper's preferences transgress his criticism of love, defined by Aquinas as the wish to make the other happy: that it is forcing one's own views upon him (OS, vol. 2, p. 237). It must be that if there is no common human nature which we can and should realise, but only mere factual tendencies to do this or that. From such an assumption, it is often inferred that we should therefore allow each to adopt his own manner of life or experiment in living. But, as Sartre saw, no such inference follows. Such a policy is itself a forcing of one's own views upon the other: even the attitude of tolerance would cause him to be "thrown forcefully into a tolerant world" and to remove from him "those free possibilities of courageous resistance, of perseverance, of self-assertion which he would have had the opportunity to develop in a world of intolerance."[8] So also, Sartre says, does the Kantian project of making the Other and his freedom ends in themselves. After all, he may not want to be free. Likewise, liberty of and for conscience, which Popper advocates, forces responsibility upon those who would prefer to have everything laid down for them. Popper believes that there is a widespread fear of freedom and personal responsibility (OS, vol. 1, p. 5). What, then, is his reason for forcing it and the Open Society upon such people instead of offering them the security of a closed society which they crave? The answer can be only that he holds that the condition of personal responsibility and living by conscience is more genuinely human and so more worthwhile than that of living by taboo and authority. But his premises prevent him from saying that.

Being based on the dualism of facts and decisions, the Open Society cannot affirm itself to be the right state for human life and an ideal towards which we ought to strive. It can be only what those who have decided for it have decided for. It cannot claim to be superior to any closed society. And, as Polanyi says (*Meaning*, p. 184), a "*wholly* open society would be a wholly vacuous one—one which could never actually exist, since it could never have any reason for existing."

Rationalism and Relativism

Yet Popper is aware that irrationalism and relativism present serious threats to free societies. He locates the origin of relativism in a desire for certainty that requires a general criterion of truth such that, if in any particular case it were fulfilled, we would know for sure that there we had found the truth. The correct realisation that there is no such criterion results in despair of ever attaining the truth about anything (OS, vol. 2, pp. 369–75). Popper's answer to this despair is, in effect, to admit it. We have no general criterion of truth; we can never know that we have arrived at the truth; we are always liable to be mistaken; but error implies truth as that of which it falls short; and we can advance towards the truth even though we cannot know that we have reached it. For what we can do is learn from our mistakes. Each error when known to be an error becomes an advance towards the truth. Consequently, we should look for our mistakes and criticise our theories, so that we can advance more quickly. Our proneness to error does not prevent us from often having a fair idea that we are closer to or further from the truth. Mistakes are absolute and what deviates from the truth is false. Therefore a statement or theory which is false remains false even though it may contain a lot of truth. Yet if it does, it is closer to the truth than others which do not contain so much truth, and so is an advance upon those others (OS, vol. 2, pp. 374–7).

In this argument, as in his theory of science, Popper will not allow that we ever attain to the truth. No theory can be proved, but false ones can be eliminated by the finding of counter-instances. Yet this depends precisely upon what it denies. If we cannot know that we right, we can never know that we are wrong. If I cannot know that "X is Y" is true, I cannot know that "'X is Z' is false" is true. If we are always liable to err, we are always liable to err in recognising our mistakes as mistakes. To learn from our mistakes, we must be sure that they *are* mistakes, or at least, as Popper says, we must have "a fair idea" that they are mistakes. But Popper denies our ability to *know* anything and to arrive at the *truth* about anything, and that must include knowing and attaining the truth about our errors.[9] Nor do I find any sign in his later writings that he ever changed his position.

In Popper one senses a deep-seated attitude of rationalist scepticism which will not allow us to *know* anything. Thus, while he rejects the consequences of such a scepticism, he still holds that to admit to definite knowledge would be to open the way to a return to dogmatism, authoritarianism, superstition, tribalism, magic, and thus the Closed Society. It was Polanyi's argument that such a scepticism is precisely that which undermines freedom and prepares the way for modern totalitarianism of one sort or another. Popper, it seems to me, also recognises the dangers of scepticism, yet cannot break its hold upon him.

We see this most clearly in his attempted defence of rationalism. He readily admits that what he calls "uncritical or comprehensive rationalism," namely, the refusal to accept anything unsupported by argument or experience, is inconsistent in being itself unsupportable by argument or experience. Furthermore, he recognises the self-contradiction of the demand not to make assumptions or presuppositions. Consequently, he proposes for adoption the attitude of "critical rationalism" which admits that irrationalism is logically tenable and that the rationalist attitude is itself based on an initial act of irrational faith in reason (OS, vol. 1, pp. 230–1). He then tries to support the choice of critical rationalism over irrationalism by spelling out some of the consequences of each. I shall pass over the details, even though he wrongly dichotomises "emotion" and "reason" and betrays signs of the worst sort of shallow rationalism in hostility to "'deeper' layers of human nature." The interesting point is that Popper presents the issue as a moral decision: that for irrationalism leading, *inter alia*, to emotionalism, violence, partiality, dogmatism, and intolerance, and that for critical rationalism leading to impartiality, responsibility, fostering of freedom, recognition of the unity of reason among mankind, and humanitarianism, to treating all men as rational. Now if there are considerations which show that the one is superior to the other, it cannot be an irrational choice. And if these particular moral considerations are what make it superior, then they too have a rational basis, or are part of the rational basis of all thought. Why, then, should Popper persist in saying that critical rationalism is founded on an irrational decision? The reason is, I suggest, that dualism of facts and standards which he never overcomes and which does make decisions about standards into arbitrary ones.

Elsewhere he repudiates what has now come to be known as "foundationalism," the assumptions that knowledge (a) must be based on necessarily true, self-evident, or incorrigible foundations, (b) must therefore be wholly correct from the start, and (c) is not a developing and self-correcting process.[10] Doubtless he would repudiate both the despairing version of contemporary post-foundationalism and Rorty's joyfully Nietzschean version in *Philosophy and the Mirror of Nature*, but in substance he draws the same conclusion, that we cannot know anything. And, like Rorty, he does not undertake a thorough revision of his own assumptions, despite the contradictions which they yield. Such a revision would start with the acknowledgment that we do know certain things, and would then seek to articulate their presuppositions and those of all knowledge, presuppositions which are *a*critically but not irrationally held, for all thought and knowledge involves them. Our faith in them is a rational faith in reason, a faith seeking its own reason, and a reason articulating that faith and its contents.[11]

If, then, the Open Society cannot *know* itself to be superior to the Closed Society, and if it rests on an irrational decision, can it claim to be worth defending? Popper has no inhibitions about not tolerating intolerance (OS, vol. 1, pp. 235, 265), which means closing the Open Society to it. But, on his assumptions, there can be no rational basis for this. Popper could be mistaken in holding that intolerance is not to be permitted, and he cannot claim to know that he is justified in believing it and acting upon it. Likewise, he will not allow that he *knows* that humanitarianism, equality before the law, and liberty are superior to indifference to human misery, legal privileges, and slavery. Hence the fatal ambiguity of the Open Society: Is it open to everything or is it based upon a commitment to certain values and therefore closed against what denies and opposes them? If the former, then it is open to its own destruction. If the latter, then it needs the will, faith, and authority to affirm, assert, defend and, if need be, impose its convictions. These are its dogmas, its articulated presuppositions, about which it cannot admit doubt and hesitation. It is clear that Popper does not doubt them, that he would not allow that they could be mistaken, and that his critical rationalism has its limits. Yet it will not allow him consistently to state *that* the Open Society is the better nor *why* it is better.

* * *

Our review of von Mises and Popper has shown the difficulties of stating a positive case for a free society within the modern framework of the dichotomy of facts and values (or decisions or standards). Von Mises could appeal only to what people want and their long-term interests, without being able to say why some should subordinate their shorter-term interests to the longer-term interests of all, and Popper's case rests upon a commitment to humanitarianism for which he can give no warrant. Hayek sought a third way between "nature" and "convention" on which to rest the case for classical liberalism, and we shall now see how far he succeeded.

Notes

1. See OS, vol. 1, pp. ix, 1, 59–61, 173.

2. See further OS, vol. 2, pp. 24–6, 303 n.10, for Popper's avowedly rationalist attitude towards the Middle Ages. Contrast Hayek, CL, pp. 162–3; LLL, vol. 1, pp. 52, 157 n.13.

   On the significance of Burke and Scott for the development of historiography, see H. Butterfield, *Man on His Past*, pp. 17–8, 68–70.

3. See Moore, *Principia Ethica*, and Hare, *The Language of Morals, Freedom and Reason*, and *Moral Thinking*. In effect, the same position was set forth by Sartre in his *Existentialism is a Humanism*.

   These and the following theses are echoed by Popper in OS, vol. 1, pp. 59–73, and vol. 2, pp. 383–6, 388–93.

4. But Moore did recognise that metaphysics can tell us in general which forms of the good can be realised and which cannot (*Principia Ethica*, pp. 68–70).

5. I owe this formulation to C. Taylor's *Hegel* (ch. 1) where its antecedents in the ancient world and its revival in the modern, are explained as result, valid or not, of a new natural science. Taylor also points out that there is an alternative interpretation of man within this cosmology, as himself just another piece of the meaningless mechanism that is the universe. In fact, this second interpretation always involves the first, for no one can apply it to himself. Kant's whole "critical" system was an endeavour to combine the two as the "noumenal" and "phenomenal" selves. We have noted how Bentham could imagine treating men, other men, as machines. In my *Education of Autonomous Man* I have shown how this cosmology and the alternative anthropologies of radical autonomy and mechanistic reductionism have informed the educational policies of Rousseau, Kant, Marx, Nietzsche, contemporary analytic philosophers, Sartre, Helvétius, and B.F. Skinner, plus Froebel and Hegel who represent, in theist and immanentist forms respectively, the Romantic reaction against it. Hegel, of course, tried to stabilise the tendencies and forces engendered by the modern cosmology by relocating self-definition upon a cosmic and wholly immanent Geist. Popper, showing scant sympathy for Hegel and his problems, misses most of the significance of Hegel's work, including the fact that he was engaged in substantially the same task as Popper himself.

   See also, H. de Lubac, *The Drama of Atheist Man* on the same basic complex of ideas in Comte and Nietzsche, and as presented and countered by Dostoyevsky.

   In my *Structure of Value*, chapter 7, I show how this notion of a necessarily valueless world is true of the inanimate universe without reference to life and mind, and, in chapters 10–12, how the latter necessarily give rise to fields and achievements of ranges of values, which, in the case of our responsible (or irresponsible) actions, necessarily include moral values.

6. Popper is seriously in error in accusing Plato of "tribalism." As Nesbit points out (*The Quest for Community*, pp. 115–6), Plato's problem was precisely that of the decline of traditional associations and the emergence of the emancipated and thus alienated and frustrated individual. His solution was to carry that process to its logical conclusion, and not to reverse it: that is, to create an absolute and total state-community to provide justice and physical, moral, and intellectual security for the individual. Hegel's modern state, furthermore, is corporatist in including within its legal and political structure the representation of "estates." And though Marx himself was a German nationalist and as contemptuous of Slavs as was Hitler, he praised the new bourgeois state for its demolition of "feudalism," and indicated that the classless society would be a totally *political* one with no associations of any kind.

7. There are other factors which exacerbate it, such as the secularisation of Christian eschatology, the full meaning of which Popper misses in his accounts of

"historicism." It is the promise of an End to history within this world and this life, a radiant future to which the present is but a means, and not just prophecies of an inevitable future, which fires the imaginations of such as Comte and Marx and their followers. Hegel promised the same but taught a Quietest acceptance of the cunning of reason in world history rather than an urgent effort to hasten the End.

The key figure in this process of secularisation is Joachim of Fiore, who prophesied the coming of a "Third Realm," that of the Holy Spirit, of joy, peace, and freedom, in which the knowledge of God is directly revealed in men's hearts, and which is about to open (the first, that of the Old Testament, was that of the Father and Law, an age of fear and servitude; the Second, of the Son and the Gospel, an age of faith and filial submission). On Joachim, see N. Cohn, *The Pursuit of the Millenium*, ch. 6, and also chs. 11–13 on the route by which the millennial rule of the saints took on the character of an egalitarian and collectivist society. See also E. Voegelin, *The New Science of Politics* and *Science, Politics and Gnosticism*.

8. *Being and Nothingness*, p. 409.
9. See Polanyi, PK, pp. 272–4, on the equivalence of belief and doubt. "I doubt X" entails either "I believe not-X" or "I believe that standard Y for knowing X has not yet been achieved," both of which involve definite affirmations: that not-X is the case, and that Y is the standard for knowing X and that, in this case, it has not yet been fulfilled.
10. "On the Sources of Knowledge and of Ignorance" in CR. Again, he shows no sign that in this he recognises a basic agreement with Hegel, who, however, thought that Absolute Knowledge could be attained and had been attained for the first time by him in his own philosophy.
11. See above, ch. 4 n. 12 on Collingwood and Polanyi.

7

The Value of the Great Society

Hayek's Utilitarianism of Institutions and Practices

From two examples of "suspended logic" which entail nihilism and the destruction of liberty, we turn to Hayek's arguments for the value of liberty. Like von Mises and Popper, Hayek frequently presents a negative case for liberty: collectivist planning is impossible and attempts at it are disastrous,[1] and consequently a free economy and society are the only practicable, prosperous, and peaceful ones. But unlike them he also develops at length positive arguments and it is they which concern us. The fullest version is to be found in Part 1 of *The Constitution of Liberty*. In brief it is that peace and prosperity, civilisation and all its benefits, result from individual liberty under the Rule of Law and a system of private property. Volumes 1 and 2 of *Law, Liberty and Legislation* extend that argument to the Great Society, that network of overlapping relations among an indefinite number of individuals who conduct trade and other affairs with each other by the mutual observation of the rules of justice, and which therefore can and do extend beyond any particular group to embrace all who are ready to act similarly. That I shall in no way dispute and shall take for granted. What I shall examine is the utilitarian account of law, justice, property, and institutions generally which Hayek uses to support it.

But before we proceed directly to examine Hayek's version of utilitarianism, which he takes from Hume, let us note another strand in his argument which is closely connected with it, the argument from human ignorance. That is part of his general and complex argument against the pretensions of social planning in all its forms, and not just in economic affairs. It has three principal applications:

1. No central planner can possibly assemble for his guidance all the knowledge that is dispersed among the population or those engaged in a spe-

cific sphere of activity, and which is not possessed by any one mind. Therefore only a free society can utilise this dispersed knowledge by allowing
each to use his own portions of it.

2. Precise predictions cannot be made regarding economic matters, and other
"complex phenomena," for the data cannot be known by anyone. All that
is possible are "explanations in principle," showing only the sorts of things
that will or will not occur, and not any predictions of the particular events
that will result, only an algebra and never an arithmetic. It follows that
what can be done is to continue or adopt, as permanent policies, those
practices and institutions which will have the sorts of results we desire
and that we should abjure any plans or schemes intended to produce particular results in particular circumstances (SPPE, chs. 1 and 2; NSPPE,
ch. 2).

3. As a corollary of (2), and because we do not and cannot know what the
future will bring, we should conduct ourselves, individually and collectively, by following general rules irrespective of the results of so doing on
particular occasions.

Hayek's utilitarianism is therefore never a "particularist," "act" or "narrow" one, which would judge each action or measure by its own results. As we shall see it, it goes beyond "generic" or "rule" utilitarianism
which evaluates kinds of action or rules of conduct by their general
results, to a utilitarianism of institutions and complex bodies of rules.

It is interesting, indeed somewhat surprising, to find that Hayek endorses the converse of these arguments: namely, that if we could know
the future, then we could dispense with rules and laws and decide each
action or measure by its own results. Thus he says of individual liberty
itself that the case for it mostly rests on our unavoidable ignorance of
many of the conditions for achieving what we seek, and then continues:

> If there were omniscient men, if we could know not only all that affects the attain-
> ment of our present wishes but also our future wants and desires, there would be
> little case for liberty. (CL, p. 29)

Again, of justice he writes:

> In a society of omniscient persons there would be no room for a conception of
> justice: every action would have to be judged as a means of bringing about known
> effects, and omniscience would presumably include knowledge of the relative
> importance of the different effects. Like all abstractions, justice is an adaptation
> to our ignorance—to our permanent ignorance of particular facts which no scien-
> tific advance can wholly remove. (LLL, vol. 2, p. 39; cf. SPPE, p. 89, and NSPPE,
> pp. 87–8)

Hayek would never concede that any of us could be omniscient. The
point of interest is that these remarks show how fundamentally utilitar-

ian is the cast of his mind. For it appears never to occur to him that justice is an intrinsic quality of a type of action, irrespective of any effects, general or particular, nor that liberty could be valuable in and for itself.

I would also suggest that his constant use of "rules," even for moral ones, is evidence of the same outlook, as it is with respect to most contemporary thinkers. For rules are primarily rules of convenience, to be adopted, altered, discarded, or not followed at the moment, for either their particular or general effects. In contrast, a law is something more, something that is authoritative and commanding and not a matter of choice. A moral rule is one I set myself because it helps me to be a better person or to avoid becoming a worse one: for example, never to enter any casino or betting shop lest I succumb to the temptation to stake money that I cannot afford to lose, or to set aside a fixed but significant proportion of my income for charitable causes so that I make sure that I have done part of my duty to those less fortunate than myself. There is nothing inherently good or bad in these practices, and others may or need not adopt them as they find convenient. In contrast, theft, fraud, and murder are inherently wrong, prohibited by the moral law, and are not matters of choice and convenience.

Hayek commits himself to a utilitarian argument for liberty because he can conceive of no other possibility. Either we argue that liberty is valuable for other things or we give no argument (FC, pp. 27–8, 70). This is the basic assumption, and error, of all utilitarianisms. As we saw in chapter 6, utilitarians constantly assume that the only alternative to their system is one of "intuitionism," of "dogmatic" and unargued intuitions of the values of things. Yet they themselves merely displace the problem onto that ultimate object for which the proximate one is said to be a good means. Either that ultimate object has a value "in itself" which, on utilitarian assumptions, can be only "intuited" or "dogmatically asserted," or we can argue for it. If we do argue for it, that can be only to show that it itself is an intermediate good as a means serving some other and ultimate end, whereat the same problem recurs. What nearly all utilitarians then resort to is an appeal to what people happen to want, as we saw in the case of von Mises and as did J.S. Mill when he said that the only proof that anything is desirable is that it is desired. There is an element of this in Hayek's argument that civilisation and all its benefits depend upon liberty for individual initiative and effort, but his position is much more complex.

Hayek rightly concludes that generic or rule utilitarianism must collapse into particularist or act utilitarianism if actions are to be evaluated on the basis of their known effects. But that would assume an omniscience regarding the effects of each action which is forever beyond us.[2] Moreover, rule utilitarianism is unworkable because the effects of any rule depend upon both its always being observed and also upon the other rules observed by both those who observe it and other members of the same society. The utility of any rule can therefore be computed only by taking for granted other rules and their observance, which are therefore not justified by their utility. Utility cannot establish the value of each single rule.

Hayek in fact provides three reasons for the use of rules, which are somewhat run together:

1. We act according to rules because we do not know the full effects of our actions in every situation. By acting according to a rule, we expect to produce similar results in similar situations. If we could always know the results we would not need rules.
2. These facts about the need for rules need not be known to the persons acting by the rules in question. The rules encapsulate a traditional and tacit knowledge of what works in the frequently recurring situations of human life or of a given society. It follows that the utility of a rule need not be immediately apparent, nor ever apparent. The point is that together they form a body of rules which generally works. And it may not be known which, in the total body, are the really efficacious ones.[3]
3. The observance of rules by persons living together itself sets up for all them a predictable order. Each knows what the others are likely to do in given types of situation, and each can plan his own action accordingly. Without regularity in human conduct, there could be no social interaction, no social order. The utility of acting according to a rule is that we always or nearly always act so, irrespective of the known or knowable effects of a particular action.[4]

Hayek's arguments can be supported by invoking Searle's distinction between "regulative" and "constituitive" rules.[5] The former regulate an already existing practice whereas the latter create or constitute a practice or institution. For example, rules of polite behaviour govern, or should govern, all our all activities with our fellows, activities which can go on independently of them, but the rules of a game define the game in question, and that game cannot exist apart from them. Now utilitarianism interprets all rules as productive generalisations: "to bring about events of type A, perform actions of type B." Hence rule-utiliarianism is always liable to collapse into act-utilitarianism when it can be seen that doing C, instead of A, will bring about B. The connection is causal and so, in human affairs, often casual. While utilitarianism may plausibly, for a while, interpret regulative rules in this way (e.g., "to avoid friction and achieve results that depend upon cooperation, behave politely to others"), no such interpretation can be applied to constituitive rules. For observing them is engaging in the activity in question: not to follow suit when one can is not to play whist or bridge. Some rules of a game can be changed without changing the whole character of the game. Those rules may be regarded as merely regulative ones or as nonfundamental constituitive rules. Likewise, many of the complex rules that govern transactions with respect to property may be merely regulative. But others are not. For, in order that we can behave politely, there must be constituitive rules which define certain modes of conduct as polite and others as impolite. Again, where there is no property, there can be no theft, and the prohibition of theft is a logical consequence of the institution of property. If anyone can take anything at any time, then no one owns anything. Even when things are communally owned, there has to be that minimal property right of the individual of his exclusive usage of something for a time, and thus, although another cannot steal it from him, yet it is possible to snatch it from him before his time is up. And, of course, anyone in the community can steal from the communal stock by appropriating without permission something for his own exclusive use. So too can a stranger *steal* from it.

Habits create order by making our conduct regular and predictable. But constituitive rules create a more extensive order by defining recurrent situations and the ways in which people should act in them, as does a code of manners. So also is each language constituted by its rules, not only those of grammar, but also those for each word, which has a meaning only as consistently used in the same way. Again, the differentiation of roles is constituted by the expectations of what anyone fulfilling a given role is to do and will usually do. Our desires and intentions are moulded into standardised actions by these expectations. As with language, we may not be focally aware of the rules that we are following, or that we are following rules at all, until someone departs from them and does not do the polite thing, speaks ungrammatically or misuses a word, or behaves strangely for a husband or wife, buyer or seller, or teacher or pupil, or until we meet a different set of rules, roles, and expectations.

Because they define institutions and practices, constituitive rules can be taken for granted when productive and merely regulative rules are being evaluated in terms of their general effects, whether the latter are always to be observed because of the general effects of actions of the relevant sort or whether they are rules of thumb to be observed or not at the individual's informed discretion. Moreover, they themselves can be evaluated only in the context of the other rules defining the relevant practice or institution, and its whole point or purpose. Consider again the rules of games and sports. They can be changed and are changed when the effects of following them lead to unfair or uninteresting results. In 1980 England's Test and County Cricket Board (TCCB) declared that wickets were to be covered when it rained once play had started. That has guaranteed spectators more play to watch in the English climate, but it has greatly reduced the chances for spin bowlers, decisive results, and the spectacle of a duel of skill between bowler and batsman. No one law of cricket makes sense without reference to the others. Again, the common law of unlimited liability for one's debts, including those incurred by companies in which one had a share, was found in the nineteenth century to restrict the formation of companies needed to provide the capital and management for the new and larger industries. Consequently, limited liability was introduced, and, in turn, that has required frequent amplification and correction by further legislation. Without it, we could not have limited liability companies. Again, foreigners are unwilling to invest in Russian businesses for there is, as yet, no law of bankruptcy and so no procedure to recover debts. None of these laws can be understood or evaluated except in the context of the whole body of company law and commercial law, and the whole ideas of ownership, contract, and tort.

It follows that the utility of constitutive rules, especially, and of regulative ones as well, is that of (a) their always being observed and the general reliance which people can place upon each other's observation of them, together with (b) the effects of the whole institution or practice which a given set of them define. This is precisely Hayek's approach, which he takes over from Hume. His is Hume's utilitarianism of a coherent set of rules and not of rules considered singly, still less of single actions.[6] As our examples show, it is the functioning and effects of each rule within and upon the whole, and of the whole, itself that matters.

A further feature of Hayek's utilitarianism, which leads him to repudiate the term itself (LLL, vol. 2, pp. 18, 22), is that it is not directed to one end. He notes how the meaning of "utility" had been changed from "usefulness," which applies to means, to denote an attribute of the ends which means serve, namely, the pleasure or satisfaction that was associated with them. The point is, rather, that utilitarianism became identified with hedonistic utilitarianism and its one goal of maximising a balance of pleasure over pain, and that in hedonistic psychology pleasure is a distinct and uniform sensation, like a glow on one's cheeks or a swelling in one's breast, which is the end product of various actions or events that happen to the self. The only usefulness that matters, for hedonistic utilitarianism, is therefore being useful for bringing about sensations of pleasure or reducing those of pain, and "utility" came to mean that specific usefulness.[7] In opposition to this narrow utilitarianism of a specific utility of a particular thing upon a given occasion, Hayek proposes the notion of a general utility of a class of actions or type of thing. It will help us to make explicit three sets of distinctions which Hayek somewhat runs together:

1. (a) actual or "episodic" usefulness (of A for bringing about B upon a *particular* occasion);
   (b) potential or "dispositional" usefulness (of A for bringing about B upon any *relevant* occasion);
2. (a) the usefulness of a particular A;
   (b) the usefulness of things of type A;
3. (a) "monotelic" usefulness, of a particular A or of things of type A, for bringing about something of type B;
   (b) "polytelic" usefulness, of a particular A or of things of type A, for bringing about things of types B to N.

A consistent specific or "act" utilitarianism must confine itself to the actual and monotelic usefulness of particular objects on particular occasions. A utilitarianism of productive rules inevitably collapses into specific or act utilitarianism, for there are always conceivable alternatives and substitutes and conceivable situations in which things will not operate as they usually do. What Hayek stresses is a combination of potential or dispositional usefulness and polytelic usefulness, the utility of types of action or practice or institution each for several different purposes. The utility of everyday tools, implements, and furniture, what Heidegger calls their "presence-at-hand" (*Vorhandenheit*), has this triple character. Hayek cites as an example the usefulness of a knife. It is useful on more than one occasion; it is not just this knife but this type of knife that has this usefulness; and it can be used for several types of purpose, not only cutting different types of thing, but other purposes as well, some of which we may not yet know. Motor cars were invented to help people get from one place to another, but they were soon found to be useful for other purposes, as when parked in secluded spots at night.

It is the last that is especially important, and into which Hayek tends to assimilate the other two categories of utility. For a liberal social order consists in the presence of rules, practices, and institutions which we all can use but each for his own purposes. We speak the same language but we do not have to express the same thoughts; we have a common currency but use it for buying, saving, and giving each in his own way; and the rules of just conduct allow each of us to pursue his own aims in life without trespassing upon the equal rights of everyone else. A liberal order is polytelic and requires equipment that can be used for a range of purposes, some as yet unknown, and in situations both known and unforeseen. Conversely, a totalitarian order is monotelic, and, as we have seen in the case of Bentham, a monotelic way of thinking both makes itself available for and encourages the imposition of a totalitarian organisation of society to achieve that one goal by a mind that claims to know all the details of the present situation and all the results that can be achieved in it. It is not common goals and common valuations of ends that matter, but agreement upon polytelic means.[8]

Utility, in Burke's words:

> must be understood, not of partial or limited, but of general and public utility, connected in the same manner with, and devised directly from, our rational nature.[9]

Such a conception of utility transcends itself. For, to begin with, the rules of just conduct and liberty itself, Hayek's principal concern, are not just useful for human well-being but are necessary to it. They have what I have called "foundational value," since they are not disposable as mere means are. They are always needed and there are no possible substitutes. This intimate relation between the necessary foundation and that which it supports almost makes the former inherently valuable. Thus at two points Hayek acknowledges that liberty has an inherent and not just an instrumental value: when he states that only in a free society can moral values develop (SPPE, p. 229); and when he argues that it is a moral principle of political action and therefore is to be regarded as a value in itself apart from whether or not its consequences are beneficial in any particular case (CL, p. 68).

Yet that sets a problem which can be resolved only by a final transcendence of utilitarianism altogether.

The Self-Transcendence of Utilitarianism

Hayek frequently quotes three passages from Hume on the necessity of observing the laws of justice on all occasions irrespective of the particular benefits of not doing so on some occasions and of the particular disadvantages of doing so on others:

> 'Tis certain that the whole plan or scheme is highly conducive, or indeed absolutely requisite, both to the support of society and the well-being of every individual.[10]

> The benefit [of justice and fidelity] is not the consequence of every individual single act; but arises from the whole scheme or system, concurred in by the whole, or the greater part of the society.[11]

> It is sufficient, if the whole plan or scheme [of the laws of property] be necessary to the support of civil society, and if the balance of good, in the main, do thereby preponderate much above that of evil.[12]

Again, Hayek frequently quotes and endorses Hume's contention that the foundations of freedom, peace, and prosperity in society are "the three fundamental laws of nature, *that of the stability of possession, of transference by consent, and of the performance of promises.*"[13]

As we shall see in Part 3, Hayek rightly considers that there are other foundations as well. For the present, the question is not their sufficiency but their justification within a utilitarian framework, even the large and liberal one that Hayek embraces.

The whole point of this utilitarianism is that the value of these laws and practices and institutions, and of any others also necessary to man's liberty and welfare in the world, depends upon their general observance by the population. The rules governing or defining them are therefore to be regarded, not as productive rules of thumb from which we may and should depart on those particular occasions when their observance is likely to prove unproductive or counterproductive, but as *laws* which are always to be followed irrespective of their consequences on particular occasions. As we have just noted, Hayek states that liberty is therefore to be regarded as a value in itself, and also, it would follow, these other practices and institutions on which it necessarily depends or which embody it. That is, the utilitarian valuation of them itself requires that they have a value that is more than that of utility.

This brings us to the central problem of utilitarianism, even the refined utilitarianism of institutions that is Hume's and Hayek's. For to attain the beneficial consequences of something we have to value it, not for those benefits, but for itself, and so gain those desired results as a by-product and not as our goal. Hayek himself argues that the greater provision of goods and services and the very coordinated order of expectations and actions arise, not as the direct objects of action, but as unintended and unknown results of observing the rules of justice as an ultimate value (LLL, vol. 1, p. 110–1). More importantly, to attain the wider result of the harmonious reconciliation of individuals' free actions and initiative, the rules of justice must be observed upon all occasions. And that means that they must be treated "not as means but as ultimate values, indeed as the only values common to all and distinct from the particular ends of the individuals" (LLL, vol. 2, p. 17; cf. CL, p. 67). Whether or not we accept that they are the only common values, we need to recognise that they are ultimate and are not means to something else. Note that this is not a matter of saying we must treat them "*as if* they are ultimate values" but "*as* ultimate values." The detached theorist may say, "These rules will have the desired effects only when people treat them *as if* they were ultimate, but really they are only means to those ends," but he himself can adopt that attitude of superior enlightenment only as a parasite on the "superstitions" and "taboos" of the unenlightened populace. Utilitarianism itself requires that we regard the rules of just conduct as laws, laws which oblige us irrespective of our will and private concerns, and which therefore oblige us in virtue of some inherent character of what they command or prohibit.[14] Certain types of action are therefore to be regarded as good or bad "in themselves." And that is to have gone beyond utilitarianism altogether.

A utilitarian valuation of just conduct, private or several property, and the keeping of promises, because they are the foundations for freedom and peaceful progress, itself requires that they are not seen and valued in utilitarian terms by the general public. The utilitarian theorist is a detached and parasitic observer, who sees others acting justly, respecting property and keeping their promises because they think that such actions are inherently right, whereas he himself is enlightened as to the true meaning and value of such conduct and attitudes. Yet his own true valuation of that action and those attitudes requires that the populace continue to think and act under the influence of the illusion that justice and fidelity are good in themselves. The utilitarian theorist is not a Nietzschean Overman who deliberately creates new values and then imposes them on the "herd," which, in its unenlightened manner, receives them on tablets of stone as if they were Natural or Divine Laws. Yet he does desire that the public continue in its non-utilitarian ways of thinking and acting while holding those ways to have a meaning and value quite other than what the public naively take them to have.

This attitude of the utilitarian theorist is an example of a more general failure in the study of human life. It comes from taking up a position of detached observation, as if men were molecules or meteorites. As Collingwood said, before he worked out the truth of the matter,

"The historian is the spectator of a life in which he does not partici-pate."[15] But, as Collingwood later realised,[16] human action is "criterio-logical." We set ourselves goals (continuing or end-states) and monitor our efforts to fulfil them. Human action has an "inside," a meaning which can be grasped only by reenactment of it, by grasping what the person thought about his situation and what he was trying to do, whether they be the actions, thoughts, and intentions of a real individual or those of an imagined and typical person. And in reenacting them in his own mind, the historian (or economist, sociologist, anthropologist, psycholo-gist, or ordinary person in everyday life) does so critically in terms of what he himself knows and believes about the situation, or type of situ-ation, and about the relevant activity and its standards. He cannot but make some evaluation of what he studies by rethinking it, of the accuracy or otherwise of a person's appreciation of his situation, of the suitabil-ity or unsuitability of his plans, of his success or failure in implement-ing them and thus in trying to achieve his goal.[17] Hume's attempts to observe, and not to rethink, the workings of the human mind meant that he failed to grasp their inner logic, and so he could see only one mental state following another by force of habit or association. He failed to rethink his own thinking. This is the error of all "value-free" studies of man, that they adopt an explicit position, which they cannot sustain, of detached observation which, as Rickert and Weber said, records the fact that men make value-judgments but which does not make them itself. As Polanyi showed,[18] such an attitude is not one of the neutrality that it pretends to be but is destructive of real value in the world by tacitly discrediting it and men's motivation by it.

Apart from any specific claims to be a detached observer of human life, a utilitarian theorist inevitably finds himself in that position be-cause his own set of values cannot accredit as valid the attitudes of those who go beyond it. We found that von Mises's supposedly "value-free" science of praxeology could only accredit and recognise the utili-tarian evaluations made by others and not those in terms of inherent and internal attributes.[19] We all make utilitarian evaluations: some things are to be judged in terms of their consequences. Given that I should do X, if Y and Z are alternative ways of doing it, I should choose the more effective: it is a doctor's duty to prescribe the most effective course of treatment, balanced when necessary against possibly harmful side-ef-fects. Utilitarianism provides the ground floor of responsible human action. Hence Max Weber's strictures upon what he called "the ethics of intention," which thinks it sufficient to mean well, because for an intention to be an intention it must, when appropriate, go beyond itself and fulfil itself in effective action. Therefore there is a necessary and indispensable truth in utilitarianism. But it necessarily transcends itself. It can tell us to do that which, when there is a choice, will be the more effective way of doing what we should. It cannot tell us what we are to do, or not to do, in the first place. Of this utilitarians are aware and try to answer in terms of goals or ends: pleasure, the greatest happiness of the greatest number, the preservation of society, peace, and progress, friendship and aesthetic experiences, or whatever. But as we have seen, particularist or act utilitarianism is impossible, and rule utilitarianism can be only a utilitarianism of productive rules, which is how it interprets moral laws, and must collapse into act utilitarianism whenever following the rule will not produce the intended results. Hence they have no logical objection to shortcuts in the way of fraud, theft, and murder, whenever these are the more effective, a logic which has not been suspended by the revolutionaries, totalitarians, and terrorists of the modern age. The result can be only a collapse of all moral standards and of society with them. Hence Hume and Hayek are right to see that the beneficial consequences of just conduct come from observing its rules on all occasions. But that is to regard them as *laws* and not just rules and therefore it is to abandon utilitarianism which makes beneficial consequences the sole principle of evaluation. Utilitarianism requires that we act within a framework of moral laws which are not regarded within a utilitarian framework. Utilitarianism either destroys or transcends itself.[20]

Liberalism, Utilitarianism, and Militarism

In order to give these last reflections a concrete substance, I propose to consider a particular activity and institution in relation to utilitarianism: war and the army.

It is particularly appropriate to consider military matters as an example, rather than, say, science which we mentioned in chapter 5 and at which we shall look again in the next chapter, for the Liberal attitude to them is bound to be a Utilitarian one. In a troubled world, armed forces are a regrettable necessity. A free society must be able to defend itself but it must not become tainted with militarism. Conversely, conservatism has often been closely allied to the traditional military classes. And socialism, even in its pacifist forms, uses a militarist vocabulary of war against this, crusades against that, and campaigns for the other.

It often generates an equivalent of a war psychosis in order to "mobilise" the populace to achieve its goals. And it likewise imposes a command structure to execute its monotelic plans.[21]

Max Scheler drew a distinction between "dispositional" (*Gesinnungs-*) and "instrumental" (*Zweck-*) militarism. Although in 1915 he had, at the behest of the German Foreign Office, argued for the former in general and the German invasion of Belgium in particular, when, in 1927, he lectured to the officers of the Weimar army, he supported the latter.[22] Considering that today the various forms of pacifism are not likely to achieve the goal of eternal peace, and rejecting claims, such as those he had himself previously made, for the positive value of war (the attitude of "dispositional militarism"), he came down in favour of an "instrumental militarism" which supports war for limited purposes and in specific circumstances but not the value of war *per se* nor of military forms. War is not necessary for heroism, and modern technological war, conscription, and total war are definitely unheroic. Nor is war necessary for avoiding effeminacy. Yet, in effect, he also proposed a sublimation of "dispositional militarism" and a surrogate for war. Arguing that history shows a trend towards a transformation of power from force to physical power to spiritual power, and thus from power over men to power over organic nature to power over things, he advocated a cooperative struggle of mankind against nature.

Scheler's "instrumental militarism" seems to be the obviously correct and sensible attitude, especially for liberals. The Politician in Vladimir Soloviev's *Three Dialogues on War, Peace and the End* expressed a similar view. Then the General spoke. Next to God and Russia, he said, he loved his work in the artillery the most. Evidently, he did not take a merely instrumental attitude towards it. It may be possible for volunteers in an emergency, and for conscripts at all times, to regard their military service in such a light, but not for the regular servicemen. Indeed, a merely mercenary army, as the Italian *condotierri* of the Renaissance showed, is unreliable. Men may risk their lives for money but no one will die for it, and mere mercenaries can be both bought and bought off. Something more is needed to make them effective fighting men, and thus able and willing to do what is required of them, especially when it comes to desperate assaults, forlorn hopes, and last stands. That something more is a sense of honour, pride in regiment or ship, and loyalty to comrades. As the Gurkhas and French Foreign Legion have proved, it is possible to create an élite fighting force by inculcating such emotions among men who have no particular attachment to the land which they serve. A utilitarian attitude towards the armed services requires that, on the whole, they do not have the utilitarian attitude themselves. They need to like the military life and to feel that it is an honourable profession.[23] The utilitarian looks suspiciously like the pacifist who condemns those who fight and die to protect his freedom to practice his pacifism. If not outrightly hypocritical, the utilitarian position is definitely parasitical.

Moreover, a non-utilitarian regard for the military life and for the armed forces is required of the general public, unless a dangerous split of contempt on either side is not to develop:

> For it's Tommy this, an' Tommy that, an' "Chuck him out, the brute!"
> But it's Saviour of 'is country; when the guns begin to shoot;
> An' it's Tommy this, an' Tommy that, an' anything you please;
> An' Tommy ain't a bloomin' fool—you bet that Tommy sees!

Ever since Cromwell and then Napoleon, modern states have too often found themselves ruled by those supposed to be their servants.

I suggest that this can be generalised. The practices and institutions upon which liberty depends require, for their effective operation and maintenance, an attitude, on the part of most of those who participate in them, that is more than utilitarian and that at least partly values them for their own sakes. They would wither or be ruined if those concerned were to espouse utilitarianism. Their utility is therefore that of a by-product, not an intended result. Even when we become aware of their beneficial consequences, we cannot make that our motive for engaging in them. Or, if we do, we shall distort and then destroy them and their benefits along with them. This is the paradox of utilitarianism, that in *all* its forms—act, rule, and institutional—it proves disutile. It can be thought by the detached spectator, but not lived by on the part of the engaged participant. The well-known paradox of happiness is but one application of the general paradox: to be happy, one must not aim at nor think much of one's happiness, but find something worthwhile and engage in it for its own sake. Happiness is a by-product of dedication to something held to be of value "in itself" and on other grounds. So too is everything valuable in this life. Utilitarianism is either self-destructive or self-transcending.

Hayek's Evolutionary Utilitarianism

Yet utilitarianism of a sort remains in one strand of Hayek's thinking about the Great Society and its value. The Great Society is a network of relationships that potentially embraces all mankind because it is the mutual observance of the rules of just conduct which are applicable to all. It overflows all boundaries and groupings of men. Hayek sees commerce as its earliest and principal element, but any common interest can bring men together and enable them cooperatively to benefit themselves by dealing justly with each other. As we shall see, Polanyi's model for a similar conception is the republic of science. Two forces are opposed to the Great Society and its expansion: *tribalism*, the division of "us" and "them" which denies universal rules of conduct; and, *constructive rationalism* which thinks of all forms of society and association in terms of monotelic organisations deliberately set up and controlled. Principally against the latter, Hayek seeks to show how laws and institutions, and especially those of the Great Society which bring with them peace and prosperity, have developed by a process of evolution which has winnowed out those less propitious to wider and lasting social orders. He is not offering any crude theory of survival of the fittest in a life-and-death struggle, but instead the argument that groups which observe these rules of just conduct will thereby build up a more effective order of actions and will prevail over others with less effective orders, not by defeating or displacing them, but by attracting new members or becoming an aristocracy whose conduct will be copied by the rest.[24] This argument raises two questions: (1) that of its factual truth; and (2) that of its function as a justification of the rules of just conduct.

In respect of the former, Hayek appears occasionally to assume that all rules, practices, and institutions of a group are implicitly oriented to the survival of that group. Those of commerce, the market, honesty, and just conduct generally prove to be the most successful. But he does acknowledge that not all rules which have evolved are conducive to the survival and increase of a population (FC, p. 20). Now we can understand "not being conducive to the survival of the group" in two ways: being detrimental to it, as are the practices inspired by envy and the fear of envy, and those of the unlimited vendetta; and being simply irrelevant to the survival of the group, as are styles of art for most of the time. Yet groups survive, though they do not prosper, even when riddled by envy and the fear of it[25] or by the unmitigated vendetta, and so no simple account of natural selection in human affairs can be given. And for many practices, such as art, it is quite irrelevant. Practices and institutions "evolve," that is, arise from what has gone before and undergo changes, and do so mostly without conscious design; but a general theory of survival and extinction cannot do justice to the diversity of the facts.

In particular, we may note how some societies and groups have survived despite, and perhaps because of, the opposition of some of their central practices to those of the Great Society. Two clear examples of this are the Hindu caste system and the Jewish law. The former probably existed in the cities of the Punjab, such as Harappa and Mohenjo-Daro, before the Aryan invasion in the fifteenth century B.C., and it certainly existed soon afterwards. And the Jewish law marks off Jews from the populations around them and preserves their identity as a distinct people, either originally as a territorial society surrounded by others, or in the Diaspora as a distinct set of people spread through other societies, precisely because it works against their assimilation into the surrounding culture and thus to some extent against the formation of a Great Society.[26]

Secondly, the factual argument, if sound, can act as a justification. The practices of being open to constructive relations with all men by means of observing the abstract rules of justice and of trading with them, can be taken as a utilitarian justification of those practices in terms of the survival of the group. Hayek's position in this respect is not clear. He often seems to be offering it as a justification but states explicitly that it is not one, yet at the same time states that the morality of the extended order (savings, property, honesty, and so on) "does enable us to survive and there is something perhaps to be said for that" (FC, p. 70). Now if it is offered as a justification, it strikes me as being a perverse one. For the groups in the survival of which men have an interest are particular ones with which they identify themselves, such as family, tribe, city, nation, and religious community—not the indefinite Great Society for which there is no image or symbol. One may be proud of one's own group for sharing in the practices of the Great Society, but the Great Society itself is not a concrete object that one can be proud of or love. It is, let us remember, a set of overlapping relationships among an indeterminate number of persons who need have nothing else in common save participation in this network.

We come to the same conclusion as before. The Great Society rests principally upon observance of the rules of justice, which have to be regarded as laws, as inherently right, and to be obeyed simply in virtue of their inherent rightness. Any external and utilitarian justification of such conduct defeats or transcends itself. Classical liberalism therefore requires an appropriate notion of the value of justice, and to Hayek's account of that we now turn.

Notes

1. Hayek (CL, p. 189 n.1) rightly criticises Polanyi's surprising complacency in this respect (LL, p. 111). Polanyi seems to have thought it sufficient to have demonstrated that central planning is impossible and was not practised in the U.S.S.R., and not to have been so much concerned about the damage—economic, political, and moral (and ecological as we now know)—done by State control of industry. State capitalism was not at all like private capitalism. Conversely, Polanyi was right to criticise *The Road to Serfdom* for implying that all socialist attempts at economic planning would result in totalitarianism. Logically they would, but fortunately non-Communist Socialists in Europe have stopped well short of that point, but not without doing much harm.

2. It is also incoherent for, by requiring each person to compute the effects of each action before he performs it, it therefore rules out action when we have no time to think about its consequences but must do straightaway what immediately strikes us as the best or least bad action. It is therefore counterproductive in emergencies: by the time we have the answer, it will be too late to do anything about it. Furthermore it also requires the agent to think out the effects of the action, B, of stopping to think out the effects of action A; but calculating the effects of B is itself an action, C, to be performed or not only after we have computed its consequences; and so on for D, the action of computing the consequences of C. It means that we can never get started.

   I am following the account of utilitarianism which Hayek gives in LLL, vol. 2, pp. 20–30. Cf. SPPE, pp. 88–91 and ch. 7; NSPPE, ch. 1; CL, p. 159.

3. Compare Burke on prejudice, which is or results in acting by rule because of an attitude that prejudges the situation as one of a given type: "Prejudice is of ready application in the emergency; it previously engages the mind in a steady course of wisdom and virtue, and does not leave the man hesitating in the moment of decision, sceptical, puzzled, and unresolved. Prejudice renders a man's virtue his habit; and not a series of unconnected acts. Through just prejudice, his duty becomes a part of his nature," *Reflections, Works*, vol. 5, p. 168.

   An example of a rule, the results of which bring great benefits but which is not recognised as producing those benefits, is the taboo among the highland tribes of New Guinea, upon eating one's own pigs and those of one's near relations, despite the importance of pigs in their diet. The result of this taboo is an extensive system of relationships of exchange of pigs which brings about peace and cooperation among many family groups and tribes. See M. Gluckman, *Politics*, p. 59, and contrast Popper's rationalistic dismissal of taboo. Gluckman gives several other examples: see especially his discussion, in chapter 3, of criss-crossing sets of relationships which give individuals an incentive in limiting vengeance and feuding because they are involved in two conflicting sets of claims.

4. Of course, knowledge of expectations based on acting by rules can be used deceptively to attain particular results, but only so far and so infrequently. Those disposed to make "psychic" bids at bridge both deceive their partners as well as their opponents on each occasion, which can land them in trouble even when they have correctly guessed the disposition of the cards. In fact, after a while, frequent psychic bidding destroys the partnership's system of conventions and the means of communicating to each other what they have.

5. *Speech Acts*, pp. 33–4.

6. Contrast von Mises: "All moral rules and human laws are means for the realization of definite ends" (HA, p. 716), which implies that each can be considered by itself in relation to its own particular purpose and effects.

7. "By utility is meant that property in any object, whereby it tends to produce benefit, advantage, pleasure, good, or happiness, (all this in the present case comes to the same thing) or (what comes again to the same thing) to prevent the happening of mischief, pain, evil, or unhappiness to the party whose interest is considered," Bentham, *Introduction to the Principles of Morals and Legislation*, p. 126.

8. Compare, on the importance in life of polytelic means, Locke's principle, in *Some Thoughts on Education*, of "frequency of use" (i.e., in adult life) for selecting what should be taught to the young. Cardinal Newman, in *The Idea of a University*, wrongly criticised Locke in this respect for making the utilitarian demand for the teaching of "useful knowledge," that is, knowledge useful for gaining a living and making one's way in the world. Although Locke did include such knowledge, he also said that what is most frequently required is knowledge of one's religious and moral duties. That transcends utilitarianism as usually understood.

   Compare, on the dangers to liberty of a monotelic way of thinking, Berlin's advocacy of a pluralism of values (see above, p. 19).

9. *Tracts on the Popery Laws, Works*, vol. 9, p. 355.

10. *Treatise*, p. 497; cf. p. 579. This and the other two are quoted at greatest length in CL, pp. 454–5 n.18.

11. *Enquiry Concerning the Principles of Morals*, appendix 3, p. 304.

12. Ibid., p. 305.

13. *Treatise*, p. 526.

14. Bentham himself failed to keep to his utilitarian assumptions: he stated that motives were not good or bad in themselves (*Introduction to the Principles of Morals and Legislation*, pp. 214, 218) but inconsistently allowed that intentions can be good or bad irrespective of their actual consequences, when what the agent thought would be the consequences of his action would have been good or bad (p. 210); that "malice will be allowed by everyone to be a bad motive" without any implication that he would except himself (p. 211); and that the absence of intention concerning consequences, and the absence of awareness or the presence of missupposal regarding circumstances, can constitute grounds of extenuation (p. 213). And in chapter 16, when he listed and classified the types of action that should be made into criminal offences, he paid no attention to consequences but only to the inherent character, the intention, of each type of action.

15. "Nature and Aims of a Philosophy of History," *Proc. Aristotelian Soc.*, vol. 25, 1924–5, p. 165.

16. *The Idea of History*, Part 5 §4. It needs to be remembered that Collingwood never completed what he saw as his life's work, *The Principles of History*, which would have dealt with the themes of Part 5 of the *Idea of History*. Parts 1–4 of the latter are the book proper and it was intended to be an historical introduction to *The Principles of History*.

17. Ibid., pp. 300–1. I have expanded this along with Polanyi's account of the matter (see PK, pp. 369–72; KB, pp. 152, 159, ch. 13; *The Study Of Man*, pp. 65–6 and Lect. 3), in *The Structure of Value*, chs. 7 and 10. Polanyi rightly argues that reenactment is also the only way to understand the behaviour of animals, and, in a way, of all organic processes, which can be understood only as we grasp their functions and thus, in each case, whether the organ, organism, or process succeeds or not in fulfilling it.

18. "The Message of the Hungarian Revolution," in KB.

   See also Hayek, NSPPE, p. 20: "The true statement that, from our understanding of causal connections between facts alone, we can derive no conclusions about the validity of values, has been extended into the false belief that science has nothing to do with values.... Scientific analysis shows that the existing factual order of society exists only because people accept certain values. With regard to such a social system, we cannot even make statements about the effect of particular events without assuming that certain norms are being generally obeyed."

That shows only that science must recognise the facts (a) that certain values are accepted and acted upon, and (b) that this is necessary to the maintenance of the social order in question. Science would still be neutral about the validity of those values themselves. But, Hayek continues (p. 22), *Wertfrei* social science discredits all values by regarding them as expressions of irrational emotions or particular material interests. "All that we can do—and must do—is to test each and every value about which doubts are raised by the standard of other values, which we can assume that our listeners or readers share with us." And it is possible "to demonstrate that what depends upon on the acceptance of values, which do not appear as the consciously pursued aims of individuals or groups, are the very foundations of the factual order, whose existence we presuppose in all our individual endeavours."

In effect, Hayek is arguing that social science is not a detached observation of the doings of mankind and must endorse certain values. But he tends to restrict values and standards to particular societies or to specific forms of society: see LLL, vol. 1, p. 112, on the neutrality of studying a society other than one's own, and having to accept certain values when giving advice on reaching particular goals in a given society.

19. See above, ch. 6, §2.
20. Collingwood developed a scheme of ethics as a scale of forms, in which each lower level transcends itself into the next higher level. In order to be itself, it must be more than itself. Collingwood's scheme had three levels: utility, right or regularian action, and duty. The "-isms" in ethics take one level as the whole truth and thus try to interpret the ones above it in its own terms, as utilitarianism turns moral laws into productive rules. But this fixing of the truth at any intermediate level proves self-destructive. See *The New Leviathan*, chs. 15–17, and, for earlier versions, D. Boucher, *The Social and Political Thought of R.G. Collingwood*, ch. 3.
21. I hope to publish an elaboration of Collingwood's scheme, which will have as its levels: utility, law, pre-moral virtues and responsibility, moral virtues and responsibility, and the person himself. This will incorporate also a sequence of levels of the person: actions, dispositions, will and intention, the "heart" or *ordo amoris*. I would also stress the opposite principle to self-transcendence: namely, self-embodiment, that each higher level, as and when appropriate, to be itself must express itself in the next lower. A moral "-ism" can err in not recognising the necessity of lower levels, as well as in not recognising that of higher ones.
21. B. de Jouvenel (*Sovereignty*, p. 64) noted two forms of socialism, the sentimental one of all as members of one family ("brothers") and positivist one of all as members of the same team. The latter usually take the form of all as workers in one factory. But the language of "comrades" reminds us that there is another possibility, that of recruits (volunteers or conscripts) in the same army, the way of specifically national socialism, but Soviet socialism regularly used military language in its economic pronouncements, propaganda, and appeals.
    Militarism characterises other forms of collectivism. Kolnai comments on Heidegger's attempt to escape the fallenness and alienation of *Dasein* in *das Mann* by way of a "resolute" Being with Others (*Being and Time*, pp. 344–5, H,

p. 298), that it amounts to "the life of a sworn band permanently at bay, or of a fortress eternally beset, or of a shift of miners permanently underground" (*The War against the West*, p. 94).

22. See "The Idea of Peace and Pacifism" (trans. M. Frings, *J. of the Brit. Soc. for Phenomenology*, vol. 7, no. 3, Oct. 1976, and vol. 8, no. 1, Jan. 1977). On his earlier work, *Der Genius des Krieges und der deutsche Krieg* (1915, reprinted 1916, 1917, *Gesammelte Werke*, Bd. 6), see Kolnai, *The War Against the West*, pp. 442–4. Scheler also published "Ueber Gesinnungs- und Zweckmilitarismus" in the volume *Krieg und Aufbau* (1916) (G. W. Bd. 4). I do not know how it stands in relation to the other two essays.

23. See J. Keegan, *A History of Warfare* p. xvi, who finds that "tribalism" is what distinguishes soldiers, and then writes: "Soldiers are not like other men; that is the lesson that I have learned from a life cast among warriors. The lesson has taught me to view with extreme suspicion all theories and representations of war that equate it with any other activity in human affairs.... War is wholly unlike diplomacy or politics because it must be fought by men whose values and skills are not those of politicians or diplomats. They are those of a world apart, a very ancient world, which exists in parallel with the everyday but does not belong to it. Both worlds change over time, and the warrior world adapts in step to the civilian. It follows, however, at a distance. The distance can never be closed, for the culture of the warrior can never be that of civilisation itself."

24. LLL, vol. 1, p. 169 n. 7. See also: SPPE, p. 67; LLL, vol. 1, pp. 44, 57, 80, 99; NSPPE, pp. 7ff.; FC, pp. 20, 70.

25. For examples see, Schoek, *Envy*, p. 30 and ch. 5. Schoek does not properly distinguish between envy itself and the fear of others' envy of oneself. The damage that envy does is twofold: that of destructive actions motivated by it, and that of efforts inhibited because of the fear that others will be envious of one's success.

26. A reductionist rationalism would explain it wholly in such terms, but it was primarily observed because it was believed to be part of God's covenant with his people. Polanyi ("Jewish Problems," *Political Quarterly*, vol. 14, Jan.-Mar. 1943; reprinted in *Society, Economics, and Philosophy*) rejected, in favour of assimilation, Zionism and the practices that would return Jews voluntarily to the ghettos, physical or cultural.

8

Justice and the Rights of the Individual

The Alleged Primacy of Injustice

"Classical Liberalism rested on the belief that there existed discoverable principles of just conduct of universal applicability which could be recognised as just irrespective of the effects of their application on particular groups" (LLL, vol. 1, p. 141). That means that the principles of justice can be recognised as right and obligatory in and by themselves. Any Utilitarian account of them either destroys them or transcends itself. Likewise, legal positivism denies any reason to law, and makes it, and justice with it, solely the command of the legislator. The only course open to liberalism, it seems, is to turn to a doctrine of Natural Law or of natural rights to give a proper foundation to the inherent claims of justice. But Hayek does not mention the last and seeks to find a third way between legal positivism and Natural Law.

Hayek regards legal positivism as the offspring of constructivist rationalism, the alternative to which he takes to be his own account of the spontaneous evolution of *nomos*. As was noted in chapter 4, Hayek argues that the explicit rules of just conduct have been articulated by judges, when called upon to settle disputes, from a communal and tacit sense of justice. Justice, therefore, is prior to law and law prior to authority, both, we may add, temporally and logically. Hayek's argument against legal positivism is that it conflates general laws with particular decrees, that it wrongly holds that the whole content of a body of law is specifically formulated and commanded by the legislator, and it declares justice to be consequent upon, and not prior to, a body of laws and to be defined by them, indeed that "justice" and "injustice" mean only what is legal and illegal, and so that law can never be unjust (LLL, vol. 2, p. 48, with references to Hobbes and Kelsen). As before, I shall take as proved Hayek's refutation of these tenets of legal positivism, and shall pass on to his own account of justice.

Yet Hayek agrees with the legal positivists on at least one point: that there are no positive criteria for justice. For justice itself, he says, is primarily negative: it is, for the most part, not doing injustice. Indeed, Hayek regards the three "sole indispensable foundations of civilisation which government must provide," namely, Peace, Freedom, and Justice, as negative (LLL, vol. 3, p. 131). That is, peace is the absence of conflict, freedom the absence of coercion, and justice the absence of injustice, and that each can only be thus defined and understood. We cannot say what justice is, but we can clearly recognise cases of injustice. We cannot set up *de novo* a set of just laws, but a body of laws which has spontaneously arisen can be improved by the removal of those laws which are now recognised as unjust because "they are not universalisable within the system of other rules whose validity is not questioned" (LLL, vol. 1, p. 54). Whereas legal positivism uses the lack of a positive criterion to ridicule the idea of justice, and to identify it with whatever laws are enforced, Hayek appeals to a tacit sense of justice, or injustice, which can progressively amend a body of law although it cannot institute any.[1]

A particular reason for regarding justice as principally negative is the belief that any positive conception could result in the organisational restructuring of society in order to secure a "social justice" of providing for what we have called entitlements. Similarly, in Part 1 we saw how "positive" conceptions can lead to a similar restructuring of society to provide for the powers or satisfactions of wants in which a "positive" conception locates liberty. Yet our criticism of the dichotomy of "positive" and "negative" conceptions, which did not concede anything to the advocates of central planning and control, suggests that a similar criticism of "negative" and "positive" conceptions of justice may be in order, a criticism which similarly will not concede anything to the partisans of "social justice." As usual, I shall take Hayek's arguments against "social justice" for granted. Mostly, they are an application of his case against constructivist rationalism with its organisational thinking, for "social justice," like legal positivism, proceeds from it or makes similar assumptions.[2]

We may agree with Hayek that it is difficult to state just what justice is although we can readily recognise what is unjust. Yet the fact that we cannot state what something is, but only what it isn't, does not prove that it is nothing in itself and only the absence or antithesis of its contraries. In theology, the negative way, of saying that God is "not this, not that," presupposes a tacit apprehension of what God is, which can be partially articulated by the "way of eminence," of saying that God is "this but eminently so."[3] Again, because we cannot say what *being* is, and every reader of Heidegger knows that he never does give a positive answer to his question at the end of his lengthy refinements of the question itself, it does not follow that *being* is only the negative of *not-being*. We can know full well what Space and Time are, and that they are something real and positive, without being able to say what they are. Similarly, without training in formal grammar, we cannot readily state the rules of our native tongue, yet we can nevertheless quickly recognise mistakes of grammar. What Hayek should have concluded is that justice, and also peace and freedom, are positive notions which we primarily grasp tacitly and may find hard to articulate.

He appends an extensive list of citations to the effect that justice principally requires us to do nothing, that is, to abstain from theft, fraud, ill-treatment, and murder, and to perform definite actions only in special circumstances, such as the repayment of debts and the fulfilment of promises (LLL, vol. 2, pp. 162–4).[4] But this is to take a rather external and behaviourist view of justice. Not to steal is not itself to act justly: I can desist from stealing for reasons, such lack of ability either to do it or to do it and get away with it, which have nothing to do with justice. Likewise with repayment of debts and fulfilment of contracts and other promises. To act justly, I must at heart have the conviction that the property and rights of others, and thus ultimately that others themselves, are to be respected and esteemed. Furthermore, *I* am not just, or am only imperfectly so, if I have to *make* myself forbear from theft, oppression, and welching on promises. Were I fully or unequivocally just, I would not even think of doing such things. Justice, like other virtues, is primarily a standing attitude which is then expressed in appropriate conduct. That conduct may often be negative, but the attitude is itself a positive acknowledgment of the rights of all men. In any case, most of us are engaged with our fellows for most of the time, and thus we bring upon ourselves many positive obligations to them.

Likewise peace and freedom are essentially positive. We have already seen that freedom necessarily has a positive aspect, of freedoms to do certain things. That is the primary one, and the negative can be defined and understood only as noninterference with it. Coercion and oppression likewise presuppose a set of positive rights and spheres of individually initiated activity, actual or potential, which can therefore be deliberately opposed, thwarted, or frustrated: you cannot oppress or coerce a robot. As for peace, that cannot be identified with the absence of open conflict:

"they make a desert and call it peace." A peaceful state of human affairs is the consequence and expression of a right order in the hearts of those concerned, of a positive appreciation of harmony, cooperation, rights, and obligations, and not just of a curb upon aggressive impulses.

Justice cannot be defined in an exhaustive list of types of specific action, although we can point to central actions. As with many other notions, it is often easier to say what it isn't rather than what it is. But that does not mean that it is essentially negative, the negation of injustice. Rather it is the positive appreciation of the rights of persons, ourselves and others equally. And, surely, that is precisely what any genuine liberalism presupposes, in contrast to all those systems of thought and politics which regard the individual wholly or principally as a member of a certain group, a fulfiler of roles, or a functionary in a social or cosmic machine. Universal principles of justice are needed because of the inherent value of the individual person himself. We shall now consider Hayek's position with respect to both of these requirements.

Hayek and Natural Law

In places, Hayek agrees with another tenet of legal positivism, that there are no universally valid principles of justice. For, he states, "if civilisation has resulted from unwanted gradual changes in morality, then no universally valid system of ethics can ever be known to us" (FC, p. 20; cf. LLL, vol. 3, p. 166). Yet the Great Society is constituted precisely by universal rules, rules applying to all, which those who do accept them must surely regard as rules to be accepted by all. If, as Hayek claims (LLL, vol. 2, pp. 145–7), the morality of the Open or Great Society is in some respects different from that of a closed society, that cannot prove that neither is right. Indeed, it is clear that he himself holds the former to be right precisely because they are universal in intent. What the facts show, if they are facts, is moral progress, a discovery of truer and wider moral principles. In this case, it is that by investment in new techniques one can do more good, by providing for the needs of many, than by giving the money to a few known neighbours.[5]

Hayek similarly rejects the idea that the principles of justice are "natural," in three senses of the word, though not in the sense of an unintended product of human action:

> as part of an external and eternal order of things, or permanently implanted in an unalterable nature of man, or even in the sense that man's mind is so fashioned once and for all that he must adopt those particular rules of conduct.

Nevertheless, he continues, this does not mean that they cannot therefore be "objective," that is, existing independently of the will of any particular person. For no one person's will has instituted, nor usually could change, the views and opinions which shape a given society. Having evolved, and not being the result of human design, they are "objectively existing" facts (LLL, vol. 2, pp. 59–60; cf. FC, p. 56 on Jacques Monod). But what is an "objectively existing" fact is that these views and opinions are held and lived by the members of the society in question, as are other and perhaps conflicting views and opinions, whether or not they are inherited or have been deliberately adopted. They are facts which we have to take into account, and are views and opinions to which, to a greater or lesser extent, we often have to conform. But that does not mean we have to agree with them, nor does it settle the question of their truth or validity. That companies in the European world have to pay commissions which are really bribes when doing any business in many parts of Africa and the Middle East, does not mean that they do or should approve of such practices. The Romans rightly suppressed any practice of human sacrifice among those whom they incorporated into their empire, and likewise the British Raj that of suttee in India.

Yet on the very same page Hayek suggests another possibility, that there may be moral principles the observance of which is necessary to any society, and therefore not open to choice. Such principles would be "natural," as being part of the nature of the object. He cites Hume:

> Though the rules of justice be *artificial*, they are not *arbitrary*. Nor is the expression improper to call them *Laws of Nature*; if by nature we understand what is common to any species, or even if we confine it to mean what is inseparable from the species. (*Treatise*, part 2, § 2; LLL, vol. 2, p. 174, n. 75)

Consequently, any such rules of justice will be found, at least in part, in every society. This is precisely the traditional doctrine of Natural Law, which holds that there are laws discoverable by all men, applicable to all men, binding upon all men, and recognised and partly observed everywhere.

Moreover, the traditional doctrine holds, with Hayek and against legal positivism, that law to be law does not have to be a command.[6] That Natural Law was often thought of as promulgated and enforced by God, is a secondary matter.[7] The whole point about Natural Law is that it can be recognised as just, right, and obligatory in and by itself. It is a rational law whose reasonableness all men are capable of recognising. It was the rise of nominalism within scholasticism, the consequence separation of will and reason in God, and the exaltation of will and power over reason, that resulted in a rejection of the whole idea of Natural Law. For God's law then became only "Divine Positive Law," what he had decreed by fiat for men to obey in fear of eternal punishment.[8] Legal positivism is, in effect and possibly historically as well, such a theological positivism minus the theology and with human sovereigns taking over the arbitrary sovereignty of the nominalist God.

As Hayek points out, legal positivism needs the notion of sovereignty, for it makes the whole content of the law to be what is willed by the sovereign. Against that he argues that sovereignty is in fact limited by a prevailing state of opinion as to what is permissible and impermissible, and by what is required for the maintenance of a spontaneous order (LLL, vol. 1, pp. 92–3; vol. 2, p. 61).

But, more fundamentally, legal positivism in the end cannot maintain its own doctrine. As Kelsen himself stated,[9] legal positivism traces all law back to "a basic norm" according to which the constitution is to be respected or the sovereign obeyed, and stops there. That means three things fatal to the claims of legal positivism to provide a complete account of a legal system:

1. The sovereign is he who has the *legal right* to rule and legislate and the courts are those which have the *legal right* to try cases, and thus that, after all, the law is prior to both, designates both, and so cannot be *in essence* the creation of either. The right to rule is essentially one of custom and prescription. Even the right to rule in virtue of conquest is one allowed by custom.
2. Legal positivism, as Kelsen, acknowledges, cannot say why the constitution is to be respected or the sovereign obeyed, or international law (itself mostly a spontaneously developed set of practices and not the decisions of international bodies) observed, that is, why "basic norms" are norms.
3. Legal positivism cannot guide any choice between competing sovereignties and bodies of law, and which is legal and which to be obeyed or observed. It cannot say, in such a case, which *is* the law.[10]

These are questions which Hayek does not explicitly raise and attempt to answer. He implies, by his account of justice and the limits that opinion places upon sovereignty, that any right to rule must respect the principles of justice and can be forfeited by flouting them. That is, legitimacy is assumed until shown to have been forfeited by grave injustice. That conservative approach seems to have been that implied by traditional Natural Law. Very different was the positive and hence radical demands made by the doctrines of natural right, as we shall see in the next section.

Hayek's account of a spontaneously evolving *nomos* corresponds with the core of the traditional doctrine of Natural Law. For Hayek credits the members of the community with a tacit sense of justice and injustice which becomes progressively but never wholly articulated, and the reasonableness of which they are assumed to be able to appreciate. The difference between his account and that of Natural Law is, as we have noted, Hayek's denial of any universally held notions of justice. What he fails to appreciate is the distinction between universally known and applicable principles and specific laws which may well be known and applicable only to and in specific times and places. What counts as property varies widely, and in modern times further types of property, such as intellectual property, have emerged and been legally recognised. But property of some sort is known everywhere—communal property is still property and can be misappropriated by those within or without the community—and so the most general principles of respect for it apply to all forms and so in all societies. What classical liberalism requires, in effect, is that the respect for the human person shown in the basic duties and virtues acknowledged in all societies,[11] be widened to all, deepened in its application to each, and made more secure, so that the person himself and his own dignity stand out more clearly. Moreover, Hayek's account of the progressive and spontaneous articulation of a tacit sense of justice can act as a useful corrective against any renewal of those rationalist tendencies that overcame Protestant theorists of Natural Law in the seventeenth and eighteenth centuries, in whose hands it became an *a priori* and deductive system.[12]

Hayek's third way between legal positivism and classical Natural Law, concedes too much to the former, in its wavering over universal moral principles, and, when that is corrected, in fact coincides with and appropriately supplements the latter.

Natural Rights

Justice is a positive notion and presupposes the value of the individual and his rights. It seems to me to be a fault of most Liberal theory that the latter is taken for granted. Indeed, the utilitarian forms of liberalism can easily be turned, as we have noted in the case of Bentham, into schemes of collectivist control and reorganisation. The individual as a complex of pleasure-pain reactions is, as B.F. Skinner said, "beyond freedom and dignity." As we noted earlier, there is no warrant at all, within utilitarianism, for Bentham's assumption, echoed by J.S. Mill and R.M. Hare, that "each is to count for one and not for more than one."[13] Bentham's principle can be only an alien element introduced into his system as a residue of inherited Christian beliefs about the value and dignity of each person in and as himself.

The doctrine of Natural Rights, formulated in the eighteenth century, appears to articulate that sense of the dignity of the individual which liberalism requires. But Hayek does not endorse it in virtue of its constructivist rationalism. For it required that society and government be founded upon (e.g., Locke, Paine), or conceived *as if* founded upon (e.g., Rousseau, Kant), a Social Contract. Society either was, or ought to be such as if it had been, the product of deliberate design, a conscious contrivance, and an organisational structure. Hence the hostility of Natural Rights theorists to tradition and prescription, to what had evolved and had not been deliberately designed. On this Hayek quotes the Abbé Sieyès's exhortation to the National Assembly, "to act like men just emerging from the state of nature and coming together for the purpose of signing a social contract" (CL, p. 57). It also set forth "self-evident" or "simple and indisputable" rights and principles as the basis of the legitimacy of government and legislation, and endorsed the Cartesian assumption that all that is not demonstrated is to be rejected (CL, pp. 64–5). And its organisational thinking led it easily to totalitarian democracy for the attainment of freedom in or through a collective purpose (CL, p. 56, with references to Talmon's *Origins of Totalitarian Democracy*).[14]

Modern compilations of rights—"civil" or "universal" rather than "natural"—also suffer from organisational and thus totalitarian tendencies, as we noted in chapter 3. Like the theories of Natural Rights, they merely present demands, and too often demands for entitlements which therefore place the burden of providing them upon unspecified others.

Moreover, the most destructive element in theories of Natural Rights, and their contemporary derivatives, is their liberation of the individual from duty. Duty was placed wholly on the side of the government, to serve the rights of the individual. Even the totalitarian version of Rousseau and his followers, emancipated the individual, as Burke complained,[15] from all those duties, "nine-tenths of the virtues," which restrain men's unruly appetites. This we see today in the demand for liberation of the individual in private life alongside subjection of him in public and economic matters to a collective and egalitarian welfare.

In the eyes of the Left, in Britain and America, one can do as one likes
with members of either sex, above the age of consent, but not with
one's money.

Natural Rights theory, and its successors, merely assert the rights of
the individual and put a moral gloss upon his unmoralised desires. What
liberalism requires is a genuine account of the dignity and duty of the
individual. We must look elsewhere for an adequate account of that.

The Value and Duty of the Individual

Hayek appreciates that liberty requires moral discipline and a sense
of personal responsibility on the part of the individual (CL, chs. 4–6).
Once again, liberty presupposes moral principles that apply to all and
can be recognised by all. Freedom itself is one of them, and, like the
others, "demands that it be accepted as a value in itself" (CL, p. 68).
But this sets a fundamental problem for liberalism which Hayek does
not overcome. On the one hand, there is the requirement of recognisable
principles of justice, the inherent value of freedom itself, the self-restraint of individuals according to "ingrained moral beliefs" (CL, p. 62,
with a reference to Burke), and respect for the dignity of the individual.
On the other, "believing in freedom means that we do not regard ourselves as the ultimate judges of another person's values" and do not
interfere with his pursuit of his own ends so long as he does not interfere with others (CL, p. 79). It would indeed be presumptuous to regard
ourselves as the ultimate judges of anything. But provisional judgments
are necessary in human life, and liberty itself requires judgments as to
what threatens it and what doesn't. That there are spheres in which we
may do more or less as we like, and that quite a variety of opinions on
certain matters does no harm and can give rise to a fair amount of good,
does not mean, as Hayek recognises, that everything goes, everywhere
and every time. The question is, Just what are the limits wherein doing
and saying what one likes must be confined in order to protect liberty
itself? Hayek clearly gives the standard liberal answer: that point where
they would impinge upon the equal liberty of others. But that, as we
saw, is difficult to define and can lead to an almost total inhibition on
saying and doing anything towards others. Moreover, if liberty is
founded, as Hayek recognises, on certain moral principles and traditions, then anything which threatens them can, in principle, be a proper
subject of public and governmental action, indirectly if not directly. To
give substance to this question, I shall mention current controversies

concerning the definition and maintenance of the family. Hayek recognises the importance of the family for the upbringing of children and the transmission of large parts of inherited culture, and, indeed, that "society is made up as much of families as of individuals" (CL, p. 90). Given that, just what "experiments in living" can be tolerated and at what point will they dissolve the family, the traditions it transmits, the discipline it inculcates, and thus the liberty which rests upon it? To these questions we shall return in Part 3. The point to be noted now is that liberty rests upon certain substantive moral beliefs and practises, and thus upon the truth of the moral principles which they embody, especially that of the dignity of the person himself. To claim, as is often done as by J.S. Mill in *On Liberty*, that we *should* respect the rights and opinions of others because none can be known to be true and that belief in the truth of one's own leads to intolerance, in fact liberates intolerance, for, on these assumptions, the principle of tolerance is just another "subjective" value and the practice of intolerance cannot be known to be false. What liberalism needs is not this self-destructive scepticism but a positive belief in the dignity and duties of the person.[16]

Now it was in an early work that Hayek came nearest to unequivocally affirming that principle. Later on the argument for liberty, as we saw in the previous chapter, is that only in a free society can the knowledge dispersed among its members be best used. Moral considerations, as just noted, enter in the form of the conditions of liberty, rather than directly as the argument for it. It is in a certain section of *The Road to Serfdom* (pp. 156–9) that he states a more directly moral argument for liberty, especially in the following:

> Freedom to order our own conduct in the sphere where material circumstances force a choice upon us, and responsibility for the arrangement of our own life according to our own conscience, is the air in which alone moral sense grows and in which moral values are daily recreated in the free decision of the individual. Responsibility, not to a superior, but to one's conscience, the awareness of a duty not exacted by compulsion, the necessity to decide which of the things one values are to be sacrificed to others, and to bear the consequences of one's own decisions, are the very essence of any morals which deserve the name. (RS, p. 157)

On the one hand, a free society enables these virtues to express themselves whereas collectivism weakens them and makes persons unwilling by their own efforts and self-sacrifices, unless everyone else will cooperate, to remedy inequities in society—one notes that socialists say that they are quite willing to pay for higher government expenditure on their pet projects *provided that* everyone else is made to pay.

On the other, it requires such attitudes and habits as personal independence and self-reliance, willingness to bear risks and to cooperate with others, noninterference with one's neighbours, tolerance of the different and odd, respect for custom and tradition, which are also weakened by collectivism (RS, pp. 157–9).[17] A free society has both a moral basis and a moral value in the moral qualities and value of the individual.

We have come a long way from von Mises's explicit scepticism and Popper's adherence to the dichotomy of facts and standards, which would destroy the liberalism based upon them, even though there are elements of utilitarianism and scepticism that Hayek has not overcome. But in the restatements of classical liberalism in the twentieth century we still await an explanation of just why the individual is so valuable that the protection of his liberty is to be the highest political good and the chief concern of government. Perhaps for that we shall need to go beyond liberalism itself. Certainly by stressing the importance of principles of justice, and the responsibility and moral conduct of the individual, Hayek in effect acknowledges that liberalism must transcend itself as a political doctrine, for the political order takes us beyond itself to the moral order upon which it rests. That was the fundamental contention of traditional Natural Law, that while political arrangements and affairs have their own sphere and will have to vary to suit each its own milieu, they depend upon fundamental and universal moral principles.[18] We now turn to Polanyi whose starting-point was the realisation that scepticism and utilitarianism provided no sure foundation for liberty, and whose conception of liberty was primarily a "positive" one of liberty for the pursuit of universal ideals which form man's calling.

Notes

1. Hayek (LLL, vol. 2, p. 159 n. 4) refers to R. Dworkin's distinction between rules and principles, and Dworkin's argument that the latter are needed to make the law complete. Hayek rejects Dworkin's assumption that the law is only a collection of laws, explicit laws, and not a system of mutually adjusted laws and in an order of rank, but otherwise agrees with the substance of Dworkin's argument. It is noteworthy that Dworkin deploys it against the positivist interpretation of judicial "discretion" in hard cases as the creation of a new law or right which is then applied retrospectively to the case in hand. Dworkin argues that even when there is no settled rule to determine the case, one party can have a right to win and that it is the judge's duty to discover the rights of the parties and not to invent new ones. What the judge does, or should do, when recognised rules fail him, is to be guided by legal principles, which are more general than rules, survive intact even when they do not prevail, and have weight and importance relative to each other, for example, freedom of contract, that none should profit by his own wrong, "the general fundamental maxims of the common law" (*Tak-*

ing Rights Seriously, chs. 2 and 3). (But it should be noted that this account sits uneasily with his later support of judicial activism against judicial restraint, op. cit., ch. 5, a position which he adopts, because like F.D. Roosevelt, who attacked the constitutionalism of the Supreme Court, he embraces a welfarist conception of liberty and thus a policy of extensive interventionism.)

2. But there is one part of Hayek's case against "social justice" which seems dubious to me. He accounts for the rise of demands for it in terms of an atavistic desire to return to that stage of prehistory in which men lived a collective existence in exclusive tribes as hunters, and therefore under the direction of chieftains who organised the activities of their groups and distributed the fruits of those activities, i.e., in a single, permanent *taxis* with little *cosmos*. The long ages, says Hayek, spent in such a state have left us with inherited emotions which the comparatively shorter periods of life in more individualist agricultural and then commercial societies have not supplanted (LLL, vol. 2, pp. 67, 146; FC, pp. 17–19, 50). But he offers no evidence for this conjecture. If we look at contemporary or recent "band" societies, which neither have domesticated cattle nor practice agriculture, we see:

   1. They are gatherers as well as, hunters, and probably depend more on gathering than hunting.

   2. Gathering is conducted individually, and so also may be hunting. Food is distributed by those who have gathered or caught it, and not centrally. There is "communism" only in the consumption of food and only in the sense that no one is allowed to go hungry and children are taught to share their food with others.

   3. Tools are individually owned but easily shared, and there are relationships and networks of gift-giving and exchange.

   4. The "band," as among the Bushmen of the Kalahari, can remain stable as a conceptual unit but vary in membership, as people both join and leave it. Or, as among the Commanche and Cheyenne, a large tribe may break up into family units during the winter and then reassemble for hunting in the summer.

   5. Smaller bands often have relationships with others, and larger tribes, like the Cheyenne, can have a complicated structure which diffuses power. There are rarely "chiefs" in the sense of individuals who are permanent heads of bands or tribes for all matters. Some tribes may have no chiefs in any sense, only wise and revered elders.

I have taken these details from Gluckman (*Politics*) and (eds.) E. Leacock and R. Lee, *Politics and History in Band Societies*. It is ironic that Leacock and Lee, both avowed Marxists, should use band societies as models of voluntary cooperation with little command or authority, as against "capitalist competition," and as proof that socialism is possible, whereas Hayek refers to hunting tribes in order to show what an organisational society or *taxis* (and therefore a socialist society) would be like, although he does also say that the members of a band do not always act communally and by command (LLL, vol. 1, p. 47). There is no sign that Leacock and Lee have misreported the facts of the bands which they themselves have studied. Of course, like Marx himself, they duck the question of whether command and authority can be eliminated in industrial society, and even more so in a communalised industrial economy.

Gluckman (*Politics*, p. 83) gives a list of different types of tribal societies, from small hunting-bands in which everyone is related to everyone else by blood or marriage to large-scale kingdoms, and warns that we cannot assume that these are stages in a line of evolution through which all larger and more complex societies have gone, nor that all mankind was first organised in hunting-bands. This is a book that Hayek has read: see LLL, vol. 1, p. 152; vol. 2, p. 165.

Hayek's conjectural prehistory appears to be false. Moreover, if it were true, we would not need to use it to explain modern demands for "social justice." We may doubt if human beings have inherited emotions in such a specific sense. It is much more plausible to point to an experience that we have all lived through: namely, that of childhood dependency upon adults when everything we had was "distributed" to us. Children are very particular about getting their fair shares and quick to spot and complain if another child has more or less. Their idea of justice is, inevitably, a distinctly distributional and "social" one. It is not atavism for a former stage of history (whether or not it was as Hayek depicts) but regression to childhood which, I suggest, explains demands for "social justice" and collective distribution of "fair shares."

It is curious that Hayek nowhere mentions another key ingredient in the demand for "social justice," namely, the "zero-sum" fallacy that all goods and wealth are permanently fixed in amount such that one person's gains can only be at another person's expense. That is, of course, the position that children see themselves in when parents are serving food at meal times or sharing out the contents of a bag of sweets, and, I suggest, adult assumptions about "zero-sums" are another regression to childish attitudes. It is the assumption in the socialist catch-phrase of "the rich get richer and the poor get poorer," despite all the evidence of increasing wealth all round. Yet, when it suits them, socialist politicians can give up this assumption and, for example, claim that "growth," which by some mysterious and never explained means they will bring about, will provide all the revenues needed for their ambitious projects.

3. See further, my *Transcendence and Immanence in the Philosophy of Michael Polanyi and Christian Theism*, ch. 4.

4. Among the quotations is one from Scheler's *Der Formalism in der Ethik* (3d ed., p. 212; Eng. trans. p. 208 n. 35). Scheler, discussing the "ideal ought" as opposed to the ought of an imperative addressed to persons in general or to particular persons, holds that "ought to be so" presupposes "is not," that the value in question is presupposed not to exist. "This ought to be," he says, can also be used inadequately to express "It is rightfully so." Consequently, he formulates the propositions quoted by Hayek, that "the order of Right" cannot state *what* ought to be or is right but only what ought not to be or is not right. The true part of this is that "right" and "what ought to be" do presuppose values and are not the sources of values: that is, that values themselves and objects, real or imagined, bearing those values are first good and *therefore* "ought to be." But unusually for him, Scheler, and perhaps the other authors cited, makes the mistake of confounding the *ordo cognoscendi* with the *ordo essendi*. In general we take what is good, correct, and right for granted, and notice and comment upon the existence of what is bad, incorrect, and wrong. Except in special circumstances, we hear or see without remarking upon them the sound of a correctly running engine, a grammatically correct and truthful utterance, the giving of correct change, and polite behaviour. What usually catches our attention is the presence of something wrong, not something right. Nor could life be lived if this were not so. The normal as rightful or correct is the normal as usual or commonly occurring, and the abnormal is the unusual and hence remarkable, at least in general though some areas of life may be exceptional. Hence the double meaning of "normal" itself. Consequently, when we say, "This ought to be" (or "He should have done that") we imply that it is not (or that he did not). Likewise, we

take intention and success for granted, and so, when we do say, "He tried to do it" or "He intended to do it," we imply failure or, in the latter, perhaps a change of mind instead. Similarly, we usually speak about what we ourselves want or need when we do not have the objects in question, for there is no reason to do so when we have them. From this many philosophers have inferred that "want" and "need" imply "have not," and some of them have drawn the logical consequence that when we have something we no longer want or need it. But consider having something and then being asked, "Do you want (or need) it?" In all reflection upon language it is necessary to look at all contexts, and not just some, and to bear in mind our propensity to take the positive for granted. Therefore, although our usage does imply that "ought to be" presupposes "is not," the logical connection between the things themselves is that "ought to be" presupposes nothing about neither the existence or nonexistence of the object in question, and so can apply equally to both.

Elsewhere (*The Eternal in Man*, p. 235), Scheler was only too aware of the fatal consequences of making the positive merely the negative of the negative, formulated by Nicholas of Cusa as *omnis determinatio est negatio* and taken up by Hegel in his doctrine of the "power of negation." (See also J. Macquarrie's Heideggerian *Principles of Christian Theology*, pp. 198–200, 234–5.) All these doctrines imply that real and finite beings emanate from a previously or otherwise undifferentiated Being, which, as Hegel said, would be indistinguishable from Nothing, so that each is what it is only by being not the others, like slices off a block of cheese. A particular application of this doctrine is the assumption that the individual person is real only as his body—either directly or indirectly by restricting his experiences to a unique section of space and time—separates him from a Mind, Intellect, or Reason which is intrinsically and ideally One and uniform. Time and again Scheler inveighed against this denial of the reality of the unique individual by such as Averroës, Spinoza (who drew the logical consequences of Descartes' assumptions), Kant (by implication), Fichte, and Hegel, and, we may add, by the whole empiricist and analytic tradition: see below, ch. 14 §1.

5. Here, like Popper, he equates *closed* with *tribal* societies, and locates the beginning of the emergence of the Open Society at the end of the Middle Ages. We have already noted the dubiousness of the latter contention, and in chapter 10 §3 shall suggest that the distinction of closed and open societies needs to be revised. Another point to note now is that it seems at times in LLL that Hayek is saying that there is no longer a need for works of charity because providing marketable goods and services is always more effective in benefiting others, but contrast what he says in CL, p. 125.

6. See A.P. d'Entrèves, *Natural Law*, ch. 4, especially pp. 76–7 and the quotations from Hooker and Aquinas.

It is interesting to note how deeply ingrained in utilitarianism was the nominalism and positivism that denies any rational content to law and hence the impossibility of obedience to it from recognising its reasonableness. For the utilitarians all law is fundamentally criminal law. According to Bentham (*Introduction*, notes added in 1789 to ch.18, pp. 430–3), every law is *coercive* (except that which is a repeal of another law), and creates an *offence*, although that which specifies the punishment is a separate law (4–7); civil law is expository (17), i.e., it only defines terms (10), the terms used in penal law. This applies also to moral law. For law is that which has a sanction attached to breaking it, and there are four forms of law each with its own type of sanction: physical and in the ordinary course of nature; political and upon the command of a judge;

moral and at the hands of chance persons in the community; and religious and by God (ibid., ch. 3, §§ 2–6, pp. 147–8). John Austin (*The Province of Jurisprudence Delimited*) defined law as rule which is commanded, and a command as an expressed desire supported by the infliction of evil. He inferred therefrom that only the commands of God and of human political superiors to their inferiors are laws properly speaking, while those enforced by mere opinion (e.g., those of honour and fashion, and all international law) are laws only improperly so called; and asserted that duty and command to be co-relative, such that one has duties only as commanded by someone else (Lect. 1, pp. 12–14; cf. pp. 142, 201). J.S. Mill (*Utilitarianism*, ch. 3) looking for the "sanctions" of utilitarianism, the motives to obey it, in the external ones of the hope of favour and fear of displeasure at the hands of God and men, and in the "internal" one of the feeling of duty or fear of the (self-inflicted) pain of disobeying it. Fear of punishment is not simply the only motive that there can be for obeying any law (perhaps with hope of reward), but is that which makes it a law in the first place.

Where, then, stands international law, which is neither commanded nor has penalties attached? Bentham replied, "With what degree of propriety rules for the conduct of persons of this description [sovereigns] can come under the appellation of laws, is a question that must rest till the nature of the thing called a law shall have been more particularly unfolded" (*Introduction*, ch. 18 §29, p. 429). But in the notes added in 1789 wherein the nature of law was "more particularly unfolded," there is no mention of international law. And his *Of Laws in General* is likewise silent upon the subject, save to remark (p. 16) that treaties among sovereigns, like those between a sovereign and his subjects, are not laws but concessions and promises. For Austin, as already noted, it is only law improperly so called.

7. For example, Cicero, *De Republica*, Bk. 2, ch. xxii, §33. Locke, as in other moral and political matters, represents a point of transition from the classical and mediaeval to the modern. In his *Essays on the Law of Nature* (165?–1664 and never published by Locke) he in fact endorses a theological positivism like that of Ockham under the guise of Natural Law. All law must be commanded by a lawgiver (pp. 111, 113, 173), and the Natural Law is that law enacted by God which can be known by the light of nature, as distinct from Revelation. But not, as we might suppose, from insight into its inherent rationality, but by inference from the natural world to the existence of God who created us and the world for some purpose and thus bound us by his law for achieving it (pp. 153–7). Obligations derive from the command which any superior has over us, and are a duty of obedience (p. 183), but we are bound by a rational apprehension of God's right as Creator and not just by fear of punishment (p. 185). But Locke gives no further specification of the Law of Nature. We can only assume that it is simply the recognition of the duty to obey God, and that further obligations are known from his revelation of his will, and so constitute "positive divine law" (p. 187). But, as with legal positivism, theological positivism cannot explain why the supreme sovereign is to be obeyed. If it is because God commands us to, then it begs the question. The Law of Nature, for Locke, therefore must be the general principle that superiors are to be obeyed and hence God above all, and nothing more.

Von Leyden, the editor of the *Essays*, suggests that Locke decided not to publish them, though requested to do so, for he had since moved to Hedonism, and quotes (p. 72) §7 from *Of Ethik in General* (1683–9): "good and bad, being relative terms, do not denote anything in the nature of the thing, but only the relation it bears to another, in its aptness and tendency to produce in it pleasure or pain." But in his *Essay on Human Understanding* Locke claimed that moral terms can be exactly defined (III, xi, 15–6) and therefore that "morality is capable of demonstration, as well as mathematics" (IV, iii, 18). But he nowhere gave such definitions and demonstrations.

8. See d'Entrèves, *Natural Law*, pp. 68–71. Edmund Burke echoed the Thomist doctrine that "in God will and reason are the same" (*Reflections, Works*, vol. 5, p. 186; see Aquinas ST, I II, 93–4). Ockham, in contrast, stated: "By the very fact that God wills something, it becomes just" (*IV Sententiae*, qq. viii–ix). The absolute sovereign of the modern age is, as Hobbes said, "a mortal god," the nominalist God secularised.

    Hayek (LLL, vol. 2, p. 174 n.74) quotes Comte and Kelsen on law as invented and commanded by God as the only alternative to law invented and willed by a human sovereign.

9. "That a norm.... is the basic norm of the national legal order does not imply that it is impossible to go beyond that norm. Certainly one may ask why one has to respect the first constitution as a binding norm. The answer might be that the fathers of the first constitution were empowered by God. The characteristic of so-called legal positivism is, however, that it dispenses with any such religious justification of the legal order. The basic norm is only the necessary presupposition of any positivistic interpretation of legal material" (*General Theory of Law and State*, p. 116).

10. On such duties and virtues, see C.S. Lewis, *The Abolition of Man*, especially its appendix and the quotations included in it.

11. See d'Entrèves, *Natural Law*, pp. 108–110, and the examples given there.

12. On Grotius, Pufendorf, Burlamqui, and Vattel, see d'Entrèves, *Natural Law*, pp.52–4. Their rationalism was taken over by the theorists of Natural Right, at whom we shall glance in a moment. Hayek (LLL, vol. 1, pp. 21, 151 n.26) comments upon their rationalist approach.

13. See above, ch. 5, n. 10.

14. On the differences between traditional Natural Law and the new doctrine of Natural Right, see d'Entrèves, *Natural Law*, pp. 54–62; Leo Strauss, *Natural Right and History*, and P. Stanlis *Edmund Burke and the Natural Law*. Hobbes deliberately took the traditional language and gave it his own and totally new meaning. Locke, in his political theory, claimed to be following Hooker and the traditional theory, but in arguing against Hobbes he in fact largely took over Hobbes's assumptions.

    One difference to which we have already referred is that the theorists of Natural Right demanded positive grounds for legitimacy of government and legislation. Thus the preamble of the *Déclaration des Droits de l'Homme et du Citoyen* requires the actions of the executive and legislative powers always to be referred back to the purpose of government, the preservation of the rights of man; Kant (*Metaphysical First Principles of the Doctrine of Right* §47, in *The Metaphysics of Morals*) states that only in terms of the Idea of an original social contract can one think of the legitimacy of a state; and Paine (*The Rights of Man* in *Common Sense and Other Political Writings*, pp. 86–7) says, "The fact therefore must be that the individual themselves, each in his own personal and sovereign right, entered into a compact with each other to produce a government; and this is the only mode in which governments have a right to arise and the only principle on which they have a right to exist." In contrast, Hooker says of human or positive laws that it is the principal use of public power to give them and that we must obey them "unless there be reason shewed which may necessarily enforce that the law of Reason or of God doth enjoin the contrary" (*Of the Law of Ecclesiastical Polity*, Bk. 1, ch. 10 §15).

As well as the tendency to totalitarian democracy, there was within Natural Rights the opposite and Libertarian one to minimal government. Thus Paine: "Government is no farther necessary than to supply the few cases to which society and civilisation are not conveniently competent; and instances are not wanting to show that everything which government can usefully add thereto has been performed by the common consent of society without government" (*Rights of Man*, p. 117). The resentment of government by others can be assuaged by either or both of less government or democratic self-government.

15. Compare Burke on the self-destructive tendencies of the theory of Natural Rights and his own cautious formulations based on traditional Natural Law:

> They have "the rights of man." Against these there can be no prescription; against these no agreement is binding: these admit no temperament, and no compromise: anything withheld from their full demand is so much of fraud and injustice. Against these their rights of men let no government look for security in the length of its continuance, or in the justice and lenity of its administration. The objections of these speculatists, if its forms do not quadrate with their theories, are as valid against such an old and beneficent government, as against the most violent tyranny, or the greenest usurpation. They are always at issue with governments, not on a question of abuse, but on a question of competency and title...
>
> Far am I from denying in theory, full as far is my heart from withholding in practice...the real rights of men...If civil society be made for the advantage of man, all the advantages for which it is made become his right. It is an institution of beneficence; and law itself is only beneficence acting by a rule. Men have a right to live by that rule; they have a right to do justice, as between their fellows, whether their fellows are in public function or ordinary occupation. They have a right to the fruits of their industry; and to the means of making their industry fruitful. They have a right to the acquisitions of their parents; to the nourishment and improvement of their offspring; to instruction in life, and to consolation in death. Whatever each man can separately do, without trespassing upon others, he has a right to do for himself; and he has a right to a fair portion of all which society, with all its combinations of skill and force can do in his favour. In this partnership all men have equal rights; but not to equal things. He that has but five shillings in the partnership, has as good a right to it, as he that has five hundred pounds has to his larger proportion. But he has not a right to an equal dividend in the product of the joint stock; and as to the share of power, authority and direction which each individual ought to have in the management of the state, that I must deny to be amongst the direct original rights of man in civil society; for I have in my contemplation the civil social man, and no other. It is a thing to be settled by convention...
>
> Men cannot enjoy the rights of an uncivil and of a civil state together. That he may obtain justice, he gives up his right of determining what it is points the most essential to him [i.e., of being judge in his own cause]....
>
> Government is a contrivance of human wisdom to provide for human *wants*. Men have a right that these wants should be provided for by this wisdom. Among these wants is to be reckoned the want, out of civil society, of a sufficient restraint upon their passions.... In this sense the restraints upon men, as well as their liberties, are to be reckoned among their rights. (*Reflections, Works*, vol. 5, pp. 119–23)
>
> These metaphysic rights entering into common life, like rays of light which

pierce into a dense medium, are, by the laws of nature, refracted from their straight line. (Ibid., p. 125)

The pretended rights of these theorists are all extremes: and in proportion as they are metaphysically true, they are morally and politically false. The rights of men are in a sort of middle, incapable of definition, but not impossible to be discerned. The rights of men in governments are their advantages; and these are often in balances between differences of good; in compromises sometimes between good and evil, and sometimes between evil and evil.... Men have no right to what is not reasonable, and what is not for their benefit. (Ibid., pp. 126–7)

See further, P. Stanlis, *Edmund Burke and the Natural Law*, and C. Parkin, *The Moral Basis of Burke's Political Thought*.

Contrast Bentham (*Anarchical Fallacies*), who totally repudiated rights as nonsense and natural rights as "nonsense upon stilts" on the grounds that only utility for the greatest happiness of the greatest number could count as right. See further, for relevant extracts from Bentham's *Anarchical Fallacies* and Burke's writings, (ed.) J. Waldon, *Nonsense Upon Stilts: Bentham, Burke and Marx on Natural Rights*.

16. Among the moral corruptions that collectivism engenders is a pervasive and begrudging envy. The "zero-sum" thinking of collectivism entails that one person's gains can only be at another's expense, and, in a régime of controls and rationing, people can improve their lot only illegally so that profits are in fact "profiteering."

17. Locke, in his first *Letter on Toleration*, argues for it on strictly Christian grounds that persecution is dealing with men by force and not charity (p. 107), and that "faith only, and inward sincerity, are the things which procure acceptance with God" (p. 124), and thus that belief cannot be forced, although he has a radical view of the Church as a merely human and voluntary association of men who are already Christian before they form or enter it (pp. 110–1). He also states that the magistrate cannot tolerate opinions contrary to human society and the moral rules for it (p. 138), nor atheists for whom oaths and covenants have no bonds and who cannot claim a pretence of religion and thus toleration in order to undermine religion (p. 140).

In contrast to those arguments, Polanyi frequently quotes a statement about the undemonstrable nature of religious truths from Locke's *Third Letter* (of which I have not been able to see a copy): "how well-grounded and great soever the assurance of faith may be wherewith it is received" but faith it is still and not knowledge, persuasion and not certainty' ("Scientific Beliefs," *Ethics*, vol. 61, Oct. 1950, p. 27). That, he says, derives toleration from doubt and is the turning of Christian faith into *mere* belief, a sign in Polanyi's eyes of the beginnings of the dangerously suspended logic of Anglo-American liberalism.

18. See Aquinas, ST I II 95 -2; Hooker, *Eccles. Polity*, Bk. 1, ch. 10 §§ 6–7.

9

Dedication or Servitude

Public Liberty

According to his own account of the matter (SFS, p. 8), Polanyi turned (or, rather, returned) to political and philosophical questions in reaction to the Marxist demand that scientific research be centrally planned, along with everything else, in order to promote the material welfare of man. To defend the freedom of science, he found that he had to reformulate the nature of freedom generally and its role in society. This context of his return to political questions gave a distinct direction to his thinking. His proximate concern was freedom for scientific research, a "positive" freedom, or, rather, an emphasis upon the positive side of freedom. And that led him to the questions of the value of science, of freedom for other human activities, and of their value. This means that he does not begin with the "negative" freedom of the individual to do as he pleases without interference by government and public opinion, a right to freedom which can only be asserted as that which we want, for, by definition, it lacks any inherent value and commitment to value. Nor does he begin with Hayek's reformulation of it as the freedom to use one's own knowledge, which permits only a utilitarian justification in terms of the greater benefit to all if individuals are allowed to act as they each think fit, although, as we have seen, Hayek also goes beyond such a conception. On the contrary, Polanyi begins with the ideals which European civilisation has pursued and for the progressive pursuit of which freedom is necessary.

In some ways his approach can be seen most clearly in his first attempt systematically to defend the freedom of science and with it freedom generally, the unpublished manuscript, *The Struggle of Man in Society*. To the totalitarian organisation of society for the pursuit of a single goal, such as power over other nations or material welfare, Polanyi

153

opposes the idea of a society based on free mental activities and not an irresponsible or merely private freedom. Freedom he takes to be:

> The policy (or behaviour) which springs from the faith that society makes sense with the ideas to which the pursuit of sympathy, justice and truth gives rise. It is an attitude cultivating all endeavours based on these tendencies, in the belief that they will all culminate in a joint result, which is thought of as the progress of civilisation. Such an ideal of freedom will be expressed in the first place by rules of procedure, by which individuals will be guided in introducing new elements into existing systems.... Established systems are based on certain fundamental principles which are being slightly modified every time that a process of growth takes place in accordance with the principles involved. Every time the principle becomes truer to its fundamental aim. This is the life of free institutions. (SMS, p. 23)

Polanyi's liberalism is primarily one of institutions, spontaneously formed and functioning, in which individuals together work out the implications of the principles which those institutions embody and serve. He explicitly rejects the interpretation of freedom as "isolation," as primarily the preservation of a private patch. That is, he says, an escape from the problem of freedom, nor is it free citizenship. Freedom lies in interaction with society, from which the individual receives and to which he gives, via "established spheres" or institutions which serve and support the activities of human life in society. The individual grows up within them and is educated by them. They develop his innate "ideal tendencies," or mental and spiritual capacities, and urge him to progress further along the paths which they have led him (SMS, p. 24).

Similarly and later, Polanyi distinguished "public" from "private" liberties (LL, pp. 157–9, 193). The former are those in which men cooperate for common purposes that are aims in themselves, such as science and religion. The latter are those in which the individual can act as he pleases without fear of punishment or censure, because the wider and social effects of his actions are considered by authority and public opinion to be negligible. Now this distinction sounds like, and roughly coincides with, J.S. Mill's distinction, in *On Liberty*, between those actions that affect others and those that do not. What concerned Mill was the delimitation and protection of the latter from intrusion by both the law and public opinion. Although, as every critic has pointed out, Mill's distinction breaks down, so that either all or no activities may be regulated by authority and public opinion, yet there is something in it. We all recognise a sphere of "private life," the extent of which cannot be precisely fixed, but which consists of those activities which we think are of no concern to others apart from those with whom we choose to share them. Thus occupation or profession fall outside private life, for in them we cannot entirely choose with whom we shall deal, even if we are self-employed or in private practice. Modern urban society makes it possible for people to live anonymously and to insulate one part of their lives from others and several from public notice. It is ironic that the pressure of public opinion, which worried Mill, was weakening in its extent just as Mill thought it was becoming unbearable. For it was quite possible to conduct many an "experiment in living" in London if the parties were discrete about it: Maida Vale was built just for that purpose.

Polanyi regards public liberty as much more important than private liberty. Both are to be protected but "it is damaging to the first that it should be demanded and its justification sought —as often happens— on the grounds of the second" (LL, pp. 158–9). That remark is clearly directed against the merely assertive individualism of such as Bentham and Paine, and of at least one level of Mill's *On Liberty*. Indeed, we note, totalitarianism and assertive individualism are suspicious of the independent institutions which claim and foster public liberties, the former because they represent foci of allegiance and solidarity outside the State and its ruling party, so that they must be incorporated within it and run by the party, and the latter because they represent just another external imposition upon the individual unless they can be reduced to wholly contractual and voluntary associations. And, Polanyi states, public and private liberties are not necessarily connected. On the one hand, both were at zero in serfdom or villeinage, and the emergence of both was brought about by the gradual establishment of fixed feudal dues and then their commutation in terms of money whereby the serf became a tenant, and able to act for and by himself in all matters. On the other, totalitarian régimes have been more concerned to deny justification and scope to public liberties than to restrict private ones. For they can see no social function in the initiatives of individuals, which they take to serve only private purposes, and so they reserve all public responsibility to the state. A liberal theory must recognise a distinction between the two and give priority to the former.

To show how private initiatives achieve public goods, Polanyi developed his theories, parallel to Hayek's accounts of *cosmos* and *taxis*, of spontaneous and corporate order, the former being polycentric and operating by individual mutual adjustments among its centres, and the latter being monocentric and operating by a plan issued from its one centre (LL, chs. 8–10). Now although Polanyi extensively applied this distinction to economic activity, in order to show how only markets and never central planning can establish and maintain an economic order, he also applied his analysis to other spheres of human activity, notably Common Law and science, especially the latter (e.g., LL, ch. 3, and pp. 162–7; KB, ch. 4). Indeed, he regarded the market, not as the archetype of spontaneous coordination by mutual adjustment of individual initiatives, but as a special and reduced form of it (KB, pp. 52, 69). Whereas markets coordinate individual efforts by competition and for the momentary material requirements of their participants, Common Law and science operate also by consultation by practitioners of one another and of the standards and accumulated knowledge of the profession, and by persuasion both within the activity and of the general public, and thus they build up permanent and progressive systems of law and scientific knowledge. A market is motivated by the expectation of gain. Similar motives, for the prestige of being the first to make an important discovery, operate in science, and act as incentives as do prices and profits in the market. But science has also a higher principle of operation, the appeal to and employment of the professional standards of science, embodied and conveyed in its traditions, by which discoveries are confirmed by the scientific community. Other branches of human culture, although not so precise and systematic in their operations and results, function in a similar manner of individual initiatives guided and supported by tradition. It is in these non-economic spontaneous orders that the value of liberty lies. Merely private liberties, in contrast, do not contribute to any spontaneous order (LL, p. 157; KB, p. 52, 69–70).

That last remark is not quite true, for surely they can result in the emergence of a market. What distinguishes the other examples of spontaneous order is the establishment of standards and the accumulation of knowledge or other achievements, a dedication to values other and higher than gain and profit.

Although it could not be set up *de novo*, Polanyi allowed that a market, and the whole system of civil law that regulates it, could become redundant if income tax were increased to 100 percent. Such might become a real possibility if a wealthy country engaged for a long time in an all-out arms race, had to cope with a permanent natural catastrophe, or increased its social services to the maximum of its income. There could be no rational allocation of resources but only the continuation of the schedule of allocation adopted at the beginning. Public liberty would then also become redundant, and if its value lay in economic management, then it would have no value in itself and hence no permanent and necessary value. Its value cannot be founded upon private wants and the operation of the market which they serve. Polanyi's argument is not that of von Mises, for whom the free market delivers what people actually want, in the longer run at least. And it goes one step beyond that of Hayek, that freedom enables individuals to use their own knowledge to the mutual benefit of all, economically and otherwise. For it bases the demand for liberty upon the inherent and permanent values of the ends which it should serve.

> Public liberty can be fully upheld as an aim in itself, insofar as it is the method for the social management of purposes that are aims in themselves. Freedom of science, freedom of worship, freedom of thought in general, are public institutions by which society opens to its members the opportunity for serving aims that are purposes in themselves. By establishing these freedoms, society constitutes itself as a community of people believing in the validity and power of things of the mind and in our obligations to these things. (LL, p. 193)

A free society Polanyi likened to the Republic of Science. Like the community of scientists, it aims at self-improvement by means of free mutual adjustment and a general authority upholding a "dynamic orthodoxy" of traditional standards yet encouraging originality. It claims to be seeking truth, and every manner of excellence in self-improvement, and so implicitly admits the right to opposition in the name of truth, provided it is that.

> The freedom of the individual safeguarded by such a society is therefore—to use the term of Hegel—of a positive kind. It has no bearing on the right of men to do as they please; but assures them the right to speak the truth as they know it. Such a society does not offer particularly wide private freedoms. It is the cultivation of public liberties that distinguishes a free society, as defined here. (KB, p. 70)

This freedom is "positive" in three senses: it is primarily the freedom to pursue self-improvement and only secondarily the freedom from interference with that pursuit; it is a freedom to strive for objects of value, and not an irresponsible or merely assertive liberty; and its aims and institutions can protect the higher levels of the individual himself against his lower ones.

Firstly, in the model of scientific and academic freedom Polanyi sees the resolution of the dangerous ambiguities of freedom (LL, ch. 3). On the one hand, freedom as freedom from external constraint, rationally bounded by the same freedom for others, is the basis of the utilitarian conception of the good as the greatest happiness of the greatest number and of the freedom that is the condition for realising it. But, notes Polanyi

(LL, p. 32), this self-assertive freedom can be used to justify many abuses, and, via its fundamental opposition to restraint, it easily turns into nihilism. (We have noted Bentham's resentful opinion that all law is evil, a necessary evil at best, because it constrains liberty.) On the other hand, the freedom of submission to impersonal obligation, exemplified in Luther's words, "I can do no other," can become like totalitarianism and actually pass over into it when the state is made the supreme guardian of the public good. This freedom requires that all recognise the transcendent ideals to which it is to be dedicated.

> This kind of freedom is not upheld for the sake of the individual. It is not maintained to satisfy anyone's desire to be left alone, or for the sake of people who want to do as they please. It is not for private use at all. A judge may enjoy discharging his office, but that is not the purpose for granting him independence. A scientist certainly enjoys the search for discovery, but again, that is a very poor reason for giving him the security of academic freedom. Nor should any businessman in the modern world believe that his property rights over capital are given for his pleasure. All freedom granted for maintaining dynamic order, is freedom for responsible action: and not for amusement or personal advantage. This is the most central doctrine of Liberalism. ("The Liberal Conception of Freedom," 1940, box 26, folder 8, pp. 8–9)

I doubt if this is the central doctrine of all liberalism, but it certainly is that of Polanyi's.[1]

We thus come to the second way in which public liberties are "positive." For it is this reference to transcendent ideals and standards which generally gives them its value, and provides the grounds on which freedom can be claimed. A free society is one whose citizens "are sensitive to the claims of conscience and are not afraid to follow them," and where "questions of conscience are generally regarded as real, and where people are on the whole prepared to admit them as legitimate motives and even to put up with considerable inconvenience or hardship, caused by acting on such motives" (LL, p. 46). Here, in the freedoms that really matter, the individual is not pursuing his merely private interests nor claiming respect from the State on those grounds. Rather,

> Freedom is demanded by the dedicated individual in view of the grounds to which he is dedicated. He speaks to the State as a liegeman of a higher master demanding homage to his master. The true antithesis is therefore between the State and the invisible things which guide men's creative impulses and in which men's consciences are naturally rooted. (LL, pp. 46–7)

It is these transcendent ideas and ideals which lift individual freedom beyond merely doing as one likes, and which give it a proper claim against unwarranted interference. Totalitarianism results from the denial of the transcendent grounds of science and scholarship, justice, religion, art, and free political discussion, leaving the State to inherit all human devotion and to define its objects.

Thirdly, a free society based on public liberties is constituted for the sake of conscience and not our private selves, for "it protects our conscience from our own greed, ambition, etc., as much as it protects it against corruption by others" (LL, p. 30). That is, its institutions, professional standards, and mutual criticism, constitute a discipline which reinforces the better judgments of their participants. But, we note, they can do this only insofar as there are transcendent ideals and as they are orientated to them. Without such ideals, there can be no better or worse judgments, no higher or lower self.

Yet, Hayek might object (CL, p. 19), has not Polanyi displaced general liberty, in which the individual can do everything but what he is specifically forbidden from doing, by a set of liberties or privileges for special groups, particularly academic institutions and learned societies, which would be compatible with a régime that forbids everything which it does not specifically allow? It is notable that Polanyi has little to say about the freedom to do as one likes. It seems to be something which has to be allowed, and with it at least some abuses of it, as a consequence of the establishment of public liberties. Yet, as we saw in chapter 3, there are problems in defining a general liberty in terms of the absence of coercion, as Hayek sought to do, and, we also noted, he in fact appeals to certain central liberties—property, movement, choice of occupation, legal status and immunity from arbitrary arrest—as jointly giving a virtual definition of that general liberty which he seeks to defend. Moreover, although Polanyi focuses upon academic liberties, especially that of science, he does explicitly generalise them to include freedom of worship and of thought in general. Together with the freedom of a market economy, which he also defends and which of itself gives plenty of scope for doing as one likes, his list of liberties tends to coincide with Hayek's general liberty, and goes beyond privileges for specific groups, such as academics, scientists, and artists, to liberties for the whole population.

The Self-Transcendence of Liberty

Polanyi realised that a utilitarian justification of the freedom science would be insufficient. For the utility of science, its employment for the bettering of man's condition, is a by-product. On the one hand, many inventions and practical discoveries have been independent of natural science, neither springing from scientific discoveries nor contributing anything, or but little, to them. On the other, science develops by its own logic as it discovers laws of nature widening in scope and penetrating deeper into the structure of the universe, both often apart from economic and technical developments and contributing little to them. Whereas natural science is cumulative, and each successive theory incorporates what was true and discards or reinterprets what was false in its predecessor, as Polanyi illustrates with the history of astronomy and mechanics from Copernicus to Einstein, there is little similar continuity in applied science. For new techniques for achieving the same purpose are frequently independent of existing ones, as gas-lamps succeeded candles and oil-lamps and were then made obsolescent by electric lighting. An obsolete technology is discarded altogether—gas mantles are no longer manufactured. And technologies are necessarily dependent upon economic developments. For nothing counts as an invention if it incurs practical disadvantages nor would be continued if, in one way or another, it proved more costly than something else. Even when there is extensive research within a technological science, in industrial laboratories and agricultural and military research institutes, their contributions to natural science are very small (LL, pp. 71–7).

Polanyi also exposed the spurious examples and specious arguments of J.G. Crowther and L. Hogben who endeavoured to show that natural science has developed in response to economic needs (LL, pp. 78–83). Their error in writing history backwards, in crediting scientists with knowledge of future applications of their discoveries even before they had made those discoveries, is in fact what a utilitarian approach to scientific research must require. For natural science to be justified by its practical applications, the likely applications of any piece of research must be foreseen before that research is undertaken. But research is research into the unknown, and so Einstein, even before conceiving his theory of relativity, would have had to envisage the use of atomic power and thus also the other discoveries on which it depended (KB, pp. 58–9). Because this requirement cannot be met, utilitarianism would stultify scientific research, even apart from the imposition of central planning which the Marxist version of it also wanted. The technological and economic applications of natural science are mostly an unforeseeable by-product of disinterested research. Even within technology itself, one invention is often an unforeseen by-product of efforts to produce something else: NASA's scientists and engineers did not build rockets and send men into space in order to produce nonstick frying-pans. As elsewhere, utilitarianism is *disutile*, and must either destroy or transcend itself. To yield practical benefits, science must be valued and practised for its own sake and without much concern for those benefits.

Moreover, the utilitarian valuation of science for its contributions to material well-being was exactly the same as the Marxist attitude to-wards it, and so offered no defence against the Marxist claim that sci-ence be subjected to central control for the collective good and not be left to the private and "selfish" interests of independent scientists and institutions. Science can thus act as a paradigm for all civilised pur-suits and for the freedom which their disinterested practice requires. They must all have an inherent value which those who participate in them cherish and cultivate. Without such values, freedom is itself val-ueless. It becomes a freedom for nothing except doing as we like. Such a freedom can claim no *moral* right to be respected, granted, and pro-tected. It will always be liable to the charge that it is an egocentric and selfish freedom, and therefore to be overruled in favour of collective goals. That the rhetoric of collectivism is illogical (for collective ego-ism is still egoism and altruism has value only as it serves another's *good*, a good that could equally be one's own) does not apparently im-pair its effectiveness. For it gives tacit moral passions an object which is more or less explicitly denied them by a purely private and valueless conception of freedom. If what is individual and private is taken, even by its defenders, to be devoid of real value, the inference will be drawn that what is collective and public is worthwhile. Without explicitly pro-claiming the collective to be good, the individual can be denounced as selfish. Only an activity held to be worthwhile in itself can morally demand freedom for its practitioners. Freedom and independence can then be given to them, not for their own private interests, but for the sake of those values and ideals to which they dedicate themselves. Oth-erwise the case for freedom is surrendered in advance.

> The proper aims of science being denied justification and even reality, the scien-tist still pursuing them is naturally held guilty of a selfish desire for his own amuse-ment. It will be logical and proper for the politician to intervene in scientific matters, claiming to be the guardian of higher interests wrongly neglected by scientists. (SFS, p. 79)

Especially in those branches of science which are less precise, Polanyi continues, a crank (like Lysenko) can catch the ear of politicians, be installed in a position of authority, and then corrupt the practice of that science. Its freedom, and then that of all science, will then be further diminished. To be protected from such interference, science and the other pursuits of civilisation, require a community acknowledging and dedicated to transcendent ideals, so that the general public, even though they may not share the interests of the practitioners of any given activity, do respect and support them in general, and do not allow their own material interests improperly to impinge upon them.

We have seen that utilitarianism either destroys or transcends itself, because what is really useful in human life is that which is primarily valued and pursued for its own sake and not for its consequences. We have now seen that freedom likewise either destroys or transcends itself. Freedom for its own sake can be only the valueless freedom of doing as we like, which can raise no moral right against collectivist and totalitarian claims. Indeed, argues Polanyi, by the processes of what he later called "moral inversion" and "a dynamo-objective coupling," people who have abandoned explicit belief in ideals such as truth, justice and charity, which their consciences would have recognised and made them feel duty-bound to defend, convert their tacit moral passions into devotion to the state or to the party that controls it, which seeks to be the final arbiter of all the interests which truth and justice are said to serve. Consequently, the choice is not one between freedom or subjection but between dedication and servitude. "A society refusing to be dedicated to transcendent ideals chooses to be subjected to servitude" (SFS, pp. 78–80).

Classical liberalism we have taken to be the doctrine that liberty is the highest political end. In the last chapter we saw that it rests upon moral foundations, of self-restraint and the practice of justice, which cannot be motivated by regarding them merely as means. Justice, the observance of the rights of others, must be taken to be good and binding in itself, apart from what results from it. And its beneficial effects, peace and the opportunities for prosperity that peace brings, are a by-product of practising justice because it is justice. Polanyi takes the self-destruction or self-transcendence of utilitarianism one very important step further, and applies it to liberty itself. We noted also that Hayek, at one moment at least, affirmed that liberty was necessary as the context for the proper moral development of the individual. Polanyi's argument is that only on grounds like that can it be defended. The liberty that matters can be only the liberty for self-dedication, not that for doing as one likes. His argument is that the pursuit of science, and of similar activities of civilised life, requires "a state of social dedication and also that only in a dedicated society can men live an intellectually and morally acceptable life." In turn, that suggests that—

> The whole purpose of society lies in enabling its members to pursue their transcendent obligations; particularly to truth, justice and charity. Society is of course also an economic organization. But the social achievements of ancient Athens compared with those of, say, Stockport—which is of about the same size as Athens was—cannot be measured by the differences in the standard of living in the two places. The advancement of well-being therefore seems not to be the real purpose of society but rather a secondary task given to it as an opportunity to fulfil its true aims in the spiritual field. (SFS, p. 83)

The political order, and with it liberty, transcends itself. For they have value only as they serve, and are not merely to be served by, a moral order beyond them. That suggests that liberty cannot remain even as the highest political good, and therefore that classical liberalism must transcend itself.

Beyond the Liberal Idea of Liberty

Those accounts of liberty which stress its "negative" character or aspect, the freedom from interference, have a problem with the value of liberty. For they make liberty primarily the freedom to do as one likes, even when it is limited by the acknowledged need for mutual restraint, and doing as one likes is, by definition, devoid of reference to value. Of course, individuals and groups can dedicate themselves and their freedom to worthwhile and meritorious concerns, but, with equal right, they can use their freedom for indolence, selfishness, or contempt for all values, provided that their outward conduct observes the restraints necessary for all to enjoy freedom. The liberty of doing as we like has no value in itself. It can therefore be disregarded by those who have a definite scheme for society, even though, like Bentham, they may also regard law and government as essentially evil because restrictive of freedom, but also estimate that even more good can be realised by such means. Those who wish to defend a "negative" conception of liberty then have to fall back upon either sheer self-assertion, as by Tom Paine, or deploy utilitarian arguments to the effect that freedom produces the goods that people in fact want, as with von Mises and, more subtly, one level of Hayek's case. Such arguments are vulnerable to the claim that they hold only "in the long run" and so long as most people observe the required restraints. For they appeal to self-interest, and thus to calculations, formalised by game theory, of what it pays me to do given certain expectations of what others will do. If, like Keynes, I believe that in the long run we are all dead, then I may not be bothered about what is likely to happen in a distant future, nor, believing that I can get away with breaking the rules while the rest observe them, may I be worried by the question, "But what if we all did that?" The moral restraints which are needed for freedom are undermined by non-moral defences of it which appeal to and encourage a purely self-regarding mentality. The moral is debased when it is valued for non-moral reasons, and its practice will soon be weakened.

That is important today when, it seems, the totalitarian threats to liberty have virtually vanished and with them the moral inversions that make unscrupulousness a virtue. Their passing does not mean that all is set fair for constitutional government, the rule of law, and internal and external peace. There is always the old Adam within us, sheer unscrupulousness that does not bother with justifications or is used to serve covert and perverted moral passions. Revolutionary totalitarianisms that feed on nihilism may well be dead and done with, but peace and liberty are still threatened by criminals and tyrants. Indeed, the collapse of communism appears too often to have given liberty principally for the crime and nationalist feuds which communist rule had suppressed. The threats to liberty peculiar to the twentieth century can easily be replaced by those which humanity has always suffered.

In contrast to these problems of "negative" conceptions, "positive" ones appear to have the advantage of beginning with a liberty needed *for* achieving a good, a good beyond individual and his purely private concerns. Theirs is a liberty *for* value, and thus from the start a liberty that has value, a liberty that can make moral claims for dedication and restraint. It is one which appeals to the motives that are needed for its practice and thus one whose rhetoric is consonant with its logic. Even classical liberalism must transcend itself and start with the positive aspect of liberty, what it is liberty *for*. In the eighteenth and nineteenth centuries, liberalism could take for granted the customary social and moral order and emphasise freedom from unnecessary restrictions and a freedom for individual initiative which would increase general welfare. But in the twentieth century it had to become aware of the foundations of liberty and take them explicitly into account. That is what we have observed in this second part of our study as we have moved from von Mises and Popper, on the one side, to Hayek and Polanyi on the other. The upshot, as we have just seen, is a movement away from the negative to the positive aspects of liberty. And that takes us beyond the usual run, at least, of liberal conceptions of liberty.

Moreover, our discussions of the value of liberty have not left the idea of liberty unaffected. I shall now sum up the revisions which have been made in understanding what liberty is.

Obviously, we have moved from emphasis upon its negative aspect, being free *from* and specifically being free from interference by government and private persons, to an emphasis upon its positive aspect, being free *to do* certain things. And what we are to be free to do can principally be only that which has a value that transcends individual likings and dislikings. Any other freedom is worthless by definition. The liberty that matters is one of self-dedication, a liberty that can claim a moral right to exist and be exercised. There can be no moral right to live irresponsibly or immorally. Consequently, the irresponsible use of liberty puts it at risk by devaluing it. Privileges are resented when they are abused, when those who have them cease to fulfil a public function and attend only to their private concerns. The same applies to the liberties enjoyed by all.

We have also moved from a simply individualist conception of liberty. For, as Polanyi makes clear, the individual cannot practice in isolation his self-dedication to transcendent ideals and ideas. Even when, unlike charity and justice, they are not directly social in aim and content, they require institutions, formal or informal, for their cultivation and traditions for their transmission. The liberty of self-dedication is therefore a liberty to practice a given activity and to do as a member of a given community or institution, such as the republic of science, the Church, a fraternity of artists, or a family. As well as the liberty of the individual himself, it is the liberty of the individual as member of such groups and institutions, and the corporate liberty of those groups and institutions.[2] It is therefore also a concrete liberty, or rather, a set of concrete liberties: for the individual to participate in these activities and their institutions, for those activities to be practised, and for those institutions to exist and direct themselves. It is a framework in which persons already find themselves or into which they enter. It is not something which they create or negotiate *de novo*, though they can seek to add to it, to correct it, and to improve it.

Secondly, it is not simply a liberty that is a set of competences and corresponding immunities, of rights that we can exercise as we choose and to do so without interference. It is a liberty that carries obligations with itself. For it is founded upon the obligation of self-dedication, and therefore is not simply a freedom to dedicate ourselves if we please, which would also be the freedom *not* to dedicate ourselves to anything. That general obligation spills over into specific obligations to maintain and further the particular groups, communities, and institutions which support and foster the activities to which we dedicate ourselves, and the wider society in which they have their home and which supports them. It is a network of mutual rights and obligations.

Now it seems to me that liberal thinkers, including even Hayek, starting with the freedom of the individual to do as he pleases or to act on his own information, confine the obligations of the individual to the negative one of not interfering with the equal liberty of others and the positive one of fulfilling his own voluntarily contracted promises. What I have not found in their work is explicit recognition of other positive duties, of general mutual aid to those in distress, and of support for the institutions of society wherein the individual lives and enjoys his freedom. The paradigm situation seems to be that of the public official or private citizen who invades the freedom of someone else and his duty not to do so. One rarely finds any mention of the case of the third party and his duty to help the victim, let alone of us all to support the institutions of a free society and the system of manners, of everyday attitudes to each other, upon which it rests. Curiously, like welfarists and socialists, they seem to see the individual as the passive recipient of the benefits of government and its policies, though, of course, they have a different notion of what those benefits should be.

Finally, the concrete system of the liberties and obligations of individuals, groups, and institutions, which is the liberty of self-dedication, is necessarily a traditional and inherited system. It cannot be explicitly defined nor established *de novo*. We can practise the activities to which we dedicate ourselves only as we grow into the accumulated knowledge embodied in its institutions and their standards. Those who set out to found a new style of painting or a new religious sect inevitably carry with them much of what they react against, and would not have the very ideas of painting or worship without the traditions against which they set themselves. Consequently, the system of liberties, with their obligations, inevitably varies according to time and place, and with different sets of traditions. It can be wider, as in the European world, or much narrower. It can be more individualist or more corporate or more collective in one place or one period than another. There cannot be one abstractly conceivable and universally realisable pattern for it.

These three features of the liberty of self-dedication, as Polanyi articulated it, take us beyond the narrowly individualist and principally "negative" conception of liberty, with which classical liberals as well as libertarians operate, to a distinctively conservative conception, as outlined in chapter 2. We shall now explore what it presupposes and further entails.

Notes

1. And also that of Tocqueville. See above ch. 4 n.10, and Brenkert's comment (*Political Freedom*, p. 247 n. 8) that in *Democracy in America* he does not give a definition of liberty but quotes Cotton Mather's: "But there is a civil, a moral, a federal liberty, which is the proper end and object of authority: it is a liberty for that only which is just and good.... This liberty is maintained in a way of subjection to authority; and the authority set over you will in all administrations for your good be quietly submitted unto, but save such as have a disposition to shake off the yoke, and lose their true liberty."

    As for Berlin's fear that emphasis upon "positive" freedom and the "better self" embodied in laws and institutions, will lead to real *unfreedom*, compare also Bosanquet, as previously mentioned, and his prescriptions which go no further than those of Hayek in the exercise of government.

    Another account, in contemporary idiom, of "positive" freedom, which also does not turn it into servitude, is given by J. Raz at the end of his *Morality of Freedom*: personal autonomy "is valuable only if exercised in pursuit of the good" (p. 381); it presupposes, not absolute self-creation and an arbitrary choice of values (à la Sartre and much Anglo-Saxon philosophy), but independently existing values which are transformed and added to by a person's projects and commitments (pp. 387–8); "positive" freedom, a capacity for creation and a range of available options, is intrinsically valuable because it is an essential ingredient in and a necessary condition of autonomous life, a capacity whose value derives from its exercise (p. 409); "negative" freedom is valuable as serving "positive" freedom (p. 410). Raz, like Hayek and Polanyi, also sees liberty as dependent upon an appropriate social background, and draws some interesting guides for policy for the protection and promotion of "positive" freedom.

2. The theoretical errors of corporatism (including guild socialism and syndicalism) are to forget that no individual can be confined within one group or institution; that formal institutions are not the only ones, still less are economic ones; that all are consumers whereas only some are producers; that no formal institution can safely have a monopoly over practitioners of the activity in question; and that the individual transcends all roles and institutions. (We shall return to the last in ch. 14). The practical error of corporatism, in its more conservative forms (e.g., Roman Catholic theory as formulated by such as Bishop Baron von Ketteler, Baron von Vogelsang, and René de la Tour du Pin, and gestured towards in Leo XIII's *De rerum novarum*), is to attempt to find a "third way" between the free market and socialism's abolition of private property and to create or recreate an "organic" society "from above," which can only defeat itself by resulting in yet more "mechanism," of ministries, boards, committees, officialdom, and *dirigisme,* as under Salazar (who only half-heartedly applied his own theory, if that) and Caetano in Portugal. Likewise, the attempt in Vichy France to apply secular and Roman Catholic corporatism, of which there had

been many examples in France in the 1930s, soon resulted in a return to traditional Colbertian *dirigisme* and mercantilism, supported by a "Plan," which has remained French policy to this day, irrespective of government and régime, and now, also with the support of German Christian Democrats and Socialists alike, is the policy of the European Union.

Part III

The Foundations and Presuppositions of Liberty

Freedom of the individual to do as he pleases, so long as he respects the other fellow's right to do likewise, plays only a minor part in this theory of freedom. Private individualism is no important pillar of public liberty. A free society is not an Open Society, but one fully dedicated to a distinctive set of beliefs.
—Polanyi, *The Logic of Liberty*, p. vi

[Man] is strong, noble and wonderful so long as he fears the voices of this firmament [of truth and greatness]; but he dissolves their power over himself and his own powers gained through obeying them, if he turns back and examines what he respects in a detached manner. Then law is no more than what the courts will decide, art but an emollient of nerves, morality but a convention, tradition but an inertia, God but a psychological necessity. Then man dominates a world in which he himself does not exist. For with his obligations he has lost his voice and his hope, and been left behind meaningless to himself.
—Polanyi, *Personal Knowledge*, p. 380

But the liberty, the only liberty I mean, is a liberty connected with order; that not only exists with order and virtue, but which cannot exist at all without them. It inheres in good and steady government, as in its substance and vital principle.
—Burke, *Speech before the Election in Bristol*, vol. 3, p. 8

There is an order that keeps things fast in their place; it is made to us, and we are made to it.
—Burke, *Speech on the Reform of Representation, Works*, vol. 10, p. 104–5

10

The Limits of Contract and Openness

From Status to Contract

The only defensible liberty is that of self-dedication. We shall now enquire as to what social foundations that requires and to what sort of society can be a free one. To those questions Popper gives the answer, an Open one; Hayek likewise, and develops the idea into that of the Great Society; and Polanyi applies the model of the republic of science. We shall take these up in turn. But there has also been a fourth answer, not given explicitly by our selected thinkers, yet elements of it are to be found in their accounts: namely, that of a contractual society.

Now the point about treating the larger society, the body politic or commonwealth, as a society (*societas*) in the original sense, is to emphasise its voluntary nature. It is, should be treated as if it were, or should be reconstructed as, a contractual association, a matter of freely adopted obligations and mutual guarantees of rights. As A. de Jasay says: contracts, as negotiated and conducted deliberately and voluntarily, are quintessentially liberal institutions.[1] Free agreement among self-responsible individuals, acting either individually or jointly in freely formed associations, is the epitome of civil liberty. It includes or presupposes those three conditions that Hayek so often quotes from Hume: *of stability of possession, of its transference by consent, and of the performance of promises*. Without individual property (including one's own labour), securely possessed, and the right to transfer one's right, there can be nothing for individual persons to make contracts about nor any means of so doing. And *contract* is the imposing of obligations upon oneself by one's own free choice, and not having them imposed upon oneself regardless of any say or choice in the matter.

Although no one today accepts the idea of an historical Social Contract, the notion that the larger society or body politic should become a voluntary and contractual association can claim support from histori-

171

cal study. In a famous passage in his *Ancient Law* Sir Henry Maine described the movement of progressive societies as—

> The gradual dissolution of family dependency, and the growth of individual obligation in its place. The Individual is steadily substituted for the Family, as the unit of which civil laws take account.... Nor is it difficult to see what is the tie between man and man which replaces by degrees those forms of reciprocity in rights and duties which have their origin in the Family. It is Contract. Starting, as from one terminus of history, from a condition of society in which all the relations of Persons are summed up in the relations of Family, we seem to have steadily moved toward a phase of social order in which all these relations arise from the free agreement of individuals.

Nowadays, Maine continues, where individuals are still dependent and subject to control by others, as are minors and those who are mentally defective or deranged, jurists now attribute this to an inability to judge their own interests and thus to make contracts. The movement of progressive societies is therefore one from "Status to Contract."[2]

What we shall now try to determine is how far this movement from Status to Contract can go and should go. The question is, Are there some limits beyond which the substitution of Contract for Status cannot go or which, if it does, it thereby defeats itself, and, if so, what are they and what are their implications? In particular, we shall have to determine how far society at large and bodies politic can be understood and lived in terms of contract and association, even though they may not have, nor could have, begun as such. Indeed, states Maine, the Law of Contract, in which the promise and the promise alone creates the obligation and gives the right to the fulfilment of the promise, is a very late development, and in archaic societies of families and households there were few opportunities for it, only those for family with family and chieftain with chieftain.[3] Furthermore, the free, self-conscious and self-responsible individual, who can make promises and contracts with others like himself, is also a late development from what we may call "primitive communalism" wherein the individual is thought of, by himself as well as others, as primarily a member of his group, family, clan, tribe, or city, whose welfare and rights prevailed over his own. In the Old Testament we can see this communalism continuing in the settled agricultural society after the conquest of Canaan. Although, as shown by the story of Naboth and his vineyard and the protest of Elijah,[4] there were individual rights to life, to property, and to its transfer by exchange or sale; yet it was still Israel, the whole people, that was the primary object of God's love; the future salvation and revival of the nation after its day of reckoning that to which the prophets, from Isaiah onwards, looked forward; and the people as a whole who continued to be collectively responsible and punishable for the misdeeds of any and of their predecessors. It was only late on that Jeremiah[5] and Ezekiel[6] proclaimed purely individual responsibility and punishment, and yet later that belief in the resurrection of the individual accompanied hope for the restoration of the nation in the Latter Days. The question, therefore, is not of the origins but of the possible destiny of society: Can Contract wholly replace Status, and can Association replace or absorb other forms of society? In Popper's terms the question becomes, Can a society become wholly open without aspects of closure? We shall investigate that below in "The Limits of Contract." In the next chapter we shall inquire, in Hayek's terms, if a Great Society can entirely absorb smaller societies, and, in Polanyi's, if the inclusive society is like the republic of science and based upon only a General Authority without a Specific Authority. Applied without qualifications, all three of these formulations would make the inclusive societies or bodies politic into voluntary associations like the specific ones within them or running across them. Any significant limits to the application of Contract will apply also to them.

The Limits of Contract

We shall now determine the limits within which the idea of Contract can be applied, and shall do so for the most part by employing Polanyi's accounts of the tacit dimensions of our thought and action. What the individual cannot choose, he cannot negotiate nor make contracts about. Any limits upon choice are therefore limits upon negotiation and contract, and signify things which cannot be the subject matter of negotiation with others nor the contents of contracts with them. What follows are some essential limits upon choice and contract.[7]

1. If all social relations were to be matters of individual choice and mutual contract, then that would presuppose that most things can be made explicit and thus negotiable, that the world and ourselves are utterly transparent to us. This is most clear in Sartre's *Being and Nothingness*, in which man is a "nothingness," a "fold in being," an empty self condemned only to choose, and to choose everything, whatever it is to be and the values by which it is to choose. But choice, as well as requiring a range of options, requires also principles and preferences *by which one chooses* and which, therefore, are not themselves chosen.

Hence Sartrean man cannot choose but can only take a blind leap into the dark. What happens in fact is that in "bad faith" he relies acritically upon principles and preferences which he thereby takes to be true and given to him apart from his choice. Neither are we wholly transparent to ourselves. We cannot tell all that we know, and what we do not and cannot explicitly know, we cannot choose. Here I shall merely refer to Polanyi's many demonstrations of these facts, and also to the parallel arguments and examples of Merleau-Ponty's *The Phenomenology of Perception*, the only other work which bases itself upon the tacit dimensions of human existence and both argues for them and from them.

2. If the self is wholly to choose itself, then, as we have seen, it cannot choose anything. Consequently it cannot choose with others and so it cannot make agreements and contracts with them. Sartre's logic is, in the main, inexorable: the empty and wholly self-choosing self paradoxically cannot form social relations with other empty and self-choosing selves. For they cannot have any consciousness of a "we." Each can only gaze at and "objectify" the other, even when attempting to apprehend and serve the other's freedom, which then becomes a "transcendence transcended." Furthermore, we may add, such wholly self-choosing selves can have nothing in common by which to choose together. For negotiation and agreement require a common language and a common understanding, of both the contents and the forms of discussion and contract. I may sign a contract which I don't understand, but I understand that I am signing a contract. Yet, if all is to be chosen and settled by free contract, then so must the language and forms within which and by means of which specific negotiations are conducted and contracts agreed. We see this in the attitudes of many to social roles. It is not sufficient, for example, that prospective husbands and wives freely choose each other. No: many now wish to define for themselves and with their spouses what it is to be married and the role that each is to play. They no longer take it for granted that the wife is to look after the house and the children, and the man to be the breadwinner. It is certainly possible for them, between themselves, to rearrange these roles by free debate and agreement. But that still presupposes that there are these roles and tasks to be done, by one, either, or both of the parties. They are the unchosen range of options from which they jointly choose. What some desire is the joint choice of that range of options, what "marriage," "wife," "husband," and so forth are to mean. If they are to do that, they still must share an already given and unchosen language and set of more general ideas by which they will together

define those terms and roles. At every point, choice, negotiation, and agreement rest upon that which is not chosen, not negotiated nor explicitly agreed. If everything is to be the subject of negotiation and contract, then negotiation and the making of contracts become impossible. Neither party would be able to speak, let alone say something which the other could understand. They would have to have talks about the language and procedures in and by which to conduct their talks about having talks about the language and procedures in and by which to conduct their talks, and so on.

3. Furthermore no contract can explicitly and precisely specify what the parties have agreed to do and the conditions in which they are to do it and in which they are allowed not to do it. Again, as Polanyi has shown, nothing can be said clearly and precisely.[8] Every utterance is defective and indeterminate to some extent, and we have to rely upon our personal judgment to be able to determine, when and as necessary, what it leaves unspecified. Therefore, whatever the qualifications and reservations added to a contract, that contract will still require further specification at some time or other. We can never anticipate every eventuality; there are some things which are so obvious that we never think to write them down; and there are always others which we know only implicitly. Hence the possibility of the very obstructive practice of working to rule, whereby the employees precisely fulfil everything stated in the rulebook, and do nothing not so stated, and so bring things to a halt. No rulebook can contain every rule that is in fact observed and required for the cooperative enterprise which it attempts to govern. Therefore in addition to explicit rules and doing exactly what one is required to do, there is also required the cooperative attitude of give and take, and willingness to do more than is precisely allotted to oneself.

4. Hence arises the paradox of contract. Contract, in the form of specified agreement, especially in writing, manifests an attitude of distrust yet requires mutual trust both in observing it and in interpreting and applying it, or mutual trust in a third party's interpretation and application of it, as when appeal is made to a court. On the one hand, if you cannot trust someone to fulfil his side of the bargain in a proper manner, you may attempt to tie him down by specifying certain definite tasks, procedures, dates, or other details. This has recently happened in Britain where the Government has been forced to specify a number of hours in the year which teachers in state schools are to work and specific duties which they are to fulfil, it being no longer possible to rely on all of them to do their work properly of their own accord.

Conversely, what is specified as the minimum soon becomes the maximum: no less is taken also to mean no more. You still have to trust the other party to do what you have specified and to use his judgment rightly in deciding in further detail how, when, and where it is to be done and not to make the specified minimum into a maximum. Max Scheler pointed out several times that reliance upon "criteria," as in all forms of modern and critical philosophy, betokens an attitude of distrust—in others, life, the world, tradition, our own tacit powers. So too does the detailed specification of the content of a contract. Yet just as we all, even "critical" philosophers, have to rely acritically on our personal powers of judgment in our knowing, so too in contracts do we have to rely on the other party's responsible exercise of his judgment in fulfilling even the most detailed contract. It is a much happier state of affairs when there is a strong tradition of responsible conduct such that many things on both sides can be confidently taken for granted and left unspecified. And the formation, strengthening, and continuation of such traditions cannot itself be a matter of contract.

5. Moreover, as Scheler argued, contract rests upon that which cannot be put into any contract. It cannot rest upon a general contract to keep contracts, or promise to keep promises. Such a general promise or contract would be merely hypothetical: I *would* be ready to do A, were you to do B. But a real contract is a matter of actual willing: I *am* ready to A, when you do B. The contract to contract, says Scheler, turns the willing of the partners into the content of the contract itself.[9] Now that would be the same error as treating "....is true" as a statement of fact and not an accreditative utterance which makes explicit the implicit endorsement of the truth of the original statement when it is ordinarily said.[10] Just as the latter error leads to the infinite regress of "'"'Snow is white' is true" is true' is true...," so too does the former lead to the infinite regress of promising to promise to promise...or contracting to contract to contract...Promises and contracts are nothing without the uncontracted and unpromised obligation to keep promises and adhere to contracts. This presupposition is not itself a matter of contract.

6. What, then, is it that promising and contracting do rest upon? The answer to this question brings us to the second set of limitations upon the scope of contracted relations: the emotional ones. According to Scheler, the level of social relations established by promises and contracts, which he terms "association," rests upon a prior level which he calls "life-community." Here he is refining a common German distinction between *Gesellschaft* and *Gemeinschaft* introduced by Tönnies. In

Scheler's description of society, or social relations in this specific sense, we recognise the Cartesian and empiricist interpretation of the individual's situation in the world and among his fellows. The individual is primarily responsible for and knows himself. All responsibility for and knowledge of others is based upon analogy with himself and his experience of himself. He knows others primarily as bodies, from the movements of which he infers minds, thoughts, and emotions like those he experiences behind his own bodily movements. Therefore he can be only *similar* to others and share *similar* experiences and interests. Between him and them there can exist only "conventions" and "contracts": that is, *artificial* and more-or-less explicitly agreed connections. There is no experienced solidarity nor *shared* experience. But this level of social connections cannot stand alone. It rests upon that of "life-community" in which persons share the same experiences and emotions, are primarily aware of themselves as members of the community, and spontaneously feel responsible for each other and the community. Promises and contracts rest upon prior experience of the spontaneous mutual solidarity and obligation which constitutes the life-community. Having had those experiences, they can then explicitly and voluntarily establish relations and obligations among themselves. For A to make a contract with B, it is not necessary that they belong to the same community, but it is necessary that each has belonged to a community and felt himself bound up with it, such as the family in which he was brought up.[11]

7. In turn this means that the sphere of contractual relations among self-responsible individuals and groups rests upon traditional and customary institutions which have not been established by contract nor can be conducted by explicit instruction. One can easily establish a new *particular* institution, such as a college, when it is customary to have institutions of that type. But it is very difficult to do so when those involved have no prior experience. I once worked in a College of Education in Nigeria, for training teachers for secondary schools. Formally it was like, and modelled on, the type of college in which I had worked in England. In reality, it operated very differently, just as Nigerians have imported lots of machinery but have no tradition of maintaining it. Now tradition is the handing on of what is already known or practised, as *authoritative* and often in a tacit manner. Since not everything can be explicitly known and stated, there are many things that cannot be explicitly taught. They are passed on from master to apprentice by imitation. The pupil must implicitly trust and acritically rely upon his

teacher in order to learn anything that either cannot be put into words at all or into a language which he has not yet learned.[12] I can contract to learn Hungarian from a teacher of that language, but, insofar as I am entirely ignorant of it, I do not know what I am letting myself in for: for example, whether what I shall be taught will be accurate or inaccurate, elementary or advanced, standard or nonstandard, or conversational or literary. And I can do that only as I and the teacher already speak another and shared language. No one can contract to learn his mother tongue.

8. In acritically learning our mother tongue, we acritically acquire the fundamental conceptions, ontology, and cosmology embodied in it.[13] Our ultimate beliefs and absolute presuppositions, which govern the ways in which we think about choice, negotiation, and contract, how to conduct them and what they can be about—if indeed we have any such ideas at all—are therefore not passed on nor acquired as the result of any contractual relationship between teachers and pupils.[14] J.S. Mill chided the religious believer on his commitment to his faith, and pointed out that if the European Christian had been born and brought up in India he would have become a Hindu. What Mill forgot was the *tu quoque*: if the European liberal and unbeliever, like Mill, had been born and brought up in India, then he also would have been a Hindu and not a liberal unbeliever.

Contract therefore has the following presuppositions and conditions which themselves are not, and cannot be, a matter of choice by the individual nor constitute the contents of contracts among individuals:

1. A set of values and standards of conduct by which one chooses.
2. A relatively determinate structure of preferences and desires within oneself with which one chooses.
3. A set of differentiated possibilities and opportunities, such as existing social roles, from which to choose, about which to make contracts, and with which to constitute associations.
4. A common language and understanding, and a minimum of shared values and standards, especially the noncontractual obligation to keep one's promises.
5. Some degree of mutual trust in each other or a third party to interpret the contract and to adjudicate disputes about it, and, in any larger or longer term association, a cooperative attitude of give-and-take which is ready to go beyond explicit obligations.
6. Therefore:
   a. an experienced emotional solidarity in a "life-community," though not necessarily in the same life-community with the other parties in any particular contract or association; and—

b. customs and traditions which mediate common language, understanding, values, standards, emotional experience, attitudes, and the other tacitly known practices of free societies, free agreements, and free associations.

Now some Liberals, of the past and the present, can be fairly charged with having taken for granted the social and customary background of liberty. Thus J. Raz states:

> Many rights were advocated and fought for in the name of individual freedom. But this was done against a social background which secured collective goods without which those individual rights would not have served their avowed purpose. Unfortunately the existence of these collective goods was such a natural background that its contribution to securing the very ends which were supposed to be served by the rights was obscured, and all too often went unnoticed.[15]

Raz continues with the example of religious freedom, which was claimed for the individual conscience but served communal peace, and since religion is also communal, is also the right of communities to pursue their own style of life as of individuals to belong to them. We shall see how the experiences of the twentieth century led Hayek and Polanyi progressively to realise and appreciate the social and customary background of freedom as exemplified by Contract and Association, and therefore either explicitly or implicitly to limit the scope of the application of those two ideas.

Openness and Closure in Society

If Contract is the preeminently liberal institution or practice, then a completely liberal society cannot exist, and no actual society can become an association throughout. Let us now examine another notion which has been used to characterise a liberal society, Openness, and see how far an Open Society is possible.

As was noted in chapter 6, Popper says little about what an Open Society actually is. One wonders, with Polanyi (*Meaning*, p. 184) if it is so open that it lacks definition. The important point about it is that it liberates and employs man's critical powers, which reject the authority of the merely established and merely traditional, which preserve those traditions which do meet standards of "freedom, humaneness, and rationality" (OS, vol. 1, pp. ix, 1), and which accept the "critical dualism" of "facts and decisions (or standards)" (OS, vol. 1, p. 59). It is also not based on kinship and common experiences, nor on many face-to-face relations, but on more "abstract" relations (OS, vol. 1, pp. 173–

4). We shall discuss the second set of characteristics in the next section, for Hayek elaborates them in his account of the Great Society.

We argued in chapter 6 that Popper's "critical dualism" is a sceptical rationalism that proves self-destructive, and would bring down with it the freedom that it is supposed to found. It a species of, or one parallel to, the Anglo-American liberalism that suspends its own logic. It cannot accredit itself nor any standards as true. Every principle which it would employ and so tacitly rely upon, it must explicitly hold to be a mere "decision." Without a firm basis somewhere that transcends individual decision or collective conventions, convention does entail arbitrariness, contrary to what Popper says.

Rationalism has always rejected tradition and custom, either in favour of an abstract, *a priori* and impersonal mechanism of deductive logic, into which the individual is absorbed, or of the individual's own self-conscious and critical reasonings, into which the former in fact collapses. As Hayek has shown, it is incompatible with liberty.[16] And we have just seen how contracts and the associations which they found also rest upon traditions which cannot be the objects of self-conscious choice and contract. Even more destructive of tradition, and therefore freedom, is a sceptical rationalism, which concludes, rightly, that its standards are not met in most or all spheres of human life and thought, so explicitly leaves us with only arbitrary decision, individual or collective, by which to conduct ourselves.

Popper has attempted to address these problems and to make a *rapprochement* between rationalism and tradition. He aimed at "a rational theory of tradition." While we cannot completely free ourselves from tradition, and can only exchange one tradition for another, we can free ourselves from its taboos by rejecting or critically accepting it. We can be ready to challenge it and everything else, including our own tradition. Rationalists themselves, among whom Popper numbers himself, need to criticise their own tradition in certain respects: its adherence to determinism, to observationalism, and to treating all social facts as intended results (CR, pp. 121–3). Traditions in society fulfil the same function as theories in science: they bring order into the world and make it predictable, and provide a starting point, something to be criticised and changed. It is impossible to start from scratch and with a clean slate. What matters most is the higher tradition of criticism itself, of challenging myths, theories and traditions, which constitutes the scientific method and outlook. Rationalists err in attacking tradition as such, but are right to attack the intolerance of traditionalism. What is needed is a tradition of tolerance, clear thinking, and speaking; a critical tradition, a tradition of reason (CR, pp. 130–5; cf. p. 376).

But how far does this accommodation of rationalism towards tradition really go? The emphasis is still upon criticism, which can in the end be only the judgment of the individual, a judgment, let us remember, which has no rational basis in Popper's account, for criticism can undercut itself and has no stability. He confesses, for example, that his own decision against violence is irrational (CR, p. 357), and that the rationalist attitude is itself irrationally chosen (OS, vol. 2, p. 230). With this rationalist individualism, we may contrast Polanyi's epistemology which, never flinching the fact of personal decision and commitment and their acritical basis, recognises that it attends away from the self to a world which anchors those commitments, that there are standards which are both self-set and inescapable while we live and think, and that tradition conveys knowledge, genuine knowledge, of the world and of those standards.

The Open Society, we recall, is open to criticism and change. It follows, from Popper's account of criticism and the dualism of facts and standards, that it is open to any criticism and any change. It has no shelter against the winds of doctrine. It cannot allow itself to have a secure faith in itself, nor a solid core which is not up for negotiation. This is an openness to self-destruction, a freedom that cannot defend itself. Popper appreciates the paradox of tolerance—that unlimited tolerance results in the disappearance of tolerance (OS, vol. 1, p. 265 n. 4). The point is that his dualism of facts and standards gives him no basis for deciding for unlimited tolerance, limited tolerance, or intolerance.

No society can be simply open. It must be closed to some things, such as those attitudes which are opposed to it. Like "negative" and "positive" liberty, openness and closure are obverse and reverse. No one has an "open mind" *simpliciter*. For a mind open to everything would be open to any every and any contradiction, and so would soon cease to be a mind. Those who claim loudly to have "open minds" in fact have minds closed to the consideration that, as G.K. Chesterton once said, the whole point of an open mind, like that of an open mouth, is to close it firmly upon something. They make it a dogma that we should have no dogma; they are prejudiced against prejudice; and they authoritatively assert that we should do without authority. What applies to the individual, applies also to society. For example, Popper associates authority and prejudice with a closed society (OS, vol. 1, p. ix). It would follow that an open society is one free of them. Yet men cannot live without authority of both kinds, that of the person who really knows something and that of the person who initiates, leads, and directs. None of us can ever know at first hand all that can be known, and as knowledge grows so too does our dependence upon the authority of others. As I have argued elsewhere and against the claim that education can and should lead us to live without authority, education is education *into* authority, into knowing what there is to be known beyond one's own knowledge, where to look for it, and on whom one may rely.[17] What Polanyi says about the role of authority in the republic of science—in maintaining standards, in admitting or refusing or even expelling members, in scrutinising new work—applies elsewhere though it may not be so rigorous. As for directive authority, both in formal and informal modes, it increases around us as life becomes more complex. Only Robinson Crusoe alone on his island lives without directive authority, and only an epistemological Crusoe, who had grown up alone and discovered all he knew for himself, would be independent of cognitive or intellectual authority. Likewise with prejudice: we cannot life nor think without prejudgments and presuppositions, such as that our sense-organs and modes of thought are generally reliable. The ideas of a presuppositionless philosophy and a presuppositionless mind that would formulate it, themselves manifest the rationalist prejudice against prejudice, and self-contradictorily presuppose that we can think without presuppositions.

A free society is a society of shared commitments, to ideas and ideals, such as truth, justice, and charity, that reach across more specific ones, and to mutual aid and support in preserving both the common framework and the specific institutions and practices. Whatever disputes may arise among specific groups, if they are to preserve their own freedom, they must support the common institutions that embody that freedom. In free societies legal processes replace private war.[18] But they work only as parties are committed to using them, to accepting the verdicts of the courts, and to the rule of law. That is not the case in many parts of the world. A free society is not founded upon neutrality but upon commitment. Judges are not neutral: they are firmly committed to the law and to doing justice and to doing it impartially. A free society depends upon a shared commitment to justice, law, its proper interpretation, the integrity of the courts, and to the enforcement of the law and the decisions of courts upon those who refuse to obey it and them. It is therefore implicitly closed against the doctrines that deny the meaning of justice, the value of law, the impartiality of judges, the right and duty of enforcement, and, beyond them, the reality and supreme importance of truth and other transcendent ideals. Or, rather, if it is not closed against them, then it will soon lose its freedom. That has happened all too often in the twentieth century when the scepticism that still lingers in Popper's "critical dualism" has been acted upon with better logic and has destroyed people's faith in justice, law, and freedom itself.

Let us now consider a specific, practical, and urgent question for a free society: immigration. Travel, even over long distances, is nowadays comparatively cheap and easy. How far can a free society afford to be open to immigration? Hayek, though recognising that precipitate policies could easily be counterproductive, nevertheless looks forward to the absence of national barriers to the free movement of peoples (LLL, vol. 2, pp. 57–8).[19] Should a free society be open to unlimited immigration, as America once was? Certainly the American example is instructive. It did no good to American liberties to allow the immigration of large numbers of Sicilians and with them the Mafia, and European liberties would not last for long if a massive wave of Islamic Arab immigration from North Africa were permitted. A free society must close itself against groups who do not value its liberties, because freedom depends on common commitments. How far they go, we shall consider later. And as Hayek is aware, the immigration of large numbers of other groups, obviously alien, can easily cause resentment. For their mere presence destroys the freedom of the indigenous population to live its accustomed life in its own country, since by reason of their very different ways and large numbers, the immigrants are unlikely to be assimilated and merged into the native population, and so will change the character of the society in which they settle. When, because of sheer weight of numbers, the Indian party won a general election in Fiji, the Fijian army, formed from native Fijians, overthrew the parliament. It was difficult not to sympathise with them. "Multiculturalism" is a policy of denying the freedom to be oneself. Any people, surely, has a right to be itself, and to protect its traditional way of life. Where very different communities already exist side by side, there are often grave problems and violent conflicts and a lack of a common framework peaceably to settle them. Prudence, and the preservation of freedom, suggests that mass immigration be carefully controlled if allowed at all.

Notes

1. *Choice, Contract, Consent: A Restatement of Liberalism*, p. 91.
   In his reformulation of contractual theory, Collingwood distinguished between "societies," founded on "contracts of society," and "nonsocial communi-

ties." Societies may be temporary or permanent, formal or informal. A temporary and informal one is that of two people who agree to take a walk together. The family, for its children, is a nonsocial community. The relation between such a nonsocial community and the larger society is a permanent and dialectical one, and not, as in the old theories of the Social Contract, a single, once-and-for-all transition from the former to the latter. Rather, the latter is always recruiting from the former (*The New Leviathan*, chs. 19, 24).

We should note that a contract needed not be negotiated: one party can offer it on a take-it-or-leave-it basis, as are most contracts of employment with government agencies or ones funded by governments.

2. *Ancient Law*, pp. 172–4.
3. Ibid., pp. 326–7.
4. I Kings 21.
5. Jer. 31: 29–30.
6. Ezek. 18.
7. What follows is taken from my paper, "The Limits of Contract" (*Polanyiana*, vol. 2, 1 and 2 combined, 1992).
8. PK, ch. 5.
9. *Formalism in Ethics*, pp. 531–2.
10. PK, pp. 254–6.
11. See *The Nature of Sympathy*, part 3, ch. 3, on the impossibility of knowing another primarily by means of analogy with one's knowledge of oneself.
12. PK, pp. 53–4, 101. See also my *Education of Autonomous Man*, ch. 7, and the references therein to my articles in *The Journal of Philosophy of Education* (see n. 17 below), developing these and other Polanyian arguments against the liberal theory of rational autonomy which dominates English-speaking philosophy of education and which would have the child taught rationally, by formal principles, to choose everything for himself and to live without authority as an adult.
13. See Polanyi, PK, pp. 47, 80, 81, 94–5, 112, 187–8; and SFS, p. 71. See also, J. Piaget, *The Child's Conception of the World*, and S. Körner, *Metaphysics: Its Structure and Functions*.
14. See Polanyi, SFS, p. 71.
15. *The Morality of Freedom*, p. 251.
16. CL, ch. 2 §9; LLL—see references in the Index to each volume; SPPE, ch. 5; FC, ch. 4.
17. "'Because I say so!' Some limitations upon the rationalism of authority," *J. of Philosophy of Education*, vol. 21, no. 1, 1987.

    On the nature and roles of "directive" authority, see chapter 2 of de Jouvenel's *Sovereignty*. Authority is "the faculty of gaining another man's assent." "In any voluntary association that comes to my notice I see the work of a force: that force is authority" (p. 29). "Man is, under Providence, apt to receive the impulsions of other men: but for this gift we should be ineducable and unadaptable. The counterpart of this receptivity is an activity. The complementary gift is the impulsive power—authority" (p. 31). For a similar and more detailed account, see C.J. Friedrich, *Tradition and Authority*.
18. The converse is also true. When legal processes are denied, private war follows. In Britain, trades-unions, for all important purposes, were placed above the law by the Trades Disputes Act of 1906. Consequently, they practised, like medieaval barons, private wars, not only against employers, but also each other.
19. Yet, unlike British Race Relations legislation, he would not compel people to welcome and mix with those who settle amongst them, and so would allow the freedom not to associate and not to contract: LLL, vol. 3, p. 195 n. 14.

11

Two Models of a Free Society

The Great Society as *Cosmos* and not *Taxis*

No inclusive society or body politic can entirely be based upon or structured by Contract, nor can a free society be an unqualifiedly Open one. But it does not therefore follow that the only alternative is a "closed" and "tribal" one, whether of the old order or of modern totalitarianism. The stark choice that Popper offers us, like that of the rationalist one between "dogmatism" and "an open mind," needs to be reconsidered. With that in mind, we shall now consider Hayek's account of the Great Society and his important distinction between a *cosmos* and a *taxis*.

Especially in volume 2 of *Law, Liberty and Legislation*, Hayek contrasts the "Great Society," his elaboration of Popper's Open Society, with previous forms of human society, in order to show how demands for "social justice" would entail a return to those earlier forms and with them a loss of the peace, freedom, and prosperity that the Great Society has brought. It is not his argument against social justice which concerns us, and which I shall take for granted, but his contrast between the Great Society and other, smaller, more intimate, and more end-orientated forms of community. I shall now summarise the main points of that contrast without specific references to the text.

Hayek employs a fundamental distinction between a *cosmos*, or what Polanyi calls a *spontaneous order*, and a *taxis*, or what Polanyi calls a *corporate order*. The former is a product of human action but not of human design. It comes into being as a result of the mutually adjusting actions of individuals, groups and organisations. It is the pattern of relationships to which those actions give rise. The latter is a designed arrangement or organisation. The specific threats to freedom which concern Hayek are those which assume that all social groupings and interactions are, or should be, deliberately designed and controlled, and thus come into the category of *taxis*. In particular, the demand for "social justice" would require deliberate organisation of those activities to which it is to be applied. The result would be a command society, like the one factory of which Lenin spoke, wherein the actions of individuals would be organised to fit a total plan conceived by a central authority and with a central scheme of awards and payments according to a scale of "needs" or "merits." Hayek thinks that the desire for "social justice" is, in effect, an atavistic one for a return to the state of a tribe of hunters under a chief who organised their activities and distributed the game which they had collectively caught. In such a band, and in later times, individuals met in face-to-face relationships and knew each other personally. They were united by working for common goals, by feelings of solidarity, and by specific obligations to each other. They shared a common way of life and, to a large extent, a common or communal life. Other examples would be the households of a farming family, with any labourers or servants that it might employ, or of a master craftsman with his family, journeymen, apprentices, and servants. Without exactly saying so, Hayek at times gives the impression that face-to-face relationships, feelings of solidarity, and specific obligations are inimical to the Great Society and thus to freedom.[1]

In contrast to *taxes* or organisations such as these, is the Great Society, which is not a closed or determinate group at all but a network of relationships among an indeterminate and open number of people who, in this respect at least, do not constitute an "us" in distinction from a "them." Those relationships are, as Popper said, "abstract," and are so in a double sense: they are often, and increasingly so today, formed among people who either do not meet at all, such as a manufacturer and the ultimate purchasers of his products, or only functionally and not personally, as when a shopper takes his purchases to the checkout in a supermarket; and they are governed by abstract and general rules and not by specific and personal obligations, bonds, and loyalties.[2] I hand £10 to this man, not because he is my impoverished cousin or my liege lord to whom I owe a yearly tribute, but because I have bought £10's worth of goods or services from him. I may know him personally or he may be a total stranger. Such facts are irrelevant. All that matters is the very general duty of buyer to pay seller, and these abstract relationships in which we now stand. Such relationships can be formed with anyone else irrespective of the groups we individually belong to. Whereas tribal society is based on the notion of kinship, cannot think of relationships and obligations in any other terms than of common descent, and consequently uses the legal fiction of adoption in order to accommodate those who are not related into the family, band, clan, or tribe,[3] the Great Society is not based on them at all but solely upon general rules that apply to everyone with whom one has some dealings. It follows that the Great Society has no inherent limits. It can and does reach across all groups, not only in its most common and frequent form of economic transactions, but in every way in which individuals can deal with each other, as fellow scientists for example, whether or not they belong to the same or any international scientific association. The Great Society is essentially open in membership and a *cosmos* without any element of *taxis*. All people in the world can in principle, and with modern communications can in fact, be brought into it. No world government is necessary for instituting it. All that matters and all that is requisite for joining it, is willingness to treat everyone else according to the abstract rules of justice and to abide by them oneself.

The Great Society is the sphere of freedom. Reversion to more concrete bonds and obligations, certainly to any great extent, would, in Hayek's view, return us to goal-oriented organisations and thus to hierarchies of command and obedience. Nostalgic longings for more face-to-face relationships, solidarity, and working together for common purposes, threaten the freedom, peace, and prosperity achieved in the modern world. The Great Society requires that we treat all alike and thus that legally enforceable duties are those which can be fulfilled towards anyone. Therefore obligations of specific help, which are possible on a small scale to a determinate number of persons whom one knows personally, are not possible towards all. The extension of such duties to more and more persons requires a corresponding contraction of their content. For example (one of my own), in a tribal society which cannot store food even when there is a surplus, individuals invest in building up relationships of mutual obligation, so that when food is short they have a wider spread of persons to approach who are bound to help them if they can.[4] Again (also my own example) in a more differentiated society, there is an obligation on those who prosper to help at least some of their relations who are less fortunate. Nowadays that obligation clashes with the impartiality required in public services. A man can do what he likes in his own business, and can appoint a less able cousin instead of a more competent stranger, though in the long run such a policy will ruin his business. But in public service that practice is nepotism, and benefits the family at the expense of the public. It can take a long time for traditions of impartiality to become established, and they can easily become overthrown by patronage and the "spoils system," where party associates rather than kinsmen are preferred over more suitable candidates.

Hayek thus presents us with two models of society: that which is a *taxis*, an organisation of working together for a common end, of command and obedience, of distributed rewards for perceived merits or needs or contributions, of felt solidarity in aiming at the common end, and of specific obligations to known individuals; and that which is a *cosmos*, of persons in largely abstract or impersonal relationships, and bound mostly or only to observe the negative rules of justice in dealing with everyone else.

I have already suggested that band societies are not, and presumably were not, quite as Hayek describes them.[5] That is an incidental point. What matters are the answers to two questions:

1. How are we to understand bodies politic and especially those of the modern world, and how do they fit into or lie outside the distinction between *cosmos* and *taxis*?
2. What combination of *cosmos* and *taxis* is necessary for the existence and preservation of freedom?

In relation to the latter, Hayek states that a government is an organisation, a *taxis*, which is compatible with the Great Society when its coercive functions are limited to maintaining the general rules needed for it, and do not include its service functions, whereby it acts like other organisations in managing the resources given to it (LLL, vol. 1, pp. 47–8). Now while it is clear that there would be little freedom in a society that was organised as a *taxis*, which is the objective of totalitarian systems, it may yet be the case that a free society is compatible with and may indeed require some elements of a *taxis* over and above that of its government functioning in the way that Hayek mentions. Let us therefore consider some human arrangements that are not full-blooded *taxes* yet clearly are not wholly *cosmoi*.

Between *Cosmos* and *Taxis*

Our first example is one of a combination of *taxis* and *cosmos*: namely, a market, which has been deliberately instituted, such as the futures market established a few years ago in London. As instituted it is a *taxis*. Of course, the rules explicitly laid down for it could not have been invented *de novo*. They, and the very ideas of a market and trading in futures, were taken from practices which had evolved spontaneously.

But the point is that, on the one hand, the market in question was deliberately established and hence in that respect is a *taxis*, while, on the other, the pattern of prices prevailing in it at any moment is a spontaneous and undesigned one, and hence a *cosmos*. Hayek allows that the spontaneous order which is the result is not the same as the spontaneous or nonspontaneous origin of the rule on which it rests (LLL, vol. 1, p. 46).

Our second set of examples are of *taxes* which operate without structures of command or collective decision, at least for much of the time. Consider a small group of people who work as a group to realise a given goal. As such, they form a *taxis*. They deliberately constitute the group and set themselves, or have set for them, the specific goal which they seek to realise. But it is possible for them to achieve their object without further commands or collective decisions but, instead, by spontaneous mutual adjustments. The conditions for this are the small size of the group and the expertise of its members which enables them to work in a familiar and perhaps routine manner. Hayek himself gives an example of such a group (the location of which I have forgotten and cannot retrace): a group of lionesses hunting. Indeed, their hunting itself appears itself to be initiated by a series of spontaneous adjustments of individual stirrings and movements. Two human examples are a quartet contrasted with an orchestra, and a group of specialist workmen each of whom performs his part of a cooperative task but without anyone acting as foreman. Even within larger organisations which have hierarchies of command or management, a lot of the work can be done by routine without definite direction. The cooperative achievement of a common goal does not always require a structure of command or direction, and, when it does, it may not require it at every point, as Hayek acknowledges even in the case of a hunting band (LLL, vol. 1, p. 47).

Let us now consider some examples of corporate associations which are organisations in that sense or to that extent, but which are not primarily orientated to the achievement of specific goals. Firstly, a household where, like the group of specialist workmen, most of the members perform their own routine tasks and spontaneously adjust themselves to each other without much in the way of one person directing them. It is like an organisation, a *taxis*, in being, not just a group of persons, but a definite unit, which at times will act as one. Yet it is not constituted to achieve specific goals, although it sets itself ones from time to time, but rather to sustain a shared way of life. Other organisations or bodies which have general purposes rather than specific goals are clubs and societies which promote an interest common to their members, for example, learned societies, and sports and social clubs. They have formal structures of officers; they organise specific events; they may set themselves specific goals. But, for the most part, they have only general purposes and are not goal-orientated. Although they are defined and distinguished by their purposes, they are some distance from Oakeshott's paradigms of "enterprise associations," such as business companies, hospitals and schools.[6] Between the two are more diffuse yet still definitely goal-orientated associations like the Red Cross.

Finally, we come to Polanyi's model of a free society, the republic of science (KB, ch. 4). This is like, or rather is, a specific segment of the Great Society. It is not a *taxis*, although it includes scientific societies and institutes, and only in totalitarian states are all scientists conscripted into specific organisations which in turn are organised into one body, just as workers are organised into trades-unions and those into one bloc. It has no overall organisational structure. Indeed, some of its members, amateurs or freelancers, may not be members of any relevant association or institute, though today that is ever less likely but is still possible with other learned republics such as that of historians. And the republic of science straddles all societies, except those closed off from the Great Society. Hence so far it is a *cosmos*. Indeed, it was Polanyi's conviction that Marxist and utilitarian attempts to organise it—to make it into a *taxis*, aimed at human welfare, of *taxes* aimed at specific goals of research to promote that end—would destroy it. Nevertheless it has some features of a *taxis*. It is not goal-orientated but it is defined by a shared but general purpose, that of the cultivation of science. Its members are members only as they are recognised as sharing that aim and competent to pursue it. A newcomer has to be accepted and may be rejected. Indeed, a member may be expelled and declared not to be a scientist, but a crank, fraud, or charlatan, if he transgresses the professional standards upheld by the fraternity of scientists.

Our review of these examples suggests that there are several possibilities between a pure case of *cosmos*, such as the Great Society, and a *taxis* which aims at the realisation of specific goals and has a structure of command or central decision to coordinate the actions of its members in order to achieve its goals. Freedom is not possible in an inclusive society modelled upon the latter. The question for us is just what elements and proportions of *cosmos* and *taxis* it requires.

From the Republic of Science to the Society of Explorers

We shall continue with Polanyi's model of the republic of science. He does not present it as an exact and complete model for society at large but only in certain of its constituents (KB, p. 49): namely (a) the necessity of freedom and the impossibility of central direction in science and society at large; (b) the need for an authority which is mutual and traditional; and (c) the combination of orthodoxy and dissent in a dynamic orthodoxy which acknowledges the reality and value of truth to which it dedicates itself.

We have already looked at the first point of comparison in chapter 9. It is the second and third that concern us now. Someone is accepted as a scientist only as he grasps and conforms to the professional standards of science by which scientists judge the scientific importance of problems and their likely solutions. These standards have a traditional authority. For no one mind can hope to encompass, let alone be competent to judge, more than a small fraction of the body of scientific work. But each specialist is engaged in mutual confirmation and criticism with others both in his own field and in neighbouring ones with which it overlaps. Consequently there is a network of mutual criticism which maintains scientific standards across the whole field, from astronomy to medicine. In entering the republic of science, each newcomer submits himself to and endorses the vast range of judgments of scientific merit made throughout the sciences, although he knows almost nothing of their subject-matter. That means that they are transmitted by tradition. Likewise, Polanyi argued earlier, the unspecifiable art of scientific research is learned by a system of apprenticeship and hence by living tradition (PK, p. 53).

Most of these standards—those of initial plausibility, accuracy, systematic importance, and the intrinsic interest of the subject-matter— tend towards conformity with the prevailing consensus or body of scientific theory. But another, that of originality, encourages dissent and revision. "The professional standards of science must impose a framework of discipline and at the same time encourage rebellion against it" (KB, p. 54). Only by requiring at least some degree of compatibility with current conceptions about the universe can the scientific community prevent dispersal of its efforts and the chasing of every hare, and maintain its standards of scientific procedure. In "The Growth of Science in Society" (KB, ch. 5) Polanyi illustrates and enlarges upon this necessary exclusion of implausible conjectures and theories with reference to the Velikovsky affair which scandalised some people who took scientists' professions of open-mindedness at face value. Of course, like everything else, it can go wrong and thus exclude theories which are later vindicated, such as Polanyi's own theory of adsorption (KB, ch. 6). It is here that Polanyi breaks entirely with the positivist separation of "the context of justification" from "the context of discovery." Science would soon get nowhere if it were to proceed by the random generation of hypotheses which were then tested. On the contrary, scientists must assess the initial plausibility of any purported discovery or theory, the likelihood of its being true.[7] They are not open-minded but employ largely tacit principles of selection and evaluation. But, precisely because science does deal with the real world and aims at a true body of theory about it, the prevailing body of theory is open to revision. Hence the recruit to the fraternity of scientists is taught both to accept the current body of theory as a true account of the universe, and that he can make its own contacts with it which may necessitate, revision, even radical revision, of that body of theory.

In this way Polanyi seeks to resolve the conflict between radicalism as typified by Tom Paine and traditionalism as expounded by Burke. He distinguishes three sorts of society: static ones (i.e., ones which do not aim to change themselves though in fact they may change); dynamic and revolutionary ones which aim at a complete and sudden renewal of themselves and hence are totalitarian; and dynamic and reformist ones, which allow thought freely to develop and reform society (PK, pp. 213–4). The second and third define the modern age. In some ways we are reminded of Popper's division between closed tribal societies and modern open ones. But Polanyi acknowledges, on the one hand, that free societies today share their dynamism with revolutionary and totalitarian ones, and, on the other, that they also share with static societies a belief in the power and worth of thought. Modern totalitarian movements are *not* reversions to "tribal" societies, even when, we may add, full allowance is given to the role of *Volkisch* elements within and around the Nazi movement. For, what a sceptical rationalism cannot consistently recognise, is the worth and power of thought, and, in particular, that premodern societies also held that belief. It assumes that before the Enlightenment were the Dark Ages. On the contrary, says Polanyi, static societies respected religion, morality, law, and all the arts in their own right, and, though they confined their pursuit each within a particular orthodoxy, the rulers accepted those orthodoxies for their own guidance. Likewise, modern free societies recognise the power and worth of truth, or deny it at their own peril. For the denial of the power and worth of truth leads, not to a restrained, tolerant liberalism, but to totalitarianisms which proclaim their denials of truth and all other ideals and obligations. What a free society therefore requires is what is found in the republic of science: a firm commitment to truth and other transcendent ideals; their embodiment in a living and authoritative tradition; and the progressive adaptation and enlargement of that tradition in the light of those ideals.

The difference between static and free societies lies in what Polanyi had distinguished yet earlier as Specific and General Authority (SFS, pp. 57–9). The former imposes specific conclusions from a central position, whereas the latter lays down only general presuppositions and leaves their interpretation and application to the individual judgment of the members of the community.

The republic of science is a "society of explorers." So too is a free society. It explores self-improvement in every respect through individual initiatives guided by traditional authority and creative self-renewal. In other spheres there is often not the same degree of basic consensus, so that rival schools, as in art, are more divided from each other and last for longer. Or, as in art again, there is not the same systematic coherence—after all, nonrepresentational works are not *about* anything, and even literary ones can be imaginary worlds rather than the one real, and the coherence that matters is that *within* each one. Yet again, as in religion (in Polanyi's time!) but not in theology, there may be not be a cult of innovation. Nevertheless, the activities of a free society will take the same general form, and the public at large will be guided by authoritative specialists, though sometimes rival ones, in each sphere (PK, pp. 220–2).

Polanyi claims that in these ways the notion of a free society aiming at its own self-improvement transcends the conflict between Paine and Burke.

It rejects Paine's demand for the absolute self-determination of each generation, but does so for the sake of its own ideal of unlimited human and social improvement. It accepts Burke's thesis that freedom must be rooted in tradition, but transposes it into a system cultivating radical progress. It rejects the dream of a society in which all will labour for a common purpose, determined by the will of the people. For in the pursuit of excellence it offers no part to the popular will and accepts instead a condition of society in which the public interest is known only fragmentarily and is left to be achieved as the outcome of individual initiatives aiming at fragmentary problems. Viewed through the eyes of socialism, this ideal of a free society is conservative and fragmented, and hence adrift, irresponsible, selfish, apparently chaotic. A free society conceived as a society of explorers is open to these charges, in the sense that they do refer to characteristic features of it. But if we recognise that these features are indispensable to the pursuit of social self-improvement, we may be prepared to accept them as perhaps less attractive aspects of a noble enterprise. (KB, p. 71)[8]

Although in other ways there may be defects in the analogy between the republic of science and the republic at large, Polanyi is right in drawing two parallels between them: that the authority of both is and must be traditional or prescriptive, and that both transcend the generations. For the individual is respectively born into or voluntarily enters into a network of obligations and commitments which he has not established, only parts of which are explicitly known by him, and the ramifications or consequences of which he cannot anticipate. And the purposes of neither cannot be achieved by one person nor one generation.

The contradiction in contract theory manifests itself also in these respects. Polanyi rejected Paine's assertion of the right of each generation to reorder society for itself. Paine asserted that right against Burke's citation of the statements of Parliament in and after the *Declaration of Right* of 1688, that it bound the nation and its heirs and successors for ever. On the contrary urged Paine:

> Every age and generation must be as free to act for itself, *in all cases*, as the ages and generation which preceded it. The vacuity and presumption of governing beyond the grave is the most ridiculous and insolent of all tyrannies.[9]

But the Social Contract itself, which Paine like Locke takes to be an historical event, has no validity today unless those who made it had the power to bind their heirs and successors, and that entails that there are noncontractual obligations and that *our* political obligations fall into that category. If, as Paine asserted, every generation is as free to act as the first, then every individual has a right *not* to contract, *not* to associate, *not* to be obliged by what some other group of individuals—in Paris or Philadelphia or wherever—happen to agree among themselves.

In every sphere of society, as well as society at large, the authority of tradition and an authority based on tradition are needed to preserve and transmit accumulated achievements which cannot be known by any single mind nor be known wholly explicitly. No part of human life can begin again from a clean slate. A famous passage in Burke's *Reflections* in effect sums up Polanyi's argument:

> Society is indeed a contract. Subordinate contracts for objects of mere occasional interest may be dissolved at pleasure—but the state ought not to be considered as nothing better than a partnership agreement in a trade of pepper and coffee, calico

or tobacco, or some other such low concern, to be taken up for a little temporary interest, and to be dissolved by the fancy of the parties. It is to be looked on with other reverence; because it is not a partnership in things subservient only to the gross animal existence of a temporary and perishable nature. It is a partnership in all science; a partnership in all art; a partnership in every virtue, and in all perfection. As the ends of such a partnership cannot be obtained in many generations, it becomes a partnership not only between those who are living, but between those who are living, those who are dead, and those who are to be born.[10]

Burke, like Polanyi, locates the purposes of society, not in safeguarding the right to do as we please, but in the cultivation of human nature or self-improvement.[11] This entails that society at large, as Burke also said, "extends in time as well as in numbers and in space."[12] Just as the individual cannot simply please himself, so too the present generation collectively cannot simply please itself. It has a heritage to maintain, to improve, and to pass on.

Polanyi, therefore, does not so much transcend the conflict between Burke and Paine, as endorse Burke's side of it. We have found substantially the same ideas of liberty and society in Polanyi and Burke, and the same conclusions drawn as to the importance of continuity, tradition, and authority. Polanyi does however speak of "radical progress" which is not quite in Burke's spirit. Perhaps this is a result of his analogy with the specific activity of science. In other spheres of life, and in society as whole, progress may consist more in closer approximation to existing standards rather than the setting of new ones. Science may be a field which offers satisfaction to one side of human nature, and to those in whom it is more prominent, namely, the desire to go out into the unknown, to explore and to adventure. Yet there is another side, that of continuity and security, of a home to return to. A society in which everything were continually changing, even though the changes were additions and improvements, would be as distorted as one which continually rehearsed an unchanging routine.

We shall now continue with the subject of the purposes of a free society. Whereas the "negative" liberty of doing as we please, sets society as a whole, and the government as its organ, only a formal purpose, of protecting that liberty, and not any substantive one, and that for many liberals is an essential constituent of its liberty, the "positive" liberty of self-dedication and self-improvement makes society a partnership in positive purposes. These are principally of a general sort rather than specific goals. The role of government is still principally that of protecting them and allowing individuals, groups, institutions, and classes to cultivate them. But, because they are positive although very general purposes, to protect them may require or permit more definite action on the part of government. For example, the question of censorship is not automatically closed. Since there is no moral case for doing as we please, there is none for reading or watching as we please. It is matter of judgment in the concrete case, and not of a principle turned into a rigid policy, as to whether more evil is done by allowing or banning certain types of publications, plays, films, and entertainments. Moreover, if a free society has certain purposes, then it is an open question, and again a matter of judgment in the concrete case, as to whether or not, and if so, as to how far and in what ways, the government may positively promote those purposes, for example, by public subsidies to institutions of education and research or even by the establishment of its own. After all, Hayek has argued for just that.

The whole of society has a heritage to maintain, to improve if it can, and to pass on. This applies to the role of government. It also applies within every special sphere of society, such as religion, learning, the arts, agriculture, and industry. This imposes special obligations upon those who are in positions of responsibility within those spheres of society. It also requires the general support of society at large. Natural science, for example, requires not only a body of specialists for its cultivation but also a general public that appreciates their work and interest, and that for its own inherent value.

> No important discovery can be made in science by anyone who does not believe that science is important in itself, and likewise no society which has no sense for scientific values can cultivate science successfully. The same applies to all cultural life: a society may be said to have a cultural life only to the extent to which it respects cultural excellence. (PK, p. 220)

Polanyi adds that this appreciation will be mostly secondhand. What anyone acknowledges as important achievements in any field will mostly depend upon the opinions of others, for he will often lack the time, the training, or the aptitude to study them himself.[13] Although the leaders of opinion may themselves be divided into rival schools or factions, there is some degree of underlying consensus which credits most of their judgments with some validity. That in turn implies the divergent standards have descended from a common stock of values and beliefs.

> This belief in an autonomous process of coherent thought is (as in science) the fundamental condition for the social cultivation of thought, guided by its own standards and prompted by its own passions. (PK, p. 222)

It was against reductionist denials of the reality and autonomy of thought that Polanyi proceeded to argue later in *Personal Knowledge* and subsequent works.[14] In the immediate context he pointed out that in a free society government and legislation follow public opinion, which in turn largely follows sets of leaders of opinion, not just because the people have decided, but because the people is deemed competent to decide *rightly*. This formation of policy by public opinion also presupposes that, despite initial conflicts, a substantial consensus can be obtained after the event for most reforms, as has happened in Britain from around 1830. If this is not possible, if large bodies of opinion continue to oppose and repudiate what has been done, then a nation is in a state of civil war and does not freely make its own law but is governed by a tyrannical majority. (Compare the history of France from 1789 to de Gaulle's establishment of the Fifth Republic and final defeat of the Organisation de l'Armée Secrète [OAS].) "In an ideal free society civic life would be continuously improved solely by the cultivation of moral principles" (PK, p. 224).

It follows that a free society is, as it were, a Society of societies, a Society for the Promotion of Self-Improvement, which can achieve its ends mostly by protecting and supporting the efforts and initiatives of individuals and other associations. That is, it does have its definite purposes but these are principally general aims rather than specific goals. It lies between the Great Society, which both includes it and pervades it, and a specific organisation aiming at specific goals.

Our reflections upon the Great Society and the Republic of Science have led us to conclude that, although a free society cannot be a *taxis* rather than a *cosmos*, yet it is one orientated to certain general aims and committed to certain distinctive beliefs. It is also one founded on tradition and traditional authority. It may be open to many things, but, to remain free, it may have to close itself firmly against others which threaten its character and existence. We have therefore given part of an answer to the second of the two questions posed at the end of "The Great Society as *Cosmos* and not *Taxis*" above, and still have to answer the first. To that we shall turn in the next chapter, wherein we shall add to our answer to the second.

Notes

1. See also Popper: the group-spirit of tribalism is not entirely lost today, nor, it seems, is wholly malign (OS, vol. 1, p.316, n.68).
2. Compare Polanyi (SMS, p. 25): Society deals with the free person impersonally

as a carrier of certain qualities. "Fairness" is dealing on the basis of a particular principle and not being influenced by extraneous circumstances.

3. See Sir Henry Maine, *Ancient Law*, pp. 134–9, and M. Gluckman's comment (*Politics*, p. 85) on apparent counterexamples.

4. See Gluckman, *Politics*, p. 13.

5. Ch. 8, n. 2.

6. *On Human Conduct*, pp. 114, 119.

7. Popper's philosophy of science, still based on a rationalist scepticism, never allows any theory to be true, and perpetuates the positivist dichotomy of discovery and justification by transposing it into that of conjecture and refutation.

8. See also PK, pp. 216–22, and TD, ch. 3.

9. *Rights of Man* I, in *Common Sense...*, pp. 76–7. The passage to which Paine objected is in the *Reflections*, *Works*, vol. 5, p. 62.

10. *Reflections*, *Works*, vol. 5, pp. 193–4. See also an earlier passage:

> [If the present generation] unmindful of what they have received from their ancestors, or of what is due to their posterity, should act as they were the entire masters.....[then] By this unprincipled facility of changing the state as often, and as much, and in as many ways, as there are floating fancies or factions, the whole chain and continuity of the commonwealth would be broken. No one generation should link with the other. Men would become little better than the flies of a summer...Personal self-sufficiency and arrogance (the certain attendants upon all those who have never experienced a wisdom greater than their own) would usurp the tribunal [left vacant by law].... No principles would be early worked into the habits...Barbarism with regard to science and literature, unskillfulness with regard to arts and manufactures, would infallibly succeed to the want of a steady education and settled principle; and the commonwealth itself, in a few generations, crumble away, be dispensed into the dust and powder of individuality, and at length be dispersed to all the winds of heaven. (pp. 181–3)

Burke also explicitly repudiated the assumption that all obligations can be based upon voluntary agreement:

> We have obligations to mankind at large, which are not in consequence of any special voluntary pact. They arise from the relation of man to man, and the relation of man to God, which relations are not matter of choice. On the contrary the force of all the pacts which we enter into with any particular person, or number of persons amongst mankind, depends upon those prior obligations. In some cases the subordinate relations are voluntary, but the duties are all compulsive. When we marry, the choice is voluntary, but the duties are not matter of choice: they are dictated by the nature of the situation. Dark and inscrutable are the ways by which we come into the world. The instincts which give rise to this mysterious process of nature are not of our making. But out of physical causes unknown to us, perhaps unknowable, arise moral duties, which, as we are perfectly well able to comprehend, we are bound indispensably to perform. Parents may not be consenting to their moral relations; but consenting or not, they are bound to a long train of duties towards those with whom they have never made a convention of any sort. Children are not consenting to their relation, but their relation, without their mutual consent, binds them to its duties. (*An Appeal from the Old Whigs to the New*, *Works*, vol. 6, pp. 201–2)

11. See also *Reflections*, *Works*, vol. 5, p. 186: "He who gave our nature to be perfected by our virtue willed also the necessary means of its perfection. He willed

therefore the state. He willed its connection with the source and original archetype of all perfection."

12. Again, I would like to quote the whole passage:

> A nation is not an idea only of local extent, and individual momentary aggregation; but it is an idea of a continuity, which extends in time as well as in numbers and in space. And this is a choice not of one day, or one set of people, not a tumultuary and giddy choice; it is a deliberate election of ages and of generations; it is a constitution made by what is ten thousand times better than choice, it is made by the peculiar circumstances, occasions, tempers, dispositions, and moral, civil, and social habitudes of the people, which disclose themselves only in a long space of time. Nor is prescription of government formed upon blind, unmeaning prejudices—for man is a most unwise and a most wise being. The individual is foolish; the multitude, for the moment is foolish, when they act without deliberation; but the species is wise, and, when time is given to it, as a species it always acts right. (*Speech on Reform of Representation, Works*, vol. 10, pp. 96–7)

13. It is here that dangerous gaps can open up between the leaders of opinion within a specific sphere and the opinions or tastes of the general public. In theology, this takes the form of a Hegelian Gnosticism in which "popular Christianity," with its beliefs in the reality of God and the historicity of the Incarnation, Atonement, and Resurrection, is reinterpreted in a nonontological and nonhistorical manner (a practice which those who undertake it do not find morally incompatible with retaining the ecclesiastical and academic positions and income which their former subscriptions to orthodoxy have enabled them to achieve). In the visual arts, it takes the form of spending public money upon, and awarding prizes to, objects which the general public derides as not being art at all.

14. Popper rightly sees relativism as the principal intellectual malady of the age (OS, vol. 2, p. 369). But as we saw in chapter 6, his critical dualism of facts and decisions not only cannot answer it but reinforces it.

12

The Obligations of a Free Society

Political Obligation

What holds a free society together? It cannot be Contract for Contract rests on noncontractual foundations. Nor can it be only the abstract rules of justice whose observance creates and defines the Open or Great Society, for that alone would leave only the morally indefensible freedom of doing as we please. At the least, a free society is, like the republic of science, constituted by self-dedication to a set of distinctive beliefs. We shall now explore what that further entails, and shall begin with political obligation, the right of government to govern and the duty of subjects to obey.

In two significant respects the republic at large is like the republic of science. Yet the analogy may fail in important as well as minor ways. One obvious difference is that the republic of science is both a voluntary and a self-selecting network. On the one hand, no one is compelled to join it and even someone born and brought up in it can at any time and immediately remove himself from it. On the other, no one has to be accepted as a scientist, and other scientists can at any time refuse to accept an applicant or effectually expel a member. For what constitutes that republic is general acceptance of and achievement within the current standards and theories of the sciences, and radical revisions of them will merit attention only as those who put them forward have already established their credentials within the current framework. The republic of science is a specialised section of society, of both specific societies and the Great Society, and is not society at large. The same applies within other activities and spheres. Even, or perhaps more so, when the prevailing consensus is upheld by a clique rather than a body of experts, admission to a publicly acknowledged status as a painter or novelist depends upon both one's own achievements and their acceptance by the leaders of opinion as art and not trash. Equally, one does not have to belong to the literary world or an artistic movement. At any moment one can leave it and drop any obligations to it.

In this respect Polanyi's model would fail, if it were intended to apply in this way, in exactly the same manner as the contractual one. Polanyi recognised that the republic of science is a voluntary society within and across bodies politic which new members do not voluntarily join at birth but into which, and into the principles of which, they are admitted and educated without reference to their wishes (SFS, p. 72). In contrast, every version of Contract theory, from Hobbes onwards, entails the contradiction of assuming, on the one hand, that all political obligation rests upon voluntary individual agreement and assent; while, on the other, of either taking the Contract to be an historical event but assuming that the obligations agreed by the original contractors are *inherited* and *not* contracted by their descendants; or of taking the Contract to be only a model but conceding that in fact society and political obligation are *not* the products of voluntary contracts. Locke, for example, had to fall back on the notion of tacit consent, on the part of anyone entering, remaining in, or using the services of a state, to explain how people in fact become subject to political and civic obligations.[1] And that was, in effect, to say that society and government are not, after all, based on or intelligible in terms of, Contract.

This, it seems to me, is one of the great weaknesses of all liberal political theory: that, in one way or another, it wishes bodies politic, or inclusive societies, to be thought of or remodelled in terms of voluntary associations within them, and, moreover, in terms of those voluntary associations of which membership is terminable at will, such as partnership agreements in matters of trade, or marriages within a framework of easy divorce, or clubs and societies formed for specific purposes. If freedom, the freedom of the individual to act as he pleases, is the greatest political good, then no corporate body, be it family, clan, Church, university, business concern, army, city, or state, can have superior claims upon the individual unless he wishes it so to have. But, precisely in order to protect his liberty and the individual from other wrongs, there must be, as all but consistent anarchists have acknowledged, a superior power somewhere whose authority does not derive from the individual's contracted agreement and can be asserted against him whatever he thinks about its legitimacy. That which enforces contracts against all comers cannot itself be a matter of contract. And therefore freedom cannot be the highest political good because it itself requires obligations whose essence does not lie in their being freely assumed. Once more we find that liberty and liberalism transcend themselves.

Only one theory of political obligation is logically coherent and fits the facts, that of "prescription," historic right, and custom. The rights of governments, of whatever description and over whatever peoples and territories, are founded, and can be founded, only upon their inheritance or assumption of existing rights. The most revolutionary régimes, despite the claims of their ideologies, tacitly act upon this principle. The French Revolutionaries, whatever they might have said about natural rights and the will of the people, did not consult every Gaston and Jacques, but assumed the rights that the deposed monarchy had built up for itself over specific territories spreading outwards from the Île de France. Moreover, if they had held referenda, that would have begged the question. For without prescriptive rights and obligations, what Gaston in Grenoble thinks and wishes has nothing to do with Jacques in Josselin. A referendum is an appeal to the people as already constituted and defined, to individuals as already members of it and already obliged to accept the decision of the majority. "The people" is not a collection of unconnected individuals, but already a corporate body defined and united by customary and hence inherited legal ties. Likewise Lenin assumed the rights of the Tsars over the lands and peoples of the Russian Empire, save what he had to concede in Poland, the Baltic republics, and Finland. In effect revolutionaries claim a right by conquest, internal conquest, while repudiating the corresponding customary obligations which a conqueror also takes over from the régime that he has defeated.

Bodies politic are not created, nor usually maintained, by choice but spontaneously as people find themselves born into them and come to identify themselves with them. Liberalism sits uneasily between a consistent anarchistic individualism which explicitly dissolves away all government, and a frank acknowledgment of the inherited and unchosen ties of prescriptive rights and obligations.

Concrete Society

This weakness of liberalism is a manifestation of a more fundamental one: namely, that of thinking in terms of abstractions. Liberalism, as we saw in Part 1, aims at defining in abstract terms a general liberty of the individual, usually to do as he pleases provided he recognises the reciprocal rights of others. While we can articulate some central immunities and competences, themselves subject to tacit qualifications and modifications, no abstract definition of liberty proves wholly successful, though some are obviously much more erroneous than others. We concluded in chapter 4, that liberty can exist and be understood only within a tradition of concrete liberties. What counts as liberty must vary from time to time and place to place, and for practical purposes a people is free if they feel and think themselves to be free.[2] Liberty, society, and the individual in the abstract do not exist, and only concrete liberties, societies, and individuals are real. Yet Liberals tend to think of "the individual," and of the "the individual" set over and against other such individuals and "the state." The "atomistic" conception of society, of which liberalism has been often accused by such as Nesbit,[3] arises in part from its abstract mode of thinking, and thus of conceiving "the individual" in general and therefore apart from the concrete society in which each real person exists, its traditions which have shaped him, and the networks of relations and obligations with and towards others wherein he lives and acts. For what it wants to do is to formulate universal or at least general principles of politics which can be applied everywhere, to every society and to each person. It is usually not enough for a liberal to defend English or other liberties. If he admires such a set of concrete liberties, then they become for him a model to be realised elsewhere. That is, he is liable to confuse policies with principles and thus to indulge in ideology to the neglect of concrete reality.[4]

This is not to deny that there are universal principles.[5] Indeed, we criticised Hayek in chapter 7 for appearing at times to deny their possibility, yet he also rightly asserts that classical liberalism depends upon them. The Great Society certainly does. They are its only cement. It is precisely that network of relationships which is brought into being by treating all men alike according to the principles of justice, a network which any man can enter at any time provided he meets that one requirement. He does not have to share any other aims or interests or be subject to any directing authority. Its law is its bond and its law is the *ius gentium*. But the "law of nations" or universal principles of fairdealing, can be only an abstraction from actual practices, some of which may come to supplant others.[6] As Hayek recognises with his arguments that no system of law can be invented *de novo* but that existing bodies of law can be amended by a tacit sense of injustice, universal principles need a concrete and therefore particular matter to inform. It is a frequently repeated but nonetheless valid criticism of Kant's formalist ethics that his Categorical Imperative presupposes systems of material or concrete laws and institutions, such as marriage and property, which, precisely because they are material and not formal, it must condemn as "heteronomous." Again, those systems are inevitably local and specific: definitions and laws about property vary from place to place and time to time. "Thou shalt not steal" is universal, but the same material act may be theft in one context and not another, as, for example, modern laws about copyright and plagiarism compared to the practices of previous ages. It follows that the Great Society can only emerge from and remain dependent upon smaller and specific societies, with their own laws and institutions. It can never absorb or replace them. At the most, one society could so expand that it would include all others within itself and replace their laws and customs by its own, what Voegelin calls "an ecumenic empire."

Similarly, one difference between the republic of science and the republic at large is that in the latter a General Authority proves, after all, not to be enough. The former cannot function with commitments only to truth, scientific method, and scientific value in the abstract. It requires also a reigning body of theory, an orthodoxy. Its content is always changing, sometimes radically, but at any one time it has a determinate content. As Polanyi said elsewhere, that our commitments are changing does not mean that we are uncommitted (PK, p. 308). But the republic of science is not permanently committed to any one theory or set of theories. A free society is not an Open one but one dedicated to a distinctive set of beliefs. But, Polanyi argues, those beliefs are like those that define science in general, the naturalistic picture of the universe as opposed to magical ones, rather than more specific beliefs. A General Authority leaves it to the individual members of the relevant society to apply and reinterpret its body of beliefs. A Specific Authority, in contrast, imposes specific beliefs from the centre. Polanyi illustrates the differences with the examples, for the former, of science, the law and Protestant theology, and, for the latter, of Roman Catholicism. He acknowledges that in law and all theology there is yet a degree of central compulsion which is not to be found in science (SFS, pp. 56–9). A free society, argues Polanyi, is like the scientific community in upholding a tradition which its members develop by individual initiatives. In this way he reinterprets Rousseau's General Will. It is not that individuals get together and commit themselves to a General Will which then sovereignly chooses it aims, for example, the cultivation of science. On the contrary, by devoting themselves to certain principles, scientists generate a community governed by them and sovereignty resides in each generation of individuals who conscientiously apply those principles to new tasks. So too the Social Contract is a commitment, not to a sovereign ruler nor a General Will, but to the service of a particular ideal, that of science (SFS, p. 64). Just as scientific tradition holds together the scientific community and guides the individual scientist in applying and reinterpreting it, so too in a free society at large the art of free discussion, transmitted by traditions of civic liberties, guides the consciences of the citizens. That art has two main principles, fairness in stating one's case and tolerance in listening to those of others. And it is embodied in free institutions, such as Parliament, the press, and the courts which protect and foster them. Those principles can be further specified as belief that truth exists, that all members of the society love it, and that they all feel obliged and can in fact pursue it. These are not explicitly held but are embodied in the institutions of a national tradition, clearly in some national traditions and not in others (SFS, pp. 67–71).

Polanyi clearly recognises two major differences between the Social Contract of the republic at large and that of the republic of science: the involuntary character of the individual's admittance to the former and of his education in its principles, and, conversely, of the greater difficulty of exclusion from it, by execution or exile. This compulsory education of new members into the principles and traditions of a free society is a proper function of its General Authority, that is, of the atomised sovereignty exercised by its members individually (SFS, pp. 71–2).

Let us consider again Polanyi's other examples of General Authority in which he allows that there is an element of central compulsion: namely, law and Protestant theology. It is the question of more specific beliefs which concerns us now. Polanyi clearly means the development of actual law and not the academic study of jurisprudence (though the two overlap and interact), which would be the exact parallel with natural science. The difference is that any body of actual law is a set of specific laws and not just legal principles. They define, permit, enforce, and debar specific acts and institutions, and together define a specific way of life. They are established by, and themselves are, a Specific Authority. Of course, they can be more or less restrictive and so define and enforce a more or less specific way of life, either generally or in certain spheres. They are more like the shared style and tastes of a school of art, marked off from other schools, than the premises of science. So too with Protestant theology, even of the most liberal kinds. As Polanyi acknowledges, it operates within the framework of the Bible.

More than that, the Reformed and Lutheran traditions impose yet more specific frameworks. Christian theology is not philosophy of religion, and the Church, the community of the faithful, is more than a body of earnest seekers after truth. Every part of the Church upholds—or professes to uphold—the creeds which give a determinate and permanent content to the faith. As authorities within the Church weaken in their own beliefs and allow apparently any opinions but those of supporting the orthodox faith and Catholic tradition, so the Church declines.

Now while a free society cannot be one that imposes a large body of highly specific beliefs, its authority cannot but be more specific than what Polanyi seems to allow. The traditions and institutions of freedom are not quite the same in the examples which he gives: England, America, Holland, and Switzerland. Dutch and Swiss law owe much to Roman Law; the Dutch have proportional representation, and the Swiss frequent and binding referenda; America and Switzerland are inherently republican and federal, England and the Netherlands monarchical and unitary. They each have been moulded by their own history, and life has a different flavour in each, perhaps also in different parts of each. Again, each is more like a school of art than a mode of inquiry uniformly practised, actually or potentially, throughout the world. Radical changes would make each other than what it is, without that continuity whereby evolutionary biology is still biology and quantum physics, physics. Again, recall the example of France and the Revolution which left deep divisions between two Frances, Royalist and Catholic versus Republican and Secularist—indeed three up to 1870, with the Napoleonic—which have been only recently reconciled. Bodies politic are like animal bodies in one way, that it can be difficult to transplant alien organs into them. A radical innovation can split a body politic permanently into two camps or parts. The Reformation divided Europe in ways which remain today. The introduction of free institutions can itself lead to divisions—Belgium from Holland in 1830, the dissolution of the Habsburg Empire in 1918, Northern and Southern Ireland in 1922, the Czech and Slovak Republics in 1992. In natural science, unity is always restored precisely because the authority is always only general.

A free society cannot be dedicated only to freedom in the abstract nor be held together only by formal commitments. It necessarily has to be committed to a concrete freedom embodied in its own specific customs, laws, and institutions, which can change but only within limits. All freedom is freedom to do or be something determinate. The Gnostic desire for an abstract and hence indeterminate freedom, a freedom to be anything, can only destroy society. Hence the paradox of "the bonds of freedom." A society free of bonds cannot be a society at all.

Positive Obligations

There is one further parallel between the republic of science and the republic at large that we can draw out although Polanyi did not. The individual scientist has particular and positive obligations to the community of scientists: that of defending it and individual scientists when they are threatened, and enforcing its standards. It is not enough for him not to fudge his results nor to criticise his fellow scientists on non-scientific grounds. Rather, he has a positive duty to discourage and even expose malpractice when he comes across it, a duty not always discharged in other professions that one could name where legalised closed shops are still allowed. Also he has a positive duty to defend the integrity of the whole community and individual members against threats and unwarranted attacks from outside, as did Polanyi himself in the face of demands for the subjection of science to a central plan to promote material welfare, and of other acts of interference.[7]

It seems to me that the paradigmatic situation for liberalism is that of one man, private citizen or bearer of public authority, encroaching upon the freedom of a second. From this situation two principles and one conclusion are drawn: the right of the latter to go his own way without interference, the duty of the former not to interfere, and the need for laws and institutions which permit the former and prevent, reduce, or give redress for the latter. It follows, as we saw that Hayek concluded, that civic duties, and perhaps moral ones also, are primarily negative duties not to interfere with others' exercise of their rights just are they are not to interfere with one's exercise of one's own. Indeed, positive duties appear to be a threat to freedom for they would restrict the time and means available for doing as one wishes. Yet Hayek himself has acted otherwise. From *The Road to Serfdom* onwards he has not merely not encroached on the liberty of others, but, like Polanyi, has actively sought by his publications, addresses, and membership of the Mont Pélerin Society, to protect and enlarge the liberty of his fellow men.

If it is generally true of liberalism and liberal thinkers that they hold our civic and moral duties to be generally ones of noninterference, then again we find it and them taking for granted a definite social background but without acknowledging its and their dependence on that background. In this case they assume a tradition of civility and a general respect for law. Let us consider another paradigmatic situation of social life. As before one person interferes with or attacks another. But this time there is also a third party. The last, surely, has a positive duty in this situation, to assist the second party and thwart the first, and not a negative one to stand aside. Now if it is claimed that this is exceptional, a liability to have do something definite only on rare occasions, then a peaceful and orderly state of society is being assumed. Liberalism, in that case, is open to the charge that it rests upon a discipline which it has not established and which now it does little to maintain. In contrast, it has been rightly said of conservatism that it is the politics of original sin. It is primarily a politics of order and the maintenance of order.

Such a charge cannot be levelled against Hayek. For although he does hold that social and civic obligations are primarily and largely negative, he does acknowledge the dependence of freedom upon traditions of discipline, restraint, and civility:

> There probably never has existed a genuine belief in freedom, and there has certainly been no successful attempt to operate a free society, without a genuine reverence for grown institutions, for customs and habits and "all those securities of liberty which arise from regulation of long prescription and ancient ways." Paradoxical as it may appear, it is probably true that a successful free society will always in a large measure be a tradition-bound society. (CL, p. 61, quoting Bishop Butler)

The immediate context of these remarks is Hayek's familiar contrast between evolutionary and constructivist ways of thinking. But on the next page he elaborates them with specific reference to traditions of restraint:

> It is indeed a truth, which all the great apostles of freedom outside the rationalistic school have never tired of emphasizing, that freedom has never worked without deeply ingrained moral beliefs and that coercion can be reduced to a minimum only where individuals can be expected as a rule to conform voluntarily to certain principles. (CL, p. 62)

In an accompanying note he refers appropriately to Burke, Madison, and Tocqueville. Yet that, apparently, is as far as Hayek goes. The question is, Is it enough? We saw in chapter 7 that a utilitarian attitude to justice defeats itself. The beneficial effects of just action can be achieved only if people act justly for the sake of justice and without thought to the consequences of so doing. Hayek's institutional utilitarianism, following that of Hume, recognises that this is so while yet holding the general effects of just conduct to be what principally matters. He appears to adopt the same position here. The significance of deeply ingrained moral beliefs, especially those which restrain the passions,[8] appears to be their effect of making liberty possible, a liberty which for Hayek is using our knowledge in our own way. Yet for such beliefs and practices to take root and be effective they must be viewed as imperative in their own right, that so to act is right and to act otherwise is wrong, in themselves and apart from any consequences in each case. It follows that it is not enough, for the establishment and maintenance of liberty, that we merely refrain from undue interference with the actions of our neighbours, but that we have positive duties to uphold and further the respect for law and order and the discipline of self-restraint, duties such as those of parents and teachers in setting good examples and instilling good habits, of all citizens in aiding each other when attacked, robbed, defrauded, or insulted, and in helping the police in the maintenance of public order. Civilisation and its institutions and practices are like buildings and machinery: without active and regular efforts to maintain them, they will decay.

In turn this reacts upon the duties of government. In principle no responsible government can stand idly by and watch with indifference a decline in standards of conduct. In life generally there is no neutrality, for life is action, and not to act is tacitly to endorse whatever then happens. The scope and possibilities of government may be severely limited; the prevention or diminution of one evil may bring about other, and perhaps greater, ones; government action may easily do more harm than good. At best its actions may have to be indirect; but in principle it has the right and the duty to intervene to maintain the conditions of civilised life and with them the possibility of a set of competences and immunities. We have already mentioned the question of censorship. There can be no *a priori* and universal case against it. No liberty of publication and free speech outweighs the duty of government and the public to uphold standards of civilised conduct. It is a matter of judgment in each concrete situation as to what can be permitted and what noxious publications and productions can be suppressed without thereby doing more harm, as for example, by bringing the whole system into ridicule and contempt through stupid and undiscriminating heavy-handedness. Again, a government cannot be neutral with regard to the structures of family life and the rearing of children. It certainly should not promote, directly or indirectly, "experiments in living" which result in children being brought up without proper models of conduct and habits of self-restraint.[9] The principal duty of government is the care and maintenance of the established laws, institutions, and customs that foster the moral life of the people.

Since civilisation in the abstract does not exist, this in turn means that a government can act only within, and in the first place to conserve, the existing framework and traditions of the society which it governs. Rights and liberties, property, family, education, and all the other features of human life vary from time to time and place to place. No one form and pattern can be imposed on all. All sane and efficacious policies are primarily conservative, or, when the conditions of civilised life have been corrupted and destroyed by revolution and totalitarianism, then policy must be primarily restorative.[10]

Society, civilisation, and freedom therefore depend upon the observance, by the public and government, of positive duties of maintaining proper ways of conducting ourselves towards each other, and, in particular, of habituating the young to them, and not just upon negative duties of noninterference. Here again liberty transcends itself. For it to come into and to continue in existence, the majority must value and work for the conditions upon which it rests. In turn that means that they must feel obliged to sustain each other, their common life and their shared freedom. And to those emotional bonds and what in turn sustains them, we shall now turn.

Notes

1. *Second Treatise*, ch. 10, §§119–21.
2. One homely example of this is the question of public and noisy celebrations. In Trinidad, while there are legal restrictions on the frequent and commercial holding of loud all-night parties in residential districts, there is a general practice of giving and tolerating them. In particular, East Indian weddings are preceded by all-night drumming, which ends at 6 A.M and resumes an hour later, these days amplified and audible a mile or more away. In Britain such practices are not accepted and neighbours can invoke the law to stop them. Wherein is freedom? In the reciprocal right to hold such parties or in the securing of quiet nights for all? In the abstract, no answer can be given. Only local custom and preferences can determine it. Hence outsiders moving into a locality with a custom different to their own must accommodate themselves to it, though they will feel constrained and not at liberty to do as they are used to doing and allowing others to do.

   Again, the question of Sunday Observance cannot be settled by thinking of liberty in the abstract. A right of all to do as each likes cuts both ways. On the one hand, if each can treat Sunday as just another day, then there is a strong chance that few or none will be able to treat it as special and not a day of business as usual. Hence the problems of Jews who wish strictly to observe their Sabbath from Friday evening to Saturday evening, and of Muslims in Europe who cannot easily all dash off—the men, that is—to the mosque at the beginning of Friday afternoon. On the other hand, for there to be a real liberty, and not a merely theoretical one, to have one day free from business as usual, there has to be strong customary or statutory restraint on what can be done on that day. This example also reminds us that liberties have frequently a communal dimension, a right of a group to follow its customary practices.

3. *The Quest for Community*, pp. 225–6.

4. Cf. Burke: "Circumstances (which with some gentlemen pass for nothing) give in reality to every political principle its distinguishing colour and discriminating effect. The circumstances are what render every civil and political scheme beneficial or noxious to mankind...Is it because liberty in the abstract may be classed among the blessings of mankind, that I am seriously to felicitate a madman, who has escaped from the protecting restraint and wholesome darkness of his cell, on his restoration to enjoyment of light and liberty?" (*Reflections*, *Works*, vol. 5, p. 14).

   "The situation of man is the preceptor of his duty" (*Speech on Fox's East India Bill*, *Works*, vol. 4, p. 44).

5. Again, compare Burke: "I never govern myself, no rational man ever did govern himself, by abstractions and universals. I do not put abstract ideas wholly out of any question because I well know, that under that name I should dismiss principles; and that without the guide and light of sound, well-understood principles, all reasonings in politics, as in everything else, would be only a confused jumble of particular facts and details, without the means of drawing out any sort of theoretical or practical conclusion' (*Speech on the Petition of the Unitarians*, *Works*, vol. 10, pp. 41–2). The sort of conservative philosophy which I am invoking is not that which, with Gray at the end of his *Liberalisms*, despairs of any general truths that transcend each particular situation, nor, with Hegel, identifies whatever has been as right at its time until the times altered.

6. Whether or not Sir Henry Maine was exactly right in arguing that the Roman notion of Natural Law is the *ius gentium*, seen in the light of a later and special theory, and that the *ius gentium* was the law common to the old Italian tribes from which immigrants had come to Rome and among whom disputes could not be settled by the application of specifically Roman Law (*Ancient Law*, pp. 53–64), something like that must happen whenever peoples with two sets of laws come into prolonged contact. A potentially universal network presupposes that it can happen.

7. With J.R. Baker he formed the Society for Freedom in Science, and then, after the Congress for Cultural Liberty in 1953, became chairman of the Committee on Science and Freedom. For details about particular efforts in respect of the latter, see the issues of *Science and Freedom*, especially nos. 1 (1954), 10 (Feb. 1958), 11 (June 1958), and 13 (Nov. 1959).

8. Cf. Burke: "I have observed that the philosophers in order to insinuate their polluted atheism into young minds systematically flatter all their passions natural and unnatural. They explode or render odious or contemptible that class of virtues which restrain the appetite. These are at least nine out of ten of the virtues. In place of all this, they substitute a virtue which they call humanity or benevolence. By this means their morality has no idea in it of restraint, or indeed of a distinct settled principle of any kind. When their disciples are thus left free and guided only by present feeling they are no longer to be depended upon for good or evil. The men who today snatch the worst criminals from justice will murder the most innocent persons tomorrow" (*Corr.*, vol. 3, p. 215). This was written in 1791 *before* the start of the Terror. Burke's most notable disciple in this respect was Irving Babbitt: see *Democracy and Leadership* and *Rousseau and Romanticism*.

9. See N. Dennis and G. Erdos, *Families without Fatherhood*, and N. Dennis, *Rising Crime and the Dismembered Family*, on the ways in which the welfare state in Britain has undermined the family and the discipline of the young, with proposals for reversing these trends.

I have noticed in most cases of child-battering, as reported in the press, that the mother seems to be a weak-willed woman who has borne the child, and perhaps others, out of wedlock and then lives with another man, and that she stands by while he maltreats the child or actively helps him. Surely, government must try to reverse the social trends that have resulted in many relationships of this type, and it cannot be neutral with regard to the structure of the family or its disappearance.

The same applies to ideologies of "child-centred" progressive education which have produced, in British state schools, a whole generation of self-centred and uneducated adolescents, and the orthodoxy of the philosophy of education peddled by the state-financed institutions of teacher-training, of "rational autonomy" for which any substantive teaching in religion, morality, and politics is "indoctrination" and hence taboo, though in their very teaching of that doctrine they "indoctrinate" their students with scepticism, relativism, secularism, and fashionable leftist opinions. See my *Education of Autonomous Man* (ch. 7) and the references therein to my articles in the *J. of Philosophy of Education*.

10. The error of the Continental reactionaries and absolutists, such as de Maistre and Bonald, was their failure to learn from Burke the lesson of the necessity of adaptation in order to conserve. Their attitude was the mirror-image of that of the revolutionaries whom they denounced. What they advocated was a futile attempt to return to the state of affairs immediately before the deluge, which obviously had grave deficiencies otherwise the deluge would not have occurred or have been so disastrous. Burke was very clear, and before 1789, that the French state needed reform, not least because of its chronic deficits. Conversely, a post-revolutionary government must try to devise institutions, laws, and policies which fit the immediate situation and build upon what survives of national and local tradition. Communism has done more far more damage in Russia than in the Baltic republics, Poland, the Czech Republic, and Hungary, both because it ruled there for longer and because the latter have had, and can remember, more secure institutions and laws. Necessarily, policies must differ in each society, as will the course of events in any case. A strong presidency, as in Mr. Yeltsin's new constitution, is the only way that Russia can be governed for the foreseeable future. But, when land has been returned to private ownership, the tradition of village self-government could be restored. That, of course, would not apply in towns and cities, and new ways of fostering cooperation will have to be tried there.

13

The Emotional Bonds of Society

Emotional Unity and the Levels of Sympathy

As we have seen, Popper, and Hayek following him, generally deprecate the experience of emotional solidarity. It smacks of "tribal society," the closed group united by the endeavour to achieve a shared and specific goal, and thus sharing the same hopes, fears, disappointments, and triumphs in that endeavour. Elements of emotional solidarity continue to exist in small groups within the Open or Great Society which rises above it and which is certainly not founded upon it. But is that a true account of the matter? It seems to me that Popper and Hayek make the common mistakes of identifying something with a specific form of itself, and of rejecting something *in toto* because of obvious abuses or malfunctions of it. One notes among many people a similar reaction against "authority" because it is identified with bullying authoritarianism. Emotional solidarity does bind together the "tribe" and any small group. It can get out of hand: a feeling of "we together" can easily become one of "us *against* them"; and one easy way to bind people together is by engendering feelings of resentment or hatred against some other group. In *1984* the objects change, but the same whipping-up of hatred towards "the enemy" continues. All totalitarian systems have used this trick, and must use it to get the people to work for a specific goal which has been set for them. Likewise, exclusive nationalisms engender or inflame resentments and fears about other groups in order to bind the nation together more closely. But to draw the inference that society is better off without emotional solidarity is like inferring from problems encountered by running a car on dirty petrol that it would go better with no petrol at all. As we shall see in a moment, a man without fellow-feeling for other men, one who does not share in their joys and sorrows, who does not feel hurt when they are hurt nor delight when they are happy, is not a citizen of any society. Moreover, without the capacity for emotional experience, he cannot act at all, except by habits and routines deposited by former experiences of emotion.[1] The cure for disorders of emotion is not their eradication but their proper direction. Nor do we have a contrast between "closed," "tribal" and small societies, on the one hand, which are bound together by shared emotions, and, on the other, "open" and "great" ones which are not, but between different sorts or levels of emotional unity in every sort of society.

Polanyi, in contrast to Popper and Hayek, does recognise the emotional basis of human life, thought, and of society, and we shall refer to his accounts as we proceed. But for a systematic survey we must turn to Max Scheler to whom reference has already been made.[2] Scheler distinguished four forms of sympathy:

1.   Emotional infection, in which B's experience of the signs of an emotion or mood in A cause B to "catch" that emotion or mood, but without knowing, in the case of an emotion, what it is directed to. In a herd of animals, one animal is alarmed at something. The others, seeing, hearing, or perhaps smelling the signs of its alarm, themselves become alarmed. In the same way panic or hysteria sweeps through a crowd. People go to parties in order to become infected by the jovial atmosphere.

2.   Emotional identification, a heightened form of emotional infection in which the other's emotions are taken as one's own. This is the attraction of spectator sports and of the vicarious wish-fulfilment offered by popular fiction and drama. In them one experiences, although secondhand and safely, the efforts, triumphs, and defeats of the protagonists. One feels the impact of a blow as the boxer reels from a punch, the satisfaction of a well-timed stroke as the batsman drives the ball effortlessly to the boundary, the heartbreak of the heroine when her lover betrays her. Emotional identification can result in emotional parasitism, either as living off the emotions of another (usually someone weaker and impressionable who can thus be used by the emotionally hungry person) in order to fill the emotional void in one's own life, or as identifying oneself so completely with the other that one has no emotions, nor thoughts, nor will of one's own but becomes a conduit for his.

3.   Community of feeling, in which A and B experience the same emotion towards the same object, as when two persons grieve over the death of the same friend.

4.   Fellow-feeling or sympathy proper, in which A shares in B's emotion towards C. Two parents standing by the grave of their child not only experience the same emotion of grief, but each is aware of and shares in the other's grief. Sympathy presupposes the ability to visualise the other's emotion. But, Scheler points out, that is not enough, for so also does cruelty. The cruel person needs to know that the other is suffering in order to enjoy, to cause, or to intensify his suffering. The merely callous person is oblivious to what the other feels.

Sympathy has a less and a more intimate form which manifests itself most clearly in the case of pity. There is pity *for* another, in which A sorrows at B's sorrow about C, and is thereby at a certain distance from and above him. Indeed, this sort of pity can cause A to do something about B's state, not for B's sake, but in order that A himself should not be saddened by it. There is also pity *with* another, in which A shares in B's sorrow at C, feels both sorrow that B is saddened by C and also his own sorrow at C.

Of these forms of sympathy in the widest sense, the first does not concern us, although Scheler maintained that it was the basis of the unity of a herd among animals and a mass or crowd among men. But herds are continuing organisations with hierarchies of leaders, whereas crowds are temporary and unstructured. Furthermore, emotional infection can break up, rather than unite, a crowd, as when panic sweeps through it and causes the people in it to rush off in different directions. As for emotional identification, that provides the basis of community of feeling and fellow-feeling. It is what we appear first to experience, before there is any clear differentiation of oneself from others, and, as Polanyi notes (PK, p. 205), there remains a deep physical sympathy with the seen bodily sufferings of others which even, as in the case of Himmler, training for merciless cruelty and domination by ideology may not overcome. But emotional identification by itself is either a state of life prior to the full emergence of the individual person or a later attempt to abolish the person by sinking back, as in hypnotic dances for example, into an undifferentiated communal feeling. And in the forms of emotional parasitism, it abolishes the person of either of the parties, the one off whose emotions the other feeds or the one who surrenders himself entirely to the other.

From these last mentioned facts, it may be inferred that the being and freedom of the individual require a liberation from all communal feeling, that he should stand proud and self-reliant in his own self-responsibility, able of his own volition to make agreements with others and bound to them only as he freely pledges himself, and not by any ties of emotion. Society is "association" and does not require any shared emotions of any form.

But any such inference is erroneous. Let us consider men without sympathy in any form. Such persons cannot be part of any society. We can see this in the case of the psychopath. As often in reflection upon human life, the abnormal is instructive by alerting us to what is otherwise so common that we take it for granted and overlook it. By the very absence of something otherwise universal, the abnormal case reveals the presence of that universal element in what is normal. What is abnormal about the psychopath is his incapacity for sympathy, even for that bodily emotional identity which makes one feel immediately the seen sufferings of others. That may be a result of an incapacity to visualise the feelings of others, and thus the effects of his actions and other events upon them, or of one to respond emotionally to them himself, or of both. Whatever the particular reason, the emotional states of others have no effect upon him. He is therefore not like the sadist who is aware of what his victims feel and enjoys it. The psychopath is an emotional monad without windows upon the hearts of others. He is actively antisocial.

What also distinguishes the psychopath is that he is active in the world. He has his own emotions, desires, and aims, all centred on himself. In that respect he is unlike the other sort of person who lacks any sympathy: namely, the one who, to avoid suffering and in despair at changing the world, has changed himself and cut off his emotional ties with the world and everything and everyone in it, and ultimately with himself. That was the way of the Hellenistic sage and the Indian ascetic. Such persons cultivate a general indifference and reduce their striving and engagement in the world. In effect, and in practice in the final stages of the Hindu scheme in which a man, having been a student and then a householder retires to solitude in the forest and then becomes a "renounced one," emotional disengagement with the world in general means emotional disengagement with others and society at large. Such persons make themselves passively asocial.[3] No society can tolerate the active man who lacks sympathy, that is the psychopath, and every society is endangered by widespread emotional and then practical withdrawal from it and indifference towards its fate. Indeed, the latter is the result of a world-weariness which, politically as in the Hellenistic world or cosmically as in India, has given up all hope of improving the world and therefore seeks retreat within it or escape from it altogether. Gnostic asceticism, as among the Manichees and Cathars, is even more radical. It is based upon a hatred of the world and therefore of what ties spirits, sparks of the One Light, to it.

That is the reverse. The obverse, and the correct inference from the facts, is that society is founded upon our general capacity for fellow-feeling, for sharing in the emotions of others, for mourning with those who grieve and rejoicing with those who rejoice. What holds men together is emotional unity. And what holds together a society of self-responsible individuals, who have emerged from undifferentiated emotional identification with each other, is community of feeling and fellow-feeling proper in which they are aware of each other as distinct but also feel themselves bound together. Consider the parable of the Good Samaritan. What the robbers lacked, and what the Priest and Levite suppressed, was sympathy with the man who was beaten, robbed, and left to die. Conversely, what the Samaritan felt was sympathy with him, despite the religious and racial antagonism between Samaritans and Jews. The whole point of the parable was not to teach an Hellenistic or Indian indifference to the world, nor a Gnostic hatred of it, but to re-awaken that general capacity for sympathy with anyone we meet which other concerns too easily dominate and put out of effect. It would be perverse to draw from it the moral that, because the Samaritan acts towards the robbers' victim as a fellow member of the Great Society and despite the mutual hostility of Jews and Samaritans, that emotional bonds are a danger to human life which would be better conducted without them. On the contrary, the Great Society has its own emotional basis, that general capacity for fellow-feeling with anyone we meet.

Let us note what it is not. It is not a sympathy or love for mankind. Mankind is not a concrete object nor can be imagined as one. There can be no genuine emotion directed towards it. The "love of humanity," as Burke saw in the case of Rousseau,[4] is a pretence which is affected precisely in order to excuse oneself from any real concern with others in the concrete. Only concrete persons exist and can be loved, never abstractions nor amorphous collections. That is why, besides the practicalities of having to operate with states as they are, the universal pretensions of socialism are narrowed and focused into the achievement of "Socialism in one country" and all socialism is a national socialism. Love for mankind is and produces nothing, but it is possible to whip up enthusiasm for a *national* Five-Year Plan. Nations are imaginable, concrete, and personified.

Our general capacity for fellow-feeling becomes focused, and is awakened by, the people we meet. To the question, "Who is my neighbour?" the answer given was not everyone or individuals in the abstract, but anyone with whom one comes to have concrete relations. What the lawyer wanted to know was who wasn't his neighbour, whom he could exclude. The point of the parable was to remind him that no one could be excluded in principle. This, then, is the basis of all social relations. Without the capacity for sympathy other people would be mere things to us and their actions mere events.

The Bonds of Particular Societies

But, of course, human life does not consist of encounters only with anonymous strangers with whom we share a general humanity and transient particular relations and concerns. Its principal context is what Burke called "the little platoon,"[5] the smaller circles of family, neighbourhood, parish, workplace, professional associations, clubs, and societies. It is curious that these groups come under suspicion from both individualists and collectivists. To the former they represent, like the state and its organs, powers and obligations which the individual has not created, unless he can form, remould, join, and leave them as he will. To the latter, they represent independent powers that rival the total concentration of all wills in one project and design: they can be permitted only as they come under central control. Radical libertarianism, whether it seeks freedom immediately or through the detour into totalitarianism, seeks freedom from what is unwilled and ultimately from what is contingent and determinate. But the little platoons are the epitome of finitude: each person is so obviously in, and shaped by one and not another, this family or household and not that, this village or town and not some other, this trade or occupation and not those. The abstract "individual" and the abstract "society" stand over against the concrete individual in the real and concrete circles in which he is born and lives, and to which he becomes attached.

The emotional ties of little platoons go beyond our general capacity for fellow-feeling. They take the form of community of feeling, of shared attachments, hopes, fears, joys, and sorrows. For there is no cohesion in a group without community of feeling. On the surface there may well be divergence, even conflict, but without an underlying commitment no group or organisation can endure. For example, if parties in dispute go before the courts that presupposes, on their part, a common commitment to the peaceful settling of disputes, to the justice of the existing system of law and to the courts as impartially interpreting and applying it. The law and its institutions decay when litigants and the public at large regard them only as something which they can use for their own advantage. No judge can take that attitude without corrupting his office at the core. For individualism, society generally, and each part of it in particular, is an exterior network or grid through which the individual negotiates his own path. It is something he uses to get what he wants. That may mean cooperation but it is only a cooperation of convenience, a temporary alliance for specific purposes.[6] The individualist is and feels himself free to make and dissolve any partnership at will, and obliged and committed only insofar as he has freely pledged himself. But, as we argued in chapter 10 §2, that attitude is parasitic upon a deeper commitment which goes beyond the letter of contract and thus upon a willingness to go beyond explicit obligations. The whole point of "working to rule" is to bring the organisation concerned to a halt.

In *Personal Knowledge* (ch. 7 §§4 and 5) we find a full acknowledgment of the emotional basis of society. Polanyi begins with "pure conviviality" or companionship, the enjoyment of the company of others for its own sake. It has its uses, and Polanyi refers to the maxim that a happy ship is an efficient ship. The comradeship of cooperation in a joint enterprise is a secondary feature, yet it becomes a second form of pure conviviality when it is expressed in a joint ritual which "affirms the convivial existence of the group as transcending the individual, both in the present and through times past" (PK, p. 211). But society at large goes beyond pure conviviality and joint enterprises. The social nature of man, and the largely tacit transmission of knowledge, practices, and culture, build up a set of common values even though the intellectual interests from which they spring are not themselves specifically directed towards other persons.

> Moreover, such sharing constitutes an orthodoxy upholding certain intellectual and artistic standards, and an undertaking to engage in the pursuits guided by them, which amounts in effect to a recognition of cultural obligations. Finally, since the passions expressed in a ritual affirm the value of group life, they declare that the group has a claim to the conformity of its members, and that the interests of group life may legitimately rival and sometimes overrule those of the individual. This acknowledges a *common good* for the sake of which deviation may be suppressed and individuals be required to make sacrifices for defending the group against subversion and destruction from outside. (PK, p. 212)

Polanyi again here echoes Burke's assertion that society is a partnership, but an enduring partnership in "all science...in all art...in every virtue and in all perfection." Society at large, says Polanyi, has four coefficients which jointly stabilise it and its institutions: sharing of convictions, sharing of fellowship, cooperation, and authority or coercion. Hayek acknowledges the third and fourth, and certain applications of the first, such as a largely tacit sense of justice and the need for moral restraint. Polanyi recognises that there is more to the first and that the second is equally necessary. These four coefficients for maintaining society are today largely differentiated and enacted by separate institutions and agencies:

(1) Universities, churches, theatres, and picture galleries, serve the sharing of convictions.... They are institutions of *culture*; (2) social intercourse, group rituals, common defence, are predominantly convivial institutions. They foster and demand *group loyalty*; (3) cooperation for a joint material advantage is the predominant feature of society as *an economic system*; (4) authority and coercion supply the *public power* which shelters and controls the cultural, convivial, and economic institutions of society. (PK, pp. 212–3)

Polanyi then continues to distinguish static, dynamic totalitarian, and dynamic free societies.

A free society is no exception to the pattern that Polanyi sketches. It too is held together by a shared and felt commitment to its continuance, to its laws and institutions, to its traditions and to its welfare. Without that commitment, and even if most people do not behave in a criminal manner, it soon becomes a lifeless shell. If people do not care about it, they will not protect and maintain it, and, like everything else in this world when left to itself, it will decline, decay, and eventually die. We see this most clearly in areas where, through indifference or fear, the population looks the other way while gangsters, drug-dealers, or terrorists take over. What Polanyi said elsewhere about professional standards in science and law, applies to every part and the whole of society. None of it can be regarded just as something which disconnected individuals use only for their own advantage. Even the market is not an exception to this rule, for it depends upon the system of law and traditions of moral restraint and fair dealing.

Government, and its specific organs such as the military, the police, the judiciary, and the civil service, are, as Hayek says, organisations or *taxes*. For their proper functioning they require felt commitments to their tasks and traditions, an *ésprit de corps*, professional pride, and a sense of public service. That implies also a felt solidarity in a common task. Of course, it can be deflected, and so what comes to matter is not the public good but the good of the organisation. The first law of every bureaucracy is to preserve itself, and the second is to expand itself. Yet one soon notices the difference between states where the civil servants have a sense of public service and those where they do not.

We noted in chapter 7 §3 the insufficiency of a merely utilitarian attitude towards the military and the danger of a gap between the attitudes of the public and of the military. The same insufficiency and gap applies to the other organs of government. A free society is policed with the consent of the public. That means not only that the police serve the public and the public good, but that the public support and aid the police. There has to be a sense of commitment to and unity in the common task of maintaining law and order, not only among the police and the judiciary, but among the general public as well. It follows that a free society itself, and not just its government, has an element of *taxis* or organisation and with it of emotional solidarity in the common task of maintaining itself. It depends upon some degree of community of feeling and mutual sympathy of the citizens with each other. And, Burke and Polanyi would add, it depends also upon a felt unity, not only within the present generation, but among the generations, a feeling of unity and co-responsibility with those who have died and those who are yet to be born. People who look, individually or collectively, only to the present and thus to their own advantage, only consume and squander and neither conserve nor build.[7]

The difference between a free and an unfree society does not lie in the bonds of emotional unity of the latter and the lack of them in the former. Indeed, modern totalitarian states have lacked such unity which is why they had to invest so much effort in propaganda and parades to whip it up. After June 1941 Stalin had to fall back upon Russian patriotism and even the Orthodox Church, and not socialist ideology, in order to sustain the war effort. The Nazis, of course, were able to build upon German national feeling. Fascism in Italy failed to generate any emotional support and soon collapsed in 1943. A free society, in contrast, is united by a spontaneous and traditional emotional solidarity.

If liberalism is open to the charge of taking for granted a peaceful order of society, so too can it be accused of taking for granted a peaceful order in the world outside. Every actual society is one among others, a power among powers. A free society is not exempt from external dangers and obligations. Inevitably it is an organisation with specific goals of self-preservation and perhaps of preserving a peaceful order in its part of the world. Without felt solidarity among its citizens, it cannot protect itself and them. Its freedom, in the end, depends upon their willingness to bear the pains, burdens, and self-sacrifices of war. France collapsed in 1940 because too many Frenchmen lacked a sense of a common destiny, mutual sympathy and thus the will to fight. Consequently, instead of taking itself, its navy, and much of its army to North Africa in order to continue the war, the French government surrendered itself to Pétain, who then surrendered to Hitler. And the felt solidarity which becomes accentuated and explicit in moments of trial and crisis, must be there, latent and quiet, in times of peace. Modern collectivisms seek to build and employ a war-psychosis in peacetime, with their campaigns for this and struggles against that. To react against that to the point of thinking that freedom consists in freedom from any emotional solidarity, is to put freedom at risk.

Indeed, as noted earlier, the isolated individual is both the product and basis of the modern absolute and total state which both forcibly emancipates him from felt attachments to traditional associations and then redirects his unfocused emotions upon itself. Excessively individualist and rationalist liberalism has ignored, to its cost, the need for men to belong to, and to feel themselves part of, something greater than themselves.

"Magic": The Maintenance of the Emotional Bonds of Society

We now come to what we have already met in Polanyi's four coefficients of society and what R.G. Collingwood called "magic." It is "the dynamo which supplies the mechanism of practical life with the emotional current that drives it." It is the technique of evoking the emotions needed for life and of discharging them into life, and is therefore found in every healthy society. "Magic art" is the art which does this by representing the emotions in question in some way or another, and includes rituals and ceremonies. Thus patriotic art evokes and canalises the emotions of loyalty to the unit or group; sports are usually rituals or have the trappings of rituals and train character (or evoke local patriotism); the ceremonials of daily life involve dressing up and acting according to prescribed manners, and thus focus the relevant emotions, such as those for married life, for life without the person who has died, or for maintaining a friendship.[8]

But, as Polanyi says (PK, p. 211), rituals incur the hostility of individualism because they celebrate a social existence which is inaccessible to the isolated individual. Even when the object of a celebration is not the group itself, as in worship, there is always a communal aspect to it: the hermit reciting his prayers is a part of the Communion of Saints. Ritual, continues Polanyi, is also denigrated by utilitarianism as useless and by romanticism, which, like Irving Babbitt, he sees to be closely related to utilitarianism, as suppressing the spontaneous feelings of the individual in favour of compulsory, standardised, and public emotions. And traditions are discredited by the awareness that we ourselves make them and yet submit to them as something external to us.

The sceptical rationalism of the modern age has thus eroded traditional rituals and with them the expression and maintenance of the emotions required for traditional society. It has replaced them, on the one hand, with what Collingwood called "amusement art," which arouses an emotion only to satisfy it imaginatively (and vicariously) in the act of arousing it or similarly discharges an existing emotion,[9] and, on the other, with the organised and faked rituals of collectivism—the rallies, banners, uniforms, parades, worship of the dead at the shrines in Red Square, "gestures of solidarity," "spontaneous demonstrations"— in which the rulers sought to generate emotional support for a new order of society imposed from above.

The consequences of this decay of emotion and "magic" were discussed by Collingwood in an unpublished essay, "Man Goes Mad."[10] Just as a man dies by refusing to eat, so he goes mad by denying the foundations of his emotional life. If emotion were to fail, civilisation would crumble into dust and men would sink back to the level of brutes. Changes in civilisation are the result of the death of certain emotions. Two types of emotion are essential to the health of a civilisation: those regarding oneself and others, and those fundamental to a particular type of civilisation. In European civilisation, which is basically agricultural, the latter are principally those regarding Nature and those regarding God. Human sanity depends on the health of fundamental human emotions, and the sanity of civilised man depends on the health of those emotions fundamental to his civilisation. For us Europeans, therefore, the vitality of the really religious emotions of patriotism and love of Nature, which are neither aesthetic nor political, is the basis of the vitality of our civilisation. But as urban technology becomes dominant, the emotions of the country dweller decline. He loses his "magical" folk-art as modern industry becomes severed from agriculture.[11] This results in modern madness, and may produce a temporary fevered and restless state of mind but no lasting vitality. The only cure is the restoration of that deep, primitive, and unconscious emotion of the man who wrestles with the soil, sees the fruits of his labour, and is satisfied.

Looking back on the twentieth century, we can see the vast damage done to European civilisation by restless and uprooted emotions. Rapid change, industrialisation, and the decline of religious belief have left men without the old patterns and sureties. But a cool, temperate scepticism is possible only for a few sheltered and detached observers of the human scene, such as Hume. For the vast majority the parable of the man exorcised of one devil, holds true: that into the empty heart will enter yet worse passions. In its milder forms, we see today a restless desire for amusements and sensations—consider the popular press and the endless stream of "news" on radio and television. At its worst, we have seen the transfer of religious emotions and energies to "immanentised eschatology," the revolutionary attempt to bring in the End by force,[12] the rise of nationalism as an alternative to fill the void, combinations of revolutionary totalitarianism and nationalism, and, more recently, unscrupulous terrorism for revolutionary and nationalist causes. All these betoken a radically disordered state of feeling in our times. To rely on disillusionment to cool men's passions in the next century would be a mistake. The appeal of revolutionary collectivism has declined dramatically, but the underlying rejection of the world will manifest itself in new ways, such as the violence and terrorism of "animal rights" movements, unless some proper emotions towards man and Nature are revived or implanted. The only defence for human dignity and liberty is a rightly ordered set of emotions which will give men the strength and patience to live, endure, and act.

Writing early in 1940, Collingwood observed that liberal and democratic principles lacked "punch" and had become mere habit, whereas fascism and nazism had tapped a source of power lacking in their opponents. Actually, as was seen in 1943, the power of fascism was a self-deceiving bluster and bravado on the part of Mussolini. And, as Polanyi observed, after Dunkirk there was a revival of national feeling in Britain which stemmed and then reversed the tide. National feeling, Polanyi concluded,

> seems to be the only sentiment today in which that responsible devotion to a community can be rooted, that bond of mutual confidence assured, which are need if reason and equity are to gain acceptance as the guides of human affairs.

The political immorality of German national tradition was thus to be seen as an aberration and "not a valid argument against the nineteenth century conception of nationhood—the nation as a source of honour and an integral international order."[13]

But can national feeling be enough? National traditions, Polanyi said in the same place, "appear as the most ample and most reliable embodiments of the principles of morality at least so far as the guidance of popular behaviour is concerned'. Now by "a national tradition" can be meant both a tradition transmitted by a nation and a tradition which has the nation as its object. Is the latter sufficient? What becomes of the worth of the individual if the nation alone is what matters? Obviously, Polanyi did not identify the two meanings of "national tradition." What, then, must form the content of a national tradition that can maintain society and especially a free society? Collingwood said that it must be an emotion directed to the nation (or other group or unit) and to nature, both of which are genuinely religious emotions. Whether that is so or not, we shall next inquire, and shall therefore close our discussion of the reformulation of liberalism with what human freedom presupposes about the nature, dignity, and destiny of man.

Notes

1. On the latter, see Scheler's description of a woman without feelings who had to live by the clock, by habit and routine, and the promptings of others ("The Meaning of Suffering" in (ed.) M. Frings, *Max Scheler: Centennial Essays*, pp. 156–7). See also the unfortunate Schneider as described in Merleau-Ponty's *The Phenomenology of Perception*, and G. Santayana's comments on people without emotions in *The Sense of Beauty*, p. 25, and my "Governance by Emotion" (*British Journal of Phenomenology*, vol. 22, no. 2, May 1991), and "Passivity and the Rationality of Emotion" (*The Modern Schoolman*, vol. 68, May 1991) in which I generalise Polanyi's account (PK, ch. 6) of the necessary role of emotion in the initiation and maintenance of scientific discovery.

2. Ch. 11 §2. See Scheler's *The Nature of Sympathy* and *Formalism in Ethics*. For a summary and discussion of Scheler's scheme, see E. Ranly, *Scheler's Phenomenology of Community*.

3. Buddhism, in its original form, presents the paradox of a discipline that aims at detachment from the world and an insubstantial self in order to end suffering, combined with a missionary effort to bring this discipline and release from suffering to other men.

4. *A Letter to a Member of the National Assembly, Works*, vol. 6, pp. 31–5. See also above, p. 167 n.7.

5. *Reflections, Works*, vol. 5, p. 100; cf. pp. 80, 352.

6. Cf. Santayana: "It was the vice of liberalism to believe that common interests covered nothing but the sum of those objects which each individual might pursue alone; whereby science, religion, art, language, and nationality itself would cease to be matters of public concern and would appeal to the individual merely as instruments. The welfare of a flock of sheep is secured if each is well fed and watered, but the welfare of a human society involves the partial withdrawal of every member from such pursuits to attend instead to memory and to ideal possessions; these involve a certain conscious continuity and organisation in the state not necessary for animal existence" (*Reason in Society*, p. 141). For further details of Santayana's criticisms of liberalism, see J. Gray, *Post-Liberalism*, ch. 2.

   See also J. Raz, *The Morality Of Freedom*, pp. 251ff., on individual rights as presupposing certain collective goods.

7. See above pp. 154–5, 157 n.10, 158 n.12.

   One notices among socialists an oscillation between the sacrifice of the present to the future, and, when their plans inevitably fail, a series of panic measures which sacrifice long-term advantage to short-term expediency. The Labour Party in Britain, for example, always has it eye on Britain's overseas investments which it would like to cash in order to finance its expansion of welfare provisions.

8. *The Principles of Art*, pp. 69–76.

9. Ibid., ch. 5.

10. Written 1936, and in the Collingwood collection in the Bodleian Library, Oxford (reference DEP 24; 38 pp.). Under the terms of his will, Collingwood's

papers are not available for publication. But a section of "Man Goes Mad" (pp. 16–28) has been published as "Modern Politics" in *R.G. Collingwood: Essays in Political Philosophy*, and other quotations and summaries from it will be found in D. Boucher, *The Social and Political Thought of R.G. Collingwood*, and W.J. Van der Dussen, *History as a Science: The Philosophy of R.G. Collingwood* (p. 268). I have relied upon these extracts from and paraphrases of the latter part of the essay (pp. 29–38) on the role of emotion.

11. See also, *The Principles Of Art*, pp. 79, 102, on the decline of folk art in Britain as a result of the agricultural depression of the 1870s, reinforced by the Education Act of 1870 which made schooling compulsory, and its replacement by a commercial amusement art of the popular press, professional spectator sports, the wireless, and the cinema (and above all today, television).

    That great English patriot, George Orwell (who changed his named from "Eric Blair," unlike the present leader of the Labour Party, as part of his protest against the "Scotchification of England"), once remarked on the blindness of leftists during the War to the feeling of Englishmen for their countryside and their revulsion at the thought of it being overrun by the Germans, a sentiment which was expressed in the wartime song, "There'll always be an England" with its picture of the lane, the thatched cottage, and the cornfield.

    If, as Collingwood says, the health of European civilisation depends partly upon a proper feeling towards Nature and if this is linked to agriculture, then our technological mastery and large populations pose a serious problem. Most people nowadays live in large cities and have little direct contact with the land. They are so used to an artificial environment that perhaps they think that human efforts can do everything. (Hence perhaps some of the feelings of social insecurity which seem to increase in proportion to the extent which insurance and the welfare state protect people against misfortune.) Moreover, farming is now agribusiness and produces more and more with fewer and fewer people. And government assistance seems to promote that trend while producing other harmful effects: the Common Agricultural Policy is a sink of corruption and dumps subsidised exports on poor countries and undermines their farmers. So where do we go from here? Can there be a revival of more intensive "organic" methods? Conservative thinkers and parties have always regarded agriculture as a special case, and not just because of their historical connection with the landed interest as against rising business interests usually represented by Liberal parties. Burke, who, as Adam Smith himself said, was the person who most clearly understood his economics, nevertheless had doubts about the policy of enclosures (as quoted by R. Kirk, *The Conservative Mind* p. 29: I have not been able to trace the reference). Disraeli opposed the repeal of the Corn Laws, yet in 1877, when cheap corn was flooding in from America and Disraeli was prime minister, he said that politically nothing could be done about it. The consequent decline of British farming cost Britain dearly in the two World Wars. See also R. Kirk, op. cit, on the conservatism of the Southern states of America, and Lord Hailsham, *The Case for Conservatism*, on national continuity and a thriving agriculture, the Jews (in Western Europe) being the one great exception. Here is one of the great problems for policy today.

12. Prefigured in the messianic movements of the late Middle Ages and the Ranters in seventeenth-century England: see, N. Cohn, *The Pursuit of the Millennium*. They were movements on a small scale, for the most part. But the Enlightenment, instead of dissipating religious emotions, bereft them of their proper objects, secularised them, and thereby generated in the mass revolutionary movements of the modern age. Cf. Burke: "Man is by his constitution a reli-

gious animal" and when he throws off religion he takes up some degrading superstition (*Reflections*, vol. 5, pp. 173–4). The decline of religious belief results generally, not in a sedate atheism, but unsatisfied emotions which chase after strange gods: pleasure, sex, drugs, art, the nation, the state, the Party, revived paganism, occultism, and witchcraft. Genuine religion and settled society provide homes for the need to belong to something greater than oneself which liberalism has too often ignored. Without them it becomes a desire to lose oneself in subpersonal collectives or drug-induced trances. Again, a free society is imperilled by homeless emotions such as these. The root, but least articulated element, of conservatism is the feeling of identity: we value our traditions and way of life because they are *ours*—they are what we are.

13. "The English and the Continent," *Political Quarterly*, vol. 14, Oct.-Dec. 1943, pp. 380–1. By "nation" we should understand that unit into which a person is born and brought up and with which he identifies himself, whether it be a tribe, city-state, province, or nation in the modern sense. When the political unit is larger and incorporates several of these, then some degree of felt unity—among themselves and to it—is required on the part of the ruling classes within each. Today that means all.

14

Ultimate Questions

The Individual in Modern Philosophy

Liberty and liberalism transcend themselves. We have seen this progressively in each part of this study as we have surveyed, in turn, the work Hayek and Polanyi. The very definition and knowledge of liberty takes us beyond the abstract formulae of any liberalism to concrete and therefore inherited liberties. The case for liberty takes us beyond valuing it, and principally its negative aspect, simply because it is, or will yield in the longer term, what people want, via an acknowledgment of its moral foundations, to redefining it principally in terms of its positive aspect and as the liberty of self-dedication to transcendent ideals. Liberty, therefore, is not after all the highest political good, and the political order transcends itself into the moral order. And a free society cannot be one free from, but one which rests upon and maintains, inherited and traditional obligations and emotional bonds. Politically, any coherent and viable liberalism must be a conservative liberalism or liberal conservatism which seeks both to maintain a traditional order of society and within it gradually to extend, as and when possible, the liberties which it has inherited. Philosophically, liberalism undermines itself if it bases itself upon a rationalist scepticism. Instead, it needs to acknowledge that it presupposes a real and knowable order of values which individuals, groups, and societies can use their liberty to cherish and pursue. We now come to the question, What further, if anything, does liberty presuppose?

In chapter 9 we endorsed Polanyi's argument that the choice we face is one, not between servitude and doing as we please, but between servitude and self-dedication. The value of liberty lies in self-dedication and self-improvement. What we must now consider is if even that is a satisfactory answer.

Polanyi's is evidently a "positive" account of liberty. So too was Bosanquet's in *The Philosophical Theory of the State*. There, his concern was to show how the individual does not stand over and against other individuals, institutions, society, and the state, but is essentially implicated in them, and that they can and do represent a better and higher level of himself below which he falls from time to time, a theme adumbrated in Polanyi's account of the republic of science. But there is more to Bosanquet's argument than what we noted at the time. For his view of the relation of one person to another and to society is essentially a metaphysical one of their substantial identity. This is hinted at and implied in *The Philosophical Theory of the State* rather than explicitly stated. For example, in the Introduction to the second edition he writes of "the supposed self-existent isolatable being," "the particular human being in his repellent isolation," an "ultra-society...above all compulsory group arrangements, and an ultra-individual.... beyond the aspect of exclusiveness, which, however falsely, clings to the current conception of individuality."[1] In the body of the book he states that

> The whole notion of man as one among others tends to break down; and we begin to see something in the one which actually identifies him with the others, and at the same time tends to make him what he admits he ought to be.[2]

Again, the interdependence of minds is "*the mind* of which the visible community is the body."[3] For, as he explicitly stated elsewhere, Bosanquet, like empiricist and analytical philosophy, assumed that a mind *is* its contents, and, unlike empiricist and analytical philosophy, drew the correct inference that minds with the same contents are, or are parts or functions of, one and the same mind.[4] For Bosanquet there is and can be ultimately only *one* individual, namely, the Whole, the Absolute. Consequently, as he also makes very clear, the value of each partial individual is that of his contribution to the Whole, his performance as a cosmic functionary. In himself he is nothing and has no value. For he is distinct from the whole only by the accidents of bodily location, without which finite minds could actually merge and unite into higher unities.

Bosanquet's liberalism is therefore somewhat ambiguous, despite the fact that its practical implications are broadly similar to Hayek's. For, if in the end the individual person is nothing substantial in himself but only an adventitious collection of experiences, just why should he be treated with respect and allowed liberty of action? Bosanquet's answer can only be the utilitarian one that, on the whole and in the long run, more good is achieved by allowing liberty to individuals than by denying it. *They*, in the end, do not matter, only what they contribute to the Whole. But if so, then, when more good can be achieved by overriding their liberty and dignity, there can be no objection to so doing. We replace defective parts in a machine with ones that are properly made and work correctly; we replace less efficient machines with more efficient ones; and, outside of cosseted bureaucracies, incompetent employees are sooner or later replaced by competent ones. I have found no explicit nor implicit repudiation in Bosanquet's writings of Hegel's frank admission of the dispensability of the finite individual when the Whole, the World Spirit, has no more use for him.[5] For all Hegel's incorporation of a level of individual rights and liberty within his rational state which will finally embody the Idea in an objective form, just as his own philosophy embodies it in a subjective form, in the end each person is but a disposable vehicle for the self-realisation of the *Weltgeist,* and intermediate levels of spirits of the time or nation can use any individual embodied spirit in whatever way best furthers the cosmic goal of the self-realisation of the Idea. Bosanquet's Absolute is a static one above time, though including time within itself, and not one coming into being in time and world-history. Yet it includes the same principle of the metaphysical and thence moral subordination of the alleged individual to higher unities and finally to the one Whole.

The revolutionary collectivisms of our age have taken the same view of the individual. Each person, each generation, is but a stage in the process of realising the End of history, and has no value in himself or in itself. It was Lenin's strength that he acted ruthlessly on these premises, and used everything and everyone around him without any sentimental attachments. Conversely, any belief in the value and freedom of the individual presupposes that each person has a substantive value in and for himself. There is no moral case for a liberalism that merely asserts what people want, either openly or dressed up as a claim to Natural Rights.

But where in modern thought do we find a conception of the real individuality and unique value of the person? Max Scheler complained time and time again, and rightly, that always it is assumed that the individual is constituted as a one among and distinct from others only by his bodily location. Either, as in behaviourism or crude materialism, he *is* his body or its movements and no more, or his body, by locating him here and now and not there and then, causes him to have different experiences from each other person. Consequently, *he* is nothing in himself and therefore can have no inherent value. Alternatively, and even more starkly, the individual in Sartre's "black" existentialism, and in contemporary analytic philosophy, is a "nothingness," a "fold in being," an empty self, condemned only to choose and thus, at every moment, to choose himself.[6]

But what about Kant and his Categorical Imperative that requires us to respect humanity in ourselves and others and never to use each other merely as means but as ends in ourselves?[7] But that is not what Kant says. What he forbids, as his subsequent examples show, is that we should not use each other just as means to *our own* ends. There is nothing at all about us not being essentially means for the realisation of something else. On the contrary, each of us has no value in and as himself. What has value, as Kant clearly states, is rational humanity. We are only temporary embodiments of it, and, in Kant's philosophy as in the empiricism and rationalism which it tries to combine, the individual is such only by the accidents of his bodily location in space and time. Ideally and really, there is but one rational process of thought, and thus one substantive mind, from which we are separated by the nonrational and morally irrelevant effects of our bodies which cause us to have different experiences. In computer-speak, there is and can be only one set of rational software: it is the pieces of hardware which cause the inputs and thus the outputs to differ from individual to individual. There is no "autonomy of the person," only the "autonomy of reason."[8] Furthermore, Kant's ethics is one of imperatives, and thus of deeds to be done. Consequently, the person has meaning only as their executor.[9] Whatever his personal politics, Kant's general philosophy offers uncertain support for human liberty.

The same applies even to Polanyi's liberty for self-dedication, as far as it explicitly goes. For what makes that liberty valuable, and to be respected, is the transcendent ideals for which it is to be used. And, in turn, the value of the individual lies in his service of those ideals, and, consequently, in what he produces within or without himself. His worth can only be that of what he produces or achieves.[10] Elsewhere I have argued that, although one plausible cosmological application of Polanyi's ontology of comprehensive entities, is a conception, akin to that of Bradley's and Bosanquet's Absolute Idealism, of the world as a whole indwelt and united by a world-soul, this cannot be carried through because it would abolish the personal coefficient that is the individual knower and agent.[11] Nevertheless, while the reality of the personal coefficient must be acknowledged, that does not entail that his value lies in himself and not in his functions and products.

What liberty and liberalism therefore need is a conception of the individual as a substance and a value in his own right, and therefore a unique, irreplaceable, and unrepeatable individuality, what Scheler called a "value-essence." European civilisation, and with it European law and liberty, is based on that idea, although its explicit philosophy has rarely recognised it and, increasingly in the modern world, has too often explicitly denied it. And when we seek for the sources of that belief, we find that, just as the political order transcends itself into the moral order, as we have already seen, so the moral order transcends itself into the theological order.

Freedom and Faith

Let us return to Collingwood's "Fascism and Nazism." I should like to quote at length two passages, the latter of which, were one to meet it unseen, one would take to be by Polanyi:

> The real ground for the "liberal" or "democratic" devotion to freedom was religious love of a God who set an absolute value on every individual human being. Free speech and free inquiry concerning political and scientific questions; free consent in issues arising out of economic activity; free enjoyment of the produce won by a man's own labour—the opposite of all tyranny and oppression, exploitation and robbery—these were ideals based on the infinite dignity or worth of the human individual; and this again was based on the fact that God loved the human individual and Christ had died for him. The doctrines concerning human nature on which liberal or democratic practice was based were not empirically derived from research into anthropological and psychological data; they were a matter of faith; and these Christian doctrines were the source from which they derived.[12]

> In the last two hundred years Christianity has suffered a curious double fate. Whatever in it is capable of logical formulation as a system of first principles has been analysed and codified and has come to function as the axioms upon which our sciences of nature and history, our practice in liberal economics and free or democratic politics—in short, all the things which make up our civilisation, are built. But whatever is not capable of logical formulation, whatever is in the nature of religious emotion, passion, faith, has been progressively exterminated, partly by ridicule and partly by force, under the names of superstition and magic. The two processes have gone hand in hand. The same men who have been most eager to formulate the principles in which Christianity has trained them have been most active in suppressing the "irrational" or emotional elements in Christianity itself.[13]

The results of this process have been a merely assertive liberalism, the liberty to do as one likes just because one likes it, and a weakening of the emotional faith that animates society and civilisation. That Collingwood identifies with religion. It is

> the passion which inspire a society to persevere in a certain way of life and to obey the rules which define it. Without a conviction that this way of life is a thing

of absolute value, and that its rules must be obeyed at all costs, the rules become dead letters and the way of life a thing of the past. The civilisation dies because the people to whom it belonged have lost faith in it.[14]

The Illuminism or Enlightenment of the eighteenth century, continues Collingwood, developed first principles which in fact derived from Christianity, but also waged war upon superstition and magic, especially as found in Christianity. In turn that led to the orthodoxy of the nineteenth century, a scientific attitude towards everything except religion. The idea of freedom was taken from Christianity but no other grounds were given for it. For example, J.S. Mill could not escape from the dilemma of utilitarianism, in which liberty is not an end in itself, or intuitionism, in which there are no grounds for anything. (We have seen that von Mises, openly, and Hayek, more subtly, are in the same position, while Popper gives no positive case for liberty at all.) The result is that today (1940) fascism and nazism have tapped a source of power—remnants of pre-Christian paganism—which free societies lack. The latters' principles have no "punch" and have become mere habit. Collingwood's conclusion is that:

> The time has long gone by when anyone who claims the title of philosopher can think of religion as a superfluity for the educated and an "opiate for the masses." It is the only known explosive in the economy of that delicate internal-combustion engine, the human mind. Peoples rich in religious energy can overcome all obstacles and attain any height in the scale of civilisation. Peoples that have reached the top of a hill by the wise use of religious energy may then decide to do without it; they can still move, but they can only move downhill, and when they come to the bottom of the hill, they stop.[15]

Of course, there was much that Collingwood had missed out in his account of how things had come to the crisis of 1940, in particular, what Voegelin calls "the immanentisation of the eschaton," the secularisation of Christian eschatology. On the one hand, it took the form of a belief in Progress, that, by and large the world was entering a new and happier state of life *in* rather than *to* which there would be yet better things to come. This was the driving force of liberalism, which held that the motive power of Progress was the liberation of the individual and his energy from customary restraints and superstitions. And there are echoes of that belief still in von Mises, Popper, and Hayek. Indeed, it is curious that, for all his repudiation of historicism, Popper has his own schema of world-history: the Dark Ages of closed and tribal societies and superstition up to the seventeenth century, when occurred the break-through to reason, science, and the Open Society.

And Hayek's ultimate case for liberty seems to be that it is the ascending line of evolutionary progress. But surely Polanyi was right to say that we cannot tell where freedom in society will lead us, and that perhaps it may lead us beyond freedom. He suggested that, for example, atomic weapons might one day be produced so cheaply that only a global police authority, strictly supervising the whole race, could sustain human existence. Hence the free pursuit of natural science may one day have to be curtailed. Likewise technological developments might render the market redundant or impossible and with it much of our judicial system. "There are many ways in which the most precious liberties of today may cease to be relevant or even admissible" (LL, pp. 197–8). Can a secular liberalism continue without a belief in Progress? On the other hand, the secularisation of Christian hope took the forms of a rebirth of pre-Christian paganism with some millenarian colouring and of an immanentised Gnosticism, a radical freedom from finitude to be achieved by total collectivisation leading dialectically to total freedom, but resulting, in fact and because of its hatred of the existing and every other order, in wanton destruction relieved only by an iron tyranny. It was these two forces which, in the twentieth century, produced the most compelling threats to liberty.

Fortunately, a rebirth of national feeling, on which even Stalin had to draw, and of that sense of a moral mission which is peculiarly American, saved liberty against fascist and nazi paganism,[16] and then, for forty or so more years outfaced the Soviet threat until it collapsed because of its own inefficiency and loss of faith. This brings us back to the point we reached at the end of the last chapter: Whence can come the emotion and faith to sustain liberty in the future?

For two things can safely be asserted: that, as at the beginning of this study Polanyi was quoted as saying, disillusionment has no positive power, and that civilisation and liberty will not go unchallenged and unthreatened in the future, either from without or from within. This answers the objection that historical derivation is one thing and logical implication another. Because European civilisation, liberty and sciences have been formed by Christian belief—in the ultimate and inherent value of the individual person himself; in the reality of the world and time; in its rational and hence intelligible structure which, being freely created, cannot be deduced *a priori* but must be discovered by observation and experimentation; in the goodness of the world and in the possibility of redeeming what is corrupted in it; in a providential order that is leading the world to a consummation beyond itself and so not to be brought in by merely human efforts nor within the world; in which also, as Leopold von Ranke said in opposition to Hegel's immanentist scheme of world-history, every age is immediate to God and has its value in itself; in the legitimacy of human government for the affairs of this world but not for the next; in the necessity of tackling the problems of the moment and not of trying to attain some atemporal Utopia; and in the desacralisation of any particular way of life and thus in the legitimacy of all, and the liberty of people to live them, so long as they do not offend that Natural Law which all can recognise without benefit of Revelation—it is sometimes supposed that they can continue substantially without it. But while habit alone can sustain human life, individually and collectively, for a time and while familiar situations recur, habit without deep conviction cannot deal with what is novel nor face up to danger and hardship. This is the fundamental problem of free societies today. What deep convictions can sustain them in the trials to come, whatever they may turn out to be?

It is a problem which Hayek recognises at the end of *The Fatal Conceit*. Mystical and religious beliefs, he writes, especially monotheistic ones, have enabled beneficial traditions to be preserved and transmitted so that the groups which have held them have grown and spread by natural or cultural selection. Consequently the loss of those beliefs in "symbolic truths," which are not true, verifiable, or testable in the same way as scientific ones are, causes great difficulties, whether they are in fact true or not and although historical connections do not entail logical ones. The only religions which have survived are those which have supported property and the family—or, we may add, which have compromised with the family as in the Hindu system of the four stages of life, with world- and self-renunciation as the last, for any thoroughgoing Gnostic rejection of procreation will soon die out. Hence there is little future for communism which opposes both, and, we may also add, for those forms of neutral liberalism and libertarianism which regard the family as but one legitimate "experiment in living" among many others.

> Perhaps most people can conceive of abstract tradition only as a personal Will. If so, will they not be inclined to find this will in "society" in an age in which more overt supernaturalisms are ruled out as superstitions?
> On that question may rest the survival of our civilisation. (FC, p. 140)

One solution can be ruled out: the utilitarianism of the Enlightenment which, dry and rationalist as in Voltaire or warm and sentimental as in Rousseau, would use religion to sustain the social order by using the threat of punishment in the next world for antisocial conduct in this. Burke saw through that as through the other delusions of his age. In an early notebook he wrote:

> If you attempt to make the end of Religion to be its utility to human society, to make it only a sort of supplement to the law, and insist principally upon this topic.... you then change its principle of operation, which consists in views beyond this life, to a consideration of another kind, and of an inferior kind; and by thus forcing it against its nature to be a political engine, you make it an engine of no efficiency at all.[17]

Years later he wrote that the rulers of England

> would be ashamed...to profess any religion in name, which, by their proceedings they appear to condemn. If by their conduct (the only language that rarely lies) they seemed to regard the great ruling principle of the moral and natural world, as a mere invention to keep the vulgar in obedience, they apprehend that by such a conduct they would defeat the politic purpose they had in view. They would find it difficult to make others believe in a system to which they manifestly gave no credit themselves.[18]

Religious faith, above all, cannot be used. It must be held as true and supremely important in itself and totally apart from any other and secular benefits it may bring. If, as Burke also held,

> All persons possessing any portion of power ought to be strongly and awfully impressed with an idea that they act in trust; and that they are to account for their conduct in that trust to the one great Master, Author and Founder of society,[19]

then that can come about only as they themselves are first convinced of the existence and justice of God. It seems that Collingwood made just this mistake, in effect. For, as already noted, he apparently deprived Christian belief of its theological content and reduced it just to an emotional force or used "religious faith" to mean any passionate conviction. Hence it is the worldly effects of faith that matter, rather than its intrinsic content and orientation.

"The Spirit bloweth where it listeth," and no man can force the hand of God. The most that human endeavours can do is to open human ears and hearts to it. This is what Polanyi realised. On several occasions he argued that the removal of the distortions of objectivism and reductionism which the modern mind has imposed upon itself, and the regaining of a saner and coherent picture of the world such as he himself tried to provide, can prepare the way for a rebirth of religious faith.[20] On the last page of *The Tacit Dimension*, he repeats the point made several times before, that no one can know where a free Society of Explorers is going. Evolution has produced mainly plants and animals which are satisfied with a brief existence. But men need "a purpose which bears on eternity." Where is it to be found?

> Truth does that; our ideals do it; and this might be enough, if could ever be satisfied with our manifest moral shortcomings and with a society which has such shortcomings fatally involved in its workings.
> Perhaps this problem cannot be resolved on secular grounds alone. But its religious solution should become more feasible once religious faith is released from pressure by an absurd vision of the universe, and so there will open up instead a meaningful world which could resound to religion. (TD, p. 92)

Polanyi's endeavour was to dissipate pictures of the world as absurd and to restore the possibility of meaning.

A religious revival, Polanyi thought, was but one of several alternative possibilities to revolutionary fanaticism based on scepticism, which he saw to be declining and which, in its most organised and menacing form, has fortunately collapsed in recent years. A rebirth of national feeling, as we have already seen, was another, although it too has its dangers; a third is a return of the sceptical tolerance of the Enlightenment in rejecting ideological strife today as originally it rejected religious conflict; and a fourth is a "more clear-sighted political conscience" like the suspended logic of Anglo-American liberalism, a civic partnership resolved on continuous reforms yet restraining its dynamism by the knowledge that to take the principles of radicalism seriously would once again lead to disaster ("Beyond Nihilism," KB, pp. 21–3). Later he added two other possibilities: romantic enlightenment and the existentialism that has descended from it and said that there could be others.[21] Between those two statements, he had suggested that it would be impossible to go back to the original Enlightenment and that it was necessary to purge it of its deficiencies:

> At our present level of consciousness we cannot build safely on the metaphysical presuppositions of a free society, while holding fast to principles of free thought and free individualism which refuse any commitment to such presuppositions. The modern mind must continue to work its own destruction, and to work it most vigorously when it is at its most incisive and most generous, so long as it fails to reach a vision of itself—and of the universe around itself—within which the unlimited demands of the modern mind can be seen to require their own framework of intrinsic limitations.[22]

But this, and the hope for a revival of a temperate reformism which suspends its logic, surely contradict what Polanyi argued elsewhere.

Logic cannot be suspended in the long term. Either people will go forward again to act upon it or they will go back and radically revise their premises.

It seems to me that, on the one hand, Polanyi recognised, in revivals of national feeling and of the reformism and dynamism of the Enlightenment in a more sober form, the principal proximate alternatives to destructive ideology, and that, on the other, he also thought that perhaps only a revival of religious faith and the Christian understanding of man and the world could be the ultimate basis of a free and orderly society, yet he himself, like many others today, could not personally take that step. That seems to me the position we are in. We have gone beyond nihilism, except as it is now diverted into other destructive passions, as in the terrorism of a few remaining Marxists, Arab nationalists, Islamic radicals, the Irish Republican Army, and some "animal rights" groups; in disillusion we have gone back to a chastened demand for reform, although there is still too much egalitarianism and *dirigisme* around; but we do not yet have a firm or even a partial hold upon the metaphysical, and (I would add) theological, presuppositions of a free society which Polanyi himself did much to articulate.

With Hayek, and even more so Polanyi, we have come a long way from the nihilism implicit in the suspended logic of the negative and sceptical liberalism manifested by von Mises and Popper. It remains, in my opinion, to take the final transpolitical step to the full-blown Christian politics of the archetypical conservatism of Edmund Burke, a step taken by Polanyi's slightly younger contemporary from Budapest, Aurel Kolnai, whose later political essays are summarised in the Appendix. Otherwise, here we must end. As Polanyi said:

> This is hardly a legitimate field for speculation; for from here onwards, thought must take the form of action. (KB, p. 23)

Notes

1. Bosanquet, *The Philosophical Theory of the State*, pp. xxxiii–xxxiv.
2. Ibid., p. 95.
3. Ibid., p. 196.
4. See *The Principle of Individuality and Value*, especially pp. 20–2, and *The Value and Destiny of the Individual*, especially pp. 260–1, 282–3, 328.
   Contrast Nozick who makes the same assumptions, plays with notions of minds splitting, but does not think at all of minds merging or reuniting (*Philosophical Explanations*, ch. 1) See Hume, *Treatise*, vol. 1, bk. 1, pt. 4 §6, on the mind as a collection of impressions and ideas.
5. See *Reason in History* (the Introduction to the *Lectures on World History*) pp. 65, 69–71, 89, 90, 91.

6. See Iris Murdoch, *The Sovereignty of Good*, ch. 1.
7. *Grundlegung*, pp. 66–7 (*The Moral Law*, p. 91).
8. See Scheler, *Formalism*, pp. 372–3.
9. Ibid., p. 184.
10. Cf. Gray, *Post-Liberalism*, p. 309, who argues against the assumptions, in what he characterises as liberalism, that only the states of minds of individuals have value, and that there are no collective or inherently public goods. For if choice and autonomy have value, then it is necessary to have a rich cultural environment in which they can be exercised and exercised in a worthwhile manner. Consequently, the practices of that environment, such as art and science, must themselves be inherently valuable, apart from what they add to the lives of any individual. Therefore the states of mind of individuals are not the only objects which have value. Furthermore, autonomous choices have value only as they range over valuable options, and so it is those practices, and not the states of mind of individuals, which are ultimately of value. Gray rightly deduces from the inherent value of cultural practices that it is they rather than its individual practitioners which should have entrenched rights. That is what Polanyi meant by "public liberties": see above, ch. 9 §1. What we are seeking is a conception in which both activities and individuals have inherent value and therefore rights.
11. *Transcendence and Immanence in the Philosophy of Michael Polanyi and Christian Theism*, ch. 6 §A.
12. "Fascism and Nazism" (*Philosophy,* 1940), reprinted in *Essays in Political Philosophy*, p. 190. See also C.J. Friedrich, *Transcendent Justice: The Religious Dimensions of Constitutionalism*.
13. Ibid, pp. 188–9. In this very passage Collingwood betrays something of the very attitude that he therein repudiates. For he omits the theological axiomatisation of Christian belief, one of the central tenets of which he himself states in the other passage quoted. Consequently, he appears to reduce Christianity to an emotional faith without an intellectual content of its own. Collingwood in his youth reacted strongly against the realism (empiricism) of Oxford philosophy, and sought an alternative firstly in a Christian philosophy (*Religion and Philosophy* 1916, but written earlier), and then in his own brand of Hegelianism (*Speculum Mentis*, 1924). Thereafter the Hegelian elements in his thinking steadily declined, and the Christian became dominant again. Yet the latter never wholly dominated the former nor the residual elements of empiricism. Consequently, Collingwood's attitude to Christianity remained ambiguous: he accepted it as the presuppositions of his other beliefs but not so much as its own doctrinal content. (See *The New Leviathan*, ch. 8, §§8:38–9 on Christianity as a religion of unsatisfied love.)

    In that, as in many other ways, he was like Polanyi. Elsewhere (*Transcendence and Immanence*, pp. 70–3). I have suggested that Polanyi's own theological position, insofar as it can be ascertained, was something like a Catholic modernism, valuing the social and moral roles of the Church and its rites, but hesitant about the articles of its faith.
14. Ibid. p. 168. Collingwood also identified religion with the holding, maintenance, and transmission of the absolute presuppositions of a civilisation as opposed to their articulation and elaboration (*Essay on Metaphysics*, pp. 197–8). But that is, on occasions, to equate it with a wholly secular function.
15. Ibid., p. 176.
16. Not that nazism was merely pagan. Hitler's "Third Reich" was coined by Moeller von der Bruck in 1923. By obscure channels it descended from the original source of all such conceptions, Joachim of Fiore, who provided a general schema

into which all manner of diverse contents could be fitted. Likewise there were other elements in Mussolini's fascism, such as futurism.

On one pagan element in nazism, see Kolnai, *The War against the West* (p. 220): its worship of Life, its heathen naturalism and vitalism. Kolnai comments, with reference also to Heidegger, that life, in that sense, also includes death as its culmination. "For the naked, vital story of life and death, the latter is the final and decisive event that moulds the phenomena of life." Cf. the cry of Millán Astray, the founder (in the 1920s) of the Spanish Foreign Legion (the "bride-grooms of death"): *Viva la muerte!*

17. "Religion of No Efficiency considered as a State Engine," in *A Note-Book of Edmund Burke*, p. 67.

18. *Reflections, Works*, vol. 5, pp. 191–2.

19. *Reflections, Works*, vol. 5, pp. 177–8. See also p. 180: "When the people have emptied themselves of all the lust of selfish will, which without religion it is utterly impossible they ever should, when they are conscious that they exercise perhaps in a higher link of the order of delegation the power which to be legitimate must be according to that eternal, immutable law, in which will and reason are the same, they will be more careful how they place power in base and incapable hands. In their nomination to office, they will not appoint to the exercise of authority, as to a pitiful job, but as to a holy function; not according to their sordid, selfish interest, nor to their wanton caprice, nor to their arbitrary will; but they will confer that power (which any man may well tremble to give or to receive) on those only, in whom they may discern that predominant proportion of active virtue and wisdom, taken together and fitted to the charge, as in the great and inevitable mixed mass of human imperfections and infirmities, is to be found."

20. For example, the end of *Personal Knowledge*; "Faith and Reason" (*J. of Religion*, Oct. 1961); *The Tacit Dimension* pp. 91–2; "Science and Religion: Separate Dimensions or Common Ground?" (*Philosophy Today*, no. 7, Spring 1963).

21. "A Postscript" in (ed.) K.A. Jelenski, *History and Hope*, p. 194 and *Society, Economics, and Philosophy*, p. 103.

22. "History and Hope," *Virginia Quarterly Review*, vol. 33, no. 2, Spring 1962, p. 195, and *Society, Economics, and Philosophy*, p. 93.

Appendix
The Conservatism of Aurel Kolnai

As stated in the Introduction, the political writings of Aurel Kolnai most clearly illustrate the argument of this study, but many of them, including all the earlier ones, have not been available to me. Dr. Francis Dunlop has kindly provided me with copies of some of the later ones.

In his *Exile and Social Thought*, Mr. Lee Congdon gives details of Kolnai's career and writings up to 1933. Kolnai was born in Budapest in 1900 into a liberal Jewish family. An atheist at the age of twelve, he admired Jászi and joined the Galilei Circle, founded by Karl and Michael Polanyi. He was attracted to psychoanalysis as a way for reforming society. He belonged to the Freudian Left as a Liberal and not a Marxist Socialist. He supported Karolyi's government and joined the silenced opposition under the Kun régime. In July 1919 he left Hungary with his parents, first to Czechoslovakia and then to Austria. In 1921 he began to read G.K. Chesterton and became a Roman Catholic in 1923–4. In 1922 he entered the University of Vienna to study philosophy, and left in 1926. In 1927 he published his doctoral dissertation, *Ethical Value and Reality*, which, among things, includes a conservative theory of reform as requiring acceptance of background. He opposed the movements to corporatism in both Austrian politics and Roman Catholic social policy. In 1930 he joined the new League of Religious Socialists and was associated with Karl Polanyi who advocated guild socialism. But in 1934 he published "Der Aufgabe des Konservatismus," opposed to the destruction of *Gemeinschaft*. At the Anschluss in 1938 he left Austria for Paris and published *The War against the West*.

In 1940 he was forced into exile for a third time and went to the United States, and then to Canada where he taught at the Laval University in Quebec. In 1959 he moved for the last time, to London, where he taught at Bedford College in the University of London. He died in June 1973.

In *The Utopian Mind and Other Papers* (pp. vi–vii) Dr. Dunlop includes Kolnai's own brief account of his intellectual development:

In a very broad sense, devoid of any "school" allegiance, I might describe my frame of mind as Aristotelian. As a student of philosophy, I was most directly influenced by modern German neo-objectivism and phenomenology (Franz Brentano, Edmund Husserl, Max Scheler, Dietrich von Hildebrand), and some kindred English and Spanish thinkers such as G.E. Moore and C.D. Broad, and Ramiro de Maeztu. Later, my philosophical thinking came to be stimulated also by some aspects of Scholasticism (Aquinas, Duns Scotus, Luis de Molina) on the one hand, contemporary British logical empiricism on the other. My political outlook has been moulded, as concerns direct and indirect literary influences, by such older classics as Vittoria, Richard Hooker, John Locke, Samuel Johnson, Edmund Burke, Tocqueville, Lord Acton and Jacob Burckhardt, and by more recent writers like Irving Babbitt, Sir Ernest Barker, Hermann Heller, Clive Bell, Wilhelm Röpke, Alfred Cobban, José Ortega y Gasset, F.A. Voigt, Christopher Hollis, C.A. Macartney, Claude Sutton and others. Particularly would I mention, in the context of the present subject matter, Karl Mannheim (*Ideology and Utopia; Diagnosis of Our Time*), Raymond Ruyer (*L'Utopie et les utopies*), and K.R. Popper (*The Open Society and Its Enemies*).

I shall now summarise Kolnai's distinctively Christian conservatism as presented in the items that I have been able to read.

In *La Divinizacion y la Suma Esclavitud del Hombre*, he argues that communism, aiming to make man totally his own master, necessarily ends by submitting him to a total slavery. It promises total emancipation—from kings, nobles, priests, capitalists, supernatural powers, and the natural roots of human frailty and contingency. It is the consummation of modernity, from the Renaissance through the rationalism of the Enlightenment, liberalism, utilitarianism, to quantitative science, mass democracy, and contemporary socialism, all focused in the French Revolution. It is the solution to the antimony of the raising of man above his natural status and his denigration to the level of mechanical materiality, an object which can be conditioned and at the same time ruled in the sovereign personification of scientific reason, released from religion and traditional ties, subject and agent of his own determination by the mechanism of his material structure and a calculable necessity, void of all meaning anterior to his own will (cf. Bentham and Skinner). It aims to raise men to a quasi "supernatural" level, only in order to subvert his natural state, by means of certain potentialities of his nature: indetermination, malleability, emptiness, the "nothing" which envelopes the nature of man. Just as in theology God is omniscient because he is the Creator, so the man-God of Marxism knows everything through a universal science, and makes the man of the future, using the "prime matter" of the proletarians who have been divested of all forms and concrete and finite possessions. Communism is the self-divinisation of man, by way of a total concentration of power, which inevitably ends in his self-enslavement. It is the fullest expression of the idea of (collective) freedom *through* the State in contrast to (individual) freedom *against* the State.

Communism is the fullest expression of, and attempt to realize, a Utopian dream. That whole outlook is examined in *Critica de las Utopias Politicas* and "La mentalité utopienne."[1] Utopias are essentially tyrannical because they are alien to human reality. They seek to lift men out of time and space, sexuality and its divergent roles for men and women, contingency, and all tensions and divisions. They are based upon a monism of value, in which one value is taken to include all the others, so that there can be no free, personal choice among them. Thence arise their oppressive atmospheres. Either the world must be changed to suit Utopian men or men must be changed to suit the world of Utopia by means of an extreme tyranny which diminishes them. They would eliminate conscience by refashioning men so that they are automatically good. The prudence of the individual would be replaced by the "human providence" of the pre-Utopian creator of Utopia. In seeking to overcome divisions among men, Utopianism creates a new and permanent one, human spontaneity which it aims to make sovereign, in the planners of Utopia, and to exclude at the same time, in those who will live in Utopia. It aims to trace "objectifications" back to a "pure humanity" and then to eliminate them. But it makes them only more overwhelming because they then represent only the decisions and directives of given human wills, instead of being "found," interpreted and adjusted to concrete situations by human reason which does not create them, and of being the support rather than the limitation of man's moral being (cf. ch. 6 above, on Popper). Because there is only *one* public will in Utopia, the "alienation" of the individual in face of will which he does not recognise as his own, is taken to the extreme just when it is supposed finally to be overcome. Utopianism cannot escape from this deep self-contradiction: the will to impose that which is most alien to man, the abolition of "alienation," upon the fundamental structure of man's links with himself, his fellows, his past and his mental categories. And the "imperfect," "prehistoric" planner, formed and encumbered by the legacy and defects of the non-Utopian past, yet claims to be the free and omnipotent creator of the perfect man of Utopia, the man who will be more than man but is yet a puppet of one less than man.

Kolnai, it can be seen, presents a radical and therefore metaphysical and theological criticism of Utopianism in general, and communism in particular, as the desire of a free and sovereign human reason, recognising nothing above and beyond itself, to recreate man and the world. Conversely, human freedom must recognise man's created status under God and Divine and moral law. It is the error of liberalism and liberal democracy, or of many of their advocates, to share the same fundamental tenets and goals of communism, and thus to be attracted to it, to present partial and inadequate criticisms of it, and to prepare the way for it. That is the argument of *Errores del Anticomunismo*.

Yet, as can be seen in "Notas Sobre la Utopia Reaccionaria,"[2] Kolnai equally repudiated the converse attempt to fix men in a supposedly perfect state of society which is thought already to have existed. That is as much a betrayal of tradition as is "progressivism" and Utopianism of the future. For tradition is inherently flexible and requires progress as its complement, just as progress presupposes tradition which has primacy over it. Conservation is the first act of life, but life and survival imply change. Reactionary Utopias negate reality in denying the need for change, progress and reform, and so copy the style of the subversive fanaticisms which they oppose. They falsify the very traditions which they seek to preserve, and, again like progressivism, aim to impose an imaginary existence upon reality. They seek to incarcerate men in a supposedly eternal reality here below, whereas the mission of tradition is to keep men, in changing and divergent conditions, in contact with a supratemporal order of values, and thus to preserve the difference between the two.

In "Privilège et liberté"[3] Kolnai criticises the egalitarian ideology of "the common man," man as good simply and purely because he is "only a man," which leads from liberal democracy to communist totalitarianism. Kolnai argues that genuine anticommunists must frankly proclaim Privilege and Hierarchy. Privilege is a way of attaining to the Good by participation in it. The Good is above and beyond man, not created by him. He therefore participates in it, and response, and not *fiat*, is man's primal act. In contrast, Emancipation and Equality propose Identity, the identity of man with himself and with others, in a single, sovereign and collective consciousness and will, emancipated from divisions, tensions, contradictions, and alienations, in which all equally share or which equally represents all. In the perspective of Participation there is, on the one hand, the Common Good, in which all can participate, but, on the other, there are also diverse private goods which are both distinct from it and cannot be reduced to one identical aspiration or will of all. Privilege, precisely because no actual set of privileges and the persons who enjoy them do nor can conform to the system of real values, represents those elements of human imperfection in relation to God and of contingency and "inexplicability" in human life which the ideology of Emancipation, Equality, and Identity wishes to overcome. A society without privilege necessarily reduces the person to zero in front of the community and simultaneously divinises him as identical with it. The outlook of "the common man" is little disposed to tolerate anything superior, different, or strange. Atheist humanitarianism has to focus upon uniformity and qualitative identity among individuals, reducing them to a common "type," because its "common good" is indeterminate since it is derived from man's own will and not from a Being or Law which transcends him. That renders the idea of "liberty under the law" a self-contradiction, for the law, being solely the will of others, is alien to me and blocks my liberty. Communism is the serious attempt to realise the only true liberty of "the common man," man raised to the rank of divinity, society identical with the individual (cf. "the Republic one and indivisible" of the French Revolution), and the State identical with society, implied in the emancipation of man from God, from the "chains which bind him," from Natural Law and the moral order, and from divisions, lack of power and imperfection.[4]

In particular, Kolnai refers to the new freedoms "from want and fear" as indications of how the mentality of "the common man" turns against liberty and towards planning. Communism can promise to fulfil the promises of Democracy because totalitarianism is implied in liberal democracy itself, in its combination of "popular sovereignty" and "the rights of the individual," each of which expresses a fundamental dimension of the sovereign self-determination of man (collectivist *through the State*, and individualist *against the State*). The delicate balance between these two is preserved, not by constitutional mechanisms, but by survivals of a different and older order in which the ideal and very idea of the unlimited self-sovereignty of man is denied and condemned. The social order of liberal democracy rests upon axioms, traditions, and habits which transcend its own framework and impose certain limits upon both popular sovereignty and individual liberty. The abstract idea of liberty, the mere *fiat* of human will and the liberty of each to do what he pleases so long as he respects the equal rights of others, cannot by itself be the basis of a liberal social order. Only "liberty under the reign of God" implies an intrinsically limited liberty, which can be developed in institutions, is inherent in the rational nature of man as a creature of God and as placed by God as a responsible agent in a moral order. The true liberty of man, including his civil liberty, his constitutional self-government and right to an equal justice, has its true place in a *conservative* idea of society, with civil liberties, autonomy of regions and other groups, and the participation of a large part of the electorate in the tasks of the State. A *liberal* conception of society sustains liberty only in contradictory fashion by resting upon conservative values which it tolerates officially but continually harasses by a dialectic immanent in liberal democracy. It is the substance—conservative, Christian, hierarchic, pluralist, realist, and "finitist"—of our civilisation which has made and sustains liberal democracy, but that substance has been practically derived of formal expression and explicit defence (cf. Collingwood, as quoted in ch. 14). The liberal idea of the absolute liberty of each individual limited only by the equally absolute liberty of others, is suicidal, for it leads to the communist (or generally collectivist) principle of the absolute liberty of the individual as the absolute power of "all" in their effective identity. Liberalism conceives the unity of human groups as a collocation of discrete "parts." But an effective compromise among men can be attained, not by mutual respect for the absolute liberty of each, but only by a common acknowledgment of real values, laws, and authorities.[5]

The historic root of liberty is Privilege and its extension from some to many. Its extension to all may appear to be its elimination, but that is not so. The rights of the citizen depend upon certain exemplary privileges, necessarily reserved to a minority. In contrast the idea of "the common man" implies Identity, the reign of one human will, which, when "noncommon" factors have been suppressed (a levelling of men to a common set of desires, a uniform mass), will represent the will of each and so will coincide with absolute justice and rationality. But in fact democracy insists on division, limitation, and cooperation based on distinction. The rule of law, respect for customs and statutes, historic and religious allegiances, the idea of governmental responsibility, the theory of checks and balances, and government by consent, all these seek to prevent any arbitrary dominion of man by man, not in levelling men into a monistic humanity of self-idolatry, but in protecting men against the arbitrary use of power. They all presuppose a difference between the common good and individual or group wills, between the governors and the governed. Likewise the ideas of the independent citizen, the franchise, and parliamentary representation presuppose distinction, diversity, inequality, and the recognition and extension of privileged positions. Marxists are right to say that social economic and therefore political privileges continues within the formal equality of liberal democracy, although they wrongly minimise the importance of that formal equality and exaggerate the role of economic inequality. For privilege is a pattern of conscious and specialised "points of interblending" between the private and the common good. Those two goods cannot be served by splitting the individual into a civic and private personality (*à la* Mill), and the coalescence of civic personalities into one, indivisible and coordinating public will aimed at the common good. This dualism within liberalism succumbs in the end to its implicit monism: the complete identification of common and private goods in "the common man." But liberty requires a diversified system of particular groups with their own perspectives, visions, virtues, loyalties, responsibilities and the like. That means privilege. Privilege is always open to abuse but the attempt to eliminate abuse by creating a meritocracy emerging from a system of competition and equal starting conditions, would require a unique centre determining everything by its own arbitrary and omnipotent will. Privilege is a means for penetrating life with higher values and aspects of the common good which essentially transcend the scope of government. It is a rampart of liberty, not just of the privileged but of all, because it safeguards the existence of relatively independent persons almost commensurable with the state, as opposed to the equal citizen of Jacobin democracy who is only an anonymous molecule of society. Privilege is therefore a limitation upon the power of the state, is limited in its own sphere, and limits other privileges. All can count as "something" because certain persons do. Privilege makes possible an unequal but real liberty. Because there are wealthy men and so centres of relatively independent capital and interests, a poor man can have his own dignity, extract himself from the collective, and can resist the power of his masters and the state much more successfully than he could defy the sole power of "the we." Liberty is more extensive and robust in a true, conservative democracy which recognises values greater than prosperity and therefore a domain of qualitative privileges other than wealth (cf. Polanyi on public liberties for groups and individuals dedicated to transcendent ideals). Even in "monopolist" capitalism the monopolists are limited by the division, independence, and competition inherent in the market. Capitalism, even if monopolistic, plutocratic, and inclined to a levelling uniformity of values, represents more essentially than socialism the cause of human dignity and political liberty for it counteracts the (collectivist) self-enslavement of man. To seek to install liberty by removing all relations of power and dependence, all hierarchies, established authorities, inequalities, and presumptions of superiority, is in reality to concentrate all power in one collective subject, supposedly embodying the "rational will" of all, on whose decrees the whole of society will depend. The only conception of political liberty opposed to this collectivism is that based on a division of social power beyond formal schemes of the separation of powers and Liberal juridical theory.[6] Privilege, though it is not a proportionate index of liberty nor the sole safeguard of it, is the ultimate and supreme presupposition of all liberty and the principle of the objectivity of value and the submission of man to God. We can secure liberty, not by abolishing power, but only by encouraging a system of distinct systems of power (cf. Brenkert on the conservative idea of liberty), lacking which there will be an omnipotent, monistic social power which will kill liberty.

From these summaries, especially the last, it can be seen that Kolnai, in terms of both philosophical presuppositions and practical politics, represents the archetypal conservatism of Edmund Burke upon which, I have argued, Hayek and Polanyi tend to converge, and that he also argues that liberalism must converge upon that conservatism if it really wishes to secure liberty. Looking back upon our examination of von Mises, Popper, and even Hayek, we can see with Kolnai's aid, as indicated in the comments which I have inserted and the notes which I have added, additional ways in which their defective liberalisms threaten liberty. But equally, Kolnai repudiated the reactionary dream of lifting human life on earth out of change, the schemes of corporatism which can lead only to more mechanism, and the fantasy of distributivism. Several property, which must be unequal in its "distribution," and the market are the necessary economic foundations of liberty. Yet liberty is also threatened, as some liberals have not appreciated, by a value-monism, usually based on a value-scepticism, which reduces all values, motives, and functions to commercial ones or which thinks that the operations of the market within a legal system can solve all our problems.

Notes

1. *La table ronde*, no. 153, Sept. 1960, Paris.
2. No details of publication; trans. from the French (*Cité Libre*, Nov. 1955, Canada).
3. *Contrepoint*, no. 21, May 1976, Paris; trans. from "Privilege and liberty," *Laval théologique et philosophique*, vol. 5, no. 1, 1949, Quebec; see also *The Utopian Mind and Other Papers*.

    Kolnai had also published, "Le cult du 'Common Man' et la gloire des Humbles" (*Université Laval Théologique et Philosophique*, 1946, Quebec) and "The meaning of the common man" (*The Thomist*, 1949, Canada), neither of which I have read.

I addition to the articles cited, I have also read "Reflexiones sobre el alzamiento húngaro" (*Revista Oriente*, vol. 7, no. 27, 1957, Madrid), and the posthumously published *The Utopian Mind and Other Papers*.

4. We may also note that a liberalism, like that of von Mises, which maintains only a formally common good, has no basis for social unity unless men in fact have identical desires, aspirations, and aims, which is what the hedonistic reductionism of utilitarianism assumes. Hence, from the other side as we saw in the case of Bentham, that identical good can be achieved for them by State action. Even Hayek is sometimes equivocal on this fundamental point, at times emphasising the divergence of human interests, with only a formal unity of mutual and equal respect for liberty under the law, while implicitly endorsing the fact of a shared and largely tacit sense of justice. The collectivisms and individualisms of the modern age both, in effect, deny any difference between the common good and private goods, and for the same reason: namely, the denial of any transcendent Law or Way for man and thus of a substantive human nature which it is our duty to realise and enhance. The collectivisms set up arbitrary notions of a common good, and identify all private goods with them, and denounce any that diverge from it as "selfish," while the individualisms identify the common good with the sum total of, or with the conditions for achieving (such as the market and the rule of law), the private goods that the population individually, freely, and arbitrarily chooses. As already suggested, individualism can easily pass over into collectivism when it is held that all or most individuals will make at least some similar choices which they will also rate as the most important of their private goods. As we saw that is what von Mises appeals to, and so, at times, does Hayek. Bentham, of course, takes it as axiomatic that all will choose pleasure and that all pleasures are commensurable and thus exchangeable. Given this factual convergence of private goods, it is an open question whether individual liberty or central direction will best realise them.

5. Kolnai tends to interpret liberalism in its more radical forms. But, in effect, he is arguing, like Polanyi, that they are implied in the explicit formulations of moderate forms of liberalism, and that in fact Liberal achievements rest upon traditional moral restraints and social distinctions which liberalism mostly takes for granted or even denies. As we have seen, the classical liberalism of Acton and Hayek contains a substantial proportion of conservative traits which are necessary to the maintenance of liberty. It has been the argument of this study, as it is that of Kolnai, that more of those traits are needed and with them the recognition and frank avowal of that need.

6. Despite his admiration for Chesterton, at this point Kolnai eschews "distributivism," as the egalitarian fetish of "property well divided," and accuses its advocates of oscillating between the reactionary Utopia of a virtual negation of society where the earth is paradisaical desert of rural family units almost isolated from each other, an idea as "atomistic" as that of liberalism despite its Roman Catholic parentage, and the reaffirmation of the omnipotent State as the guarantor of an equal and uniform distribution of private property. Likewise he had earlier repudiated corporatism.

Bibliography

Acton, Lord. 1972. *Essays on Freedom and Power*, edited by G. Himmelfarb. Gloucester, MA: Peter Smith.

Allen, R.T. 1992. *The Education of Autonomous Man*. Guildford: Ashgate.

———. 1993. *The Structure of Value*. 1993. Guildford: Ashgate.

———. 1992. *Transcendence and Immanence in the Philosophy of Michael Polanyi and Christian Theism*. Lewiston, NY: Edwin Mellen.

Aron, R. 1970. *An Essay on Freedom*. Cleveland, OH: World Pub. Co.

Austin, J. 1954. *The Province of Justice Defined*. London: Weidenfeld and Nicolson.

Babbitt, I. [1919]1979. *Democracy and Leadership*. Indianapolis, IN: Liberty Classics.

———. [1924]1955. *Rousseau and Romanticism*. Cleveland, OH: World Pub. Co.

Bák, J.M., ed. 1991. *Liberty and Socialism: Writings of Libertarian Socialists in Hungary* 1884–1919. Savage, MD: Rowman and Littlefield.

Bentham, J. 1989. *First Principles Preparatory to a Constitutional Code*, edited by P. Schofield. Oxford: Clarendon Press.

———. 1960. *A Fragment on Government* and *An Introduction to the Principles of Morals and Legislation*. Oxford: Blackwell.

———. 1970. *Of Laws in General*, edited by H.L.A. Hart. London: Athlone Press.

Berlin, I. 1969. *Four Essays on Liberty*. London: Oxford University Press.

Bosanquet, B. 1923. *The Philosophical Theory of the State*, 4th ed. London: Macmillan.

———. 1912. *The Principle of Individuality and Value*. London: Macmillan.

———. 1913. *The Value and Destiny of the Individual*. London: Macmillan.

Boucher, D. 1989. *The Social and Political Thought of R.G. Collingwood*. Cambridge: Cambridge University Press.

Brenkert, G.G. 1991. *Political Freedom*. London: Routledge.

Bullock, A. 1991. *Hitler and Stalin: Parallel Lives*. London: Harper Collins.

Burke, E. 1844. *Correspondence*, 4 vols. London: Rivington.

———. 1908. *Speeches and Letters on American Affairs*. London: Dent.

———. 1826–7. *Works*, 16 vols. London: Rivington.

Cohn, N. 1970. *The Pursuit of the Millennium*, 3d ed. London: Temple Smith.

Collingwood, R.G. 1940. *Essay on Metaphysics*. Oxford: Clarendon Press.

————. 1967. *Essays in the Philosophy of Religion*, edited by M.L. Rubinoff. Chicago: Quadrangle Books.

————. 1989. *Essays on Political Philosophy*, edited by D. Boucher, Oxford: Clarendon Press.

————. 1946. *The Idea of History*, edited by T.M. Knox, Oxford, Clarendon Press.

————. [1942]1993. *The New Leviathan*. Oxford: Clarendon Press.

————. 1938. *The Principles of Art*. Oxford: Clarendon Press.

————. 1916. *Religion and Philosophy*. London: Macmillan.

————. 1924. *Speculum Mentis*. Oxford: Clarendon Press.

Congdon, L. 1991. *Exile and Social Thought*. Princeton, NJ: Princeton University Press.

Dennis, N. 1993. *Rising Crime and the Dismembered Family*. London: Institute of Economic Affairs.

Dennis, N., and Erdos, G. 1992. *Families without Fatherhood*. London: Institute of Economic Affairs.

Dussen, H. van der. 1981. *History as Science: the Philosophy of R.G. Collingwood*. The Hague: Nijhoff.

Dworkin, R. 1977. *Taking Rights Seriously*. London: Duckworth.

Friedrich, C.J. 1972. *Tradition and Authority*. London: Macmillan.

————. 1964. *Transcendent Justice: The Religious Dimension of Constitutionalism*. Durham, NC: Duke University Press.

Frings, M., ed. 1974. *Max Scheler: Centennial Essays*. The Hague: Nijhoff.

Gluckman, M. 1965. *Politics, Law and Ritual in Tribal Societies*. Oxford: Blackwell.

Gray, J. 1995. *Enlightenment's Wake*. London: Routledge.

————. 1989. *Liberalisms*. London: Routledge.

————. 1993. *Post-Liberalism*. London: Routledge.

Hailsham, Lord. 1959. *The Case for Conservatism*, 2d ed. Harmonsworth: Penguin.

Hare, R.M. 1962. *Freedom and Reason*. Oxford: Clarendon Press.

————. 1952. *The Language of Morals*. Oxford: Clarendon Press.

————. 1981. *Moral Thinking*. Oxford: Clarendon Press.

Hayek, F.A. 1960. *The Constitution of Liberty*, London, Routledge.

————. 1979. *The Counter Revolution of Science*, 2d ed. Indianapolis: Liberty Press.

————. 1988. *The Fatal Conceit, Collected Works*, vol. 1. London: Routledge.

————. 1982. *Law, Liberty and Legislation*, 3 vols., rev. ed. London: Routledge.

————. 1976. *New Studies in Philosophy, Politics and Economics*, London: Routledge.

————. 1944. *The Road to Serfdom*. London: Routledge.

————. 1967. *Studies in Philosophy, Politics and Economics*, London: Routledge.

Hegel, G.W.F. 1975. *Reason in History*, translated by Nisbet. Cambridge: Cambridge University Press.

Heidegger, M. 1978. *Being and Time*, translated by Macquarrie and Robinson. Oxford: Blackwell.

Henshall, N. 1992. *The Myth of Absolutism*. London: Longman.

Hooker, R. 1975. *Of the Law of Ecclesiastical Polity*, abridged ed. London: Sidgwick and Jackson.

Hume, D. 1894. *Enquiries Concerning Human Understanding and the Principles of Morals*, edited by Selby-Bigge. Oxford: Clarendon Press.

———. [1888] 1978. *Treatise of Human Nature*, edited by Selby-Bigge, 2d ed. Oxford: Clarendon Press.

Jasay, A. de. 1991. *Choice, Contract, Consent*. London: Institute of Economic Affairs.

Jelenski, K.A., ed. 1963. *History and Hope*. New York: A. Praeger.

Jonas, H. 1963. *The Gnostic Religion*, 2d ed. Boston, MA: Beacon Press.

Jouvenel, B. de. 1957. *Sovereignty*, translated by Huntington. Cambridge, Cambridge University Press.

Kant, I. 1991. *The Metaphysics of Morals*, translated by McGregor, Cambridge: Cambridge University Press.

———. 1948. *The Moral Law*, translated by Paton. London: Hutchinson.

Keegan, J. 1993. *A History of Warfare*. London: Hutchinson.

Kelsen, H. 1991. *The General Theory of Law and State*, translated by Hartney. Oxford: Clarendon Press.

Kirk, R. 1954. *The Conservative Mind*. London: Faber.

Kolnai, A. 1938. *The War against the West*. London: Gollancz.

———. 1952. *La Divinizacion y la Suma Esclavitud del Hombre*. Madrid: Ateneo.

———. 1952. *Errores del Anticomunismo*, translated by Pons. Madrid: Ediciones Rialp; originally published as "Quelques erreurs fondamentales sur le communisme," *La Revue de l'Université Laval*, 1946.

———. 1959. *Critica de las Utopias Politicas*. Madrid: Ateneo.

———.1995. *The Utopian Mind and Other Papers*, edited by F. Dunlop. London: Athlone Press.

Körner, S. 1984. *Metaphysics: Its Structure and Functions*, Cambridge: Cambridge University Press.

Laqueur, W., and Mosse, G., eds. 1974. *Historians in Politics*, London: Sage Publications.

Leacock, E., and Lee, R., eds. 1982. *Politics and History in Band Societies*. Cambridge: Cambridge University Press.

Lewis, C.S. 1978. *The Abolition of Man*. Glasgow: Collins.

Locke, J. 1954. *Essays on the Law of Nature*, edited and translated by W. von Leyden. Oxford: Clarendon Press.

———. 1965. *Letter on Toleration*. New York: Collier Macmillan.

———. 1960. *Two Treatises on Civil Government*, edited by Laslett. Cambridge: Cambridge University Press.

————. 1968. *Some Thoughts on Education*. London: Oxford University Press.

Lubac, H. de. 1949. *The Drama of Atheist Man*, translated by Riley. London: Sheed and Ward.

Macquarrie, J. 1966. *Principles of Christian Theology*. London: S.C.M. Press.

Maine, H. 1906. *Ancient Law*, 10th ed., edited by F. Pollock. London: John Murray.

Mannheim, K. 1940. *Man and Society in an Age of Reconstruction*, London: Kegan Paul.

Merleau-Ponty, M. 1962. *The Phenomenology of Perception*, translated by Smith. London: Routledge.

Mill, J.S. 1972. *Utilitarianism, On Liberty, and Representative Government*. London: Dent.

Mises, L. von. 1949. *Human Action*. London: Wm. Hodge & Co.

————. 1951. *Socialism*, translated by Jonathan Cape, rev. ed. London: Kahane.

Moore, G.E. 1903. *Principia Ethica*. Cambridge: Cambridge University Press.

Murdoch, I. 1970. *The Sovereignty of Good*. London: Routledge.

Nesbit, R.A. 1953. *The Quest for Community*. New York: Oxford University Press.

Newman, J.H. 1957. *The Idea of a University* in *Newman: Prose and Poetry*, edited by Tillotson. London: Rupert Hart-Davis.

Nietzsche, F. 1954. *The Twilight of the Idols* in *The Portable Nietzsche*, translated by Kaufmann. New York: Viking Press.

————. 1968. *The Will to Power*, translated by Kaufmann and Hollingdale. New York: Vintage Books.

Nozick, R. 1974. *Anarchy, State and Utopia*. Oxford: Blackwell.

————. 1981. *Philosophical Explanations*. Oxford: Clarendon Press.

Oakeshott, M. 1975. *On Human Conduct*. Oxford: Clarendon Press.

Paine, T. 1953. *Commonsense and Other Political Writings*. Indianapolis, IN: Bobbs-Merrill.

Parkin, C. 1956. *The Moral Basis of Burke's Political Thought*. Cambridge: Cambridge University Press.

Piaget, J. 1929. *The Child's Conception of the World*, translated by Tomlinson. London: Routledge.

Polanyi, M. 1969. *Knowing and Being*. London: Routledge.

————. 1951. *The Logic of Liberty*. London: Routledge.

————. 1975. *Meaning*. Chicago: Chicago University Press.

————. 1958. *Personal Knowledge*. London: Routledge.

————. 1946. *Science, Faith and Society*. London: Routledge.

————. 1997. *Society, Economics, and Philosophy: Selected Articles*, edited by R.T. Allen. New Brunswick, NJ: Transaction Publishers.

————. 1959. *The Study of Man*. London: Routledge.

————. 1964. *The Tacit Dimension*. London: Routledge.

Popper, K. 1969. *Conjectures and Refutations*, 3d ed. London: Routledge.

————. 1962. *The Open Society and its Enemies*, 2 vols., 5th ed. London: Routledge.

————. 1960. *The Poverty of Historicism*, 2d ed. London: Routledge.

Ranly, E. 1966. *Scheler's Phenomenology of Community*. The Hague: Nijhoff.

Raz, J. 1986. *The Morality of Freedom*. Oxford: Clarendon Press.

Rorty, R. 1979. *Philosophy and the Mirror of Nature*. Princeton, NJ: Princeton University Press.

Runciman, S. 1947. *The Mediaeval Manichee*. Cambridge: Cambridge University Press.

Ryan, A., ed. 1979. *The Idea of Freedom*. Oxford: Oxford University Press.

Santayana, G. 1962. *Reason in Society*. New York: Collier Books.

————. 1961. *The Sense of Beauty*. New York: Collier Books.

Sartre, J-P. 1958. *Being and Nothingness*, translated by Barnes. London: Methuen.

————. 1948. *Existentialism is a Humanism*, translated by Mairet. London: Methuen.

Scheler, M. 1963–82. *Gesammelte Werke*. Bern: A. Franke Verlag.

————. 1960. *The Eternal in Man*, translated by Noble. London: SCM Press.

————. 1973. *Formalism in Ethics*, translated by Frings and Funk. Evanston, IL: Northwestern University Press.

————. 1954. *The Nature of Sympathy*, translated by Heath. London: Routledge.

————. 1973. *Selected Philosophical Essays*, translated by Lachterman. Evanston, IL: Northwestern University Press.

Schoek, H. 1969. *Envy*, translated by Glenny and Ross. London: Secker and Warburg.

Searle, J. 1969. *Speech Acts*. London: Cambridge University Press.

Skinner, B.F. 1972. *Beyond Freedom and Dignity*. New York: Bantam Books.

————. 1953. *Science and Human Behaviour*. New York: Free Press.

Stanlis, P. 1958. *Edmund Burke and the Natural Law*. Ann Arbor, MI: University of Michigan Press.

Strauss, L. 1953. *Natural Right and History*. Chicago: Chicago University Press.

Talmon, J.L. 1952. *The Origins of Totalitarian Democracy*. London: Secker and Warburg.

Taylor, C. 1975. *Hegel*. Cambridge: Cambridge University Press.

Voegelin, E. 1975. *From Enlightenment to Revolution*. Durham, NC: Duke University Press.

————. 1952. *The New Science of Politics*. Chicago: Chicago University Press.

————. 1966. *Science, Politics and Gnosticism*. Chicago: Regnery-Gateway.

Waldon, J., ed. 1987. *Nonsense upon Stilts: Bentham, Burke and Marx on Natural Rights*. London: Methuen.

Webb, S. and B. 1936. *Soviet Communism: A New Civilisation?* 2 vols. London: Longmans.

Index